Cross-Cultural Perspectives on Policy and Practice

Routledge Research in Education

Cross-Cultural Perspectives on Policy and Practice

Decolonizing Community Contexts

**Edited by Jennifer Lavia
and Michele Moore**

Routledge
Taylor & Francis Group
New York   London

First published 2010
by Routledge
270 Madison Ave, New York, NY 10016

Simultaneously published in the UK
by Routledge
2 Park Square, Milton Park, Abingdon, Oxon OX14 4RN

Routledge is an imprint of the Taylor & Francis Group, an informa business

© 2010 Taylor & Francis

Typeset in Sabon by IBT Global.
Printed and bound in the United States of America on acid-free paper by IBT Global.

Library of Congress Cataloging-in-Publication Data

Cross-cultural perspectives on policy and practice: decolonizing community contexts /
edited by Jennifer Lavia and Michele Moore.
    p. cm.—(Routledge research in education)
    Includes bibliographical references and index.
    1. Education—Cross-cultural studies.   2. Education and state—Cross-cultural
studies.   3. Education—Parent participation—Cross-cultural studies.   4. Educational
change—Cross-cultural studies.   5. Indigenous peoples—Education—Cross-cultural
studies.   I. Lavia, Jennifer.   II. Moore, Michele.
    LB14.7.C76 2009
    306.43'2—dc22
    2009018025

ISBN10: 0-415-99769-0 (hbk)
ISBN10: 0-203-87100-6 (ebk)

ISBN13: 978-0-415-99769-0 (hbk)
ISBN13: 978-0-203-87100-3 (ebk)

This book is dedicated to all those individuals and communities who struggle to be heard

Contents

Preface

> No name is yours until you speak it; somebody returns your call and
> suddenly, the circuit of signs, gestures, gesticulations, is established
> and you enter the territory of the right to narrate. You are part of a
> dialogue that may not, at first, be heard or heralded—you may be
> ignored—but your personhood cannot be denied. In another's coun-
> try that is also your own, your person divides, and in following the
> forked path you encounter yourself in a double movement . . . once as
> stranger, and then as friend. (Homi Bhabha 1994, xxv).

This is a book whose time has come, whose production is a signifier of the
urgent and unfinished business to reposition the idea of community and
consider implications of change for a wide audience of those committed to
pioneering an agenda for social justice within educational organisations
and their wider communities.

   *Cross-Cultural Perspectives in Policy and Practice: Decolonizing Com-
munity Contexts* provides a critical space in which struggles for indigenous
knowledge within a community context are articulated, valued, heard and
responded to. Taking change as its focus, discursive engagements within
the text acknowledge that the origins and significance of change are frequently found to be unsettling. The book seeks to promote advocacy of
change which recognises the importance of an informed engagement with
cross-cultural issues in order to foreground those missing perspectives that
are often marginalised, silenced, ignored or denied.

   All contributors are concerned with how the process of change can bridge
the gap between social justice and exclusion. Each of the chapters develops its
own critical understanding of the implications of changing policy and practice for those within and working with the educational organizations and
communities under discussion. Theoretical perspectives, innovative practice
and policy are interrogated in each of the chapters as they explore how community is experienced and interpreted within a range of cultural settings.

   This book also brings together understandings of change agendas that
forge sustainable, inclusive and just communities. Autobiography, citizenship, resistance, peacemaking, critical literacies and second-chance opportunities are examples of unifying themes throughout. The impact of change
for those within or working with educational organisations and communities is therefore considered, from a number of different perspectives,
informed by the personal, professional and research experiences of change
encountered by its authors.

REFERENCE

Bhabha, H. (1994). *Location of Culture*. London: Routledge.

Acknowledgments

The writing of a book such as this is never an individual endeavor. Its final production represents months (and years) of sharing and collaborations. This book is a collective effort that emerged out of several critical moments of dialogue held at the Academy, in various airports, on public transport and via a range of electronic means.

We owe a debt of gratitude to the various communities who are represented in the text, who allowed us to be with them, travel with them, learn with them, teach with them, listen with them and write with them.

Sincere thanks are conveyed to all the contributors, who were gracious enough to endure very short deadlines and push the boundaries of their own practice.

To the publishers we are especially thankful for the guidance and support along the way.

Throughout writing and editing of the book, our families have been eternally supportive. Their encouragement along the journey has been more than can be expected and for this we extend our heartfelt and special thanks.

Introduction
Education, Community and Change

Jennifer Lavia and Michele Moore

OPENING THOUGHTS

Education continues to be a contested site and field of inquiry requiring ongoing interrogation and reinterpretation. Its shifting terrain is impacted upon by the pervasiveness of globalization to exercise normalizing and reforming agendas across cultures and contexts on the one hand, and on the other hand, the transnationalization of education is itself throwing up dialogic spaces and opportunities for change. We see this dynamic process occurring particularly in the link between education and community and the ways in which each entity becomes a constituent part of the other. Education occurs in community. Its responsive or transformational function is determined within theatres of agency, where contending voices struggle to be heard and recognized. Consequently, the book, *Cross-Cultural Perspectives on Policy and Practice: Decolonizing Community Contexts*, exemplifies a community of researchers, educators, scholars, critics and activists whose representations "shift the terrains of knowledge" (Mutua & Swadener, 2004: 1), re-positioning and recasting new discursive spaces which recognize and value indigenous knowledge and culturally ethical research practice.

Each of the chapters, while presenting specific cross-cultural sites of research, makes no claim to these as being finished, complete or constant. Indeed, the unity within the book is to be found in the sensitive, scholarly yet accessible treatment of troubling and problematic social realities of change, which question the effects of colonizing policies and practices upon "spaces of marginalization" (Smith, 1999: 4). These sites are represented not merely from a point of marginalization but also as sites of knowledge production and change; creativity and wisdom; and, resistance and hope (Smith, 1999).

AIM OF THE BOOK

The aim of the book is to examine the notion of community and the quality of engagement that occurs within community. The motivation and concern that gave rise to the book begin with a commitment to social justice and the necessity to pursue such an agenda within educational settings. This concern is shared by the contributors to the book who themselves have exemplified in their research and practice a consistent and high regard for indigenous knowledge and a practice that is embedded within participatory research.

We posed five key questions that have emerged as a guiding theoretical and conceptual framework for the book: (a) What do we mean in theoretical and practical terms by "decolonizing community contexts"? (b) Why is the process of decolonizing in relation to understanding communities important? (c) What are the possibilities offered by a decolonizing approach to understanding communities? (d) What is the link between education and community development? (e) To what extent is this link central to a decolonizing process? We do not pose these questions lightly or only for the purpose of developing the discourses within this particular text. Rather, the demand of this undertaking is to challenge common assumptions about the location of knowledge and to recognize this undertaking as central to those who are concerned with histories and experiences of exclusion and oppression. Each chapter addresses some or all of these questions through discourses that are reflective of the specific context/s in which the researchers are working.

We also recognize the need for a rethink of community in light of globalization. As Rizvi states:

> It is clear that no community is entirely unaffected by the global processes. Even if people do not recognize their effects, it is hard for me to see how subjectivities and social relations can remain unaltered by global shifts, produced by increasing levels of travel, access to the global media, the changing nature of work and the shifting modes of social imagination.
>
> (Rizvi, 2006: 19)

SHIFTING TERRAIN OF COMMUNITY: TOWARDS DECOLONIZATION

> Community is the antagonist supplement of modernity, threatening the claims of civility; in the transnational world it becomes the border-problem of the diasporic, the migrant, the refugee.
>
> (Bhabha, 1994: 330)

Communities are neither fixed nor homogeneous. Rather as Bhabha suggests, critical interpretations position community in opposition to hegemonic, ahistorical, acritical, definitions. In this book community is constructed in different ways with each chapter reflecting on its own contextual nuances yet responding to the aforementioned theoretical framework made explicit through the five key questions, and also reflecting on issues such as: researcher positionality, research priorities and contexts; points of tension and access; and personal and public development. Community is referenced in this text through the use of policy and practice examining how these references are narrated through discourses on inclusion, patterns of migration, reclamation of academic, intellectual and cultural spaces, re-emergence of indigenous thought, performative and aesthetic discourses and expressions of new ways to being, thinking and living together.

Similarly, the term "decolonization" occupies a contested terrain. Its more popular link within geopolitics for example, suggests a form of undoing and righting the wrongs of colonial governance in which occupational and oppressive external forces give way coercively or otherwise, to a process of national and ethnic self-determination and independence. While important to our understanding of how knowledge has been colonized, to limit the discourse to only this definition is to apply temporal stricture to the debate. On the one hand such discourse is limited to temporal arguments in which time and space are presented as rigid histories of conquest, conformity and distance. On the other hand, a temporal discourse provides the basis for identifying (rather than avoiding) an array of dispositions that have shaped how specific communities are engaged and represented.

In our view, decolonization refers to a process that recognizes the historical circumstances of communities and how those historical circumstances can be interrogated at different levels. Decolonization occupies a deconstructed terrain in which histories and biographies intersect and are repositioned. We draw upon Linda Tuhiwai Smith's work on indigenous communities in which she articulates that "in a decolonizing framework, decolonization is part of a much larger intent" (Tuhiwai Smith, 1999: 3); researching communities in this light requires collaborative engagements involving conscious practice constructed around wider issues of social justice and self-determination.

Moving beyond any narrow understanding of community, we critically embrace Appardurai's (2001) appeal to "deparochialize" globalization. Appadurai's appeal elaborated by Lingard (2006) thus:

> The new multi-modal and multi-directional circuits of power associated with globalization, and related flows of students and researchers, challenge many of our theoretical, epistemological and methodological assumptions about doing educational research. The educational research imagination needs to be exercised to meet these challenges of globalization.
>
> (p. 287)

Appradurai makes the case for the need to re-examine, re-present, re-position, indeed, re-imagine research in light of the shifting terrain of global flows. Here he argues for "epistemological diffidence" as a necessary undertaking of deparochialization where, as Edward Said claims the positional superiority of Western knowledge pervaded through epistemic certainty is decentred and challenged by minority and indigenous voices. Globalization in this sense is to be understood as invasive, constantly changing: meaning and understanding; texts and sub-texts; the global and the local; and transforming the nature, effects and affects of social relations.

Appadurai (2001) calls for "grassroots globalization" in which the internationalization of the work of non-governmental organizations in setting policy and research agendas on their own terms. That is what he calls bottom-up globalization. In advancing his interest in how deparochialization agendas become manifest, Appadurai (2009) refers to the development of a capacity to hope. The desire to aspire and develop a capacity to hope can be added to Bourdieu's articulation of the development of social and cultural capital and Amartya Sen's notion of capabilities. These articulations foreground the centrality of human agency.

One of the responsibilities which this book undertakes is to unearth and represent research evidence of the stories and perspectives of communities and groups that have been historically and traditionally silenced and marginalized, and who consider themselves to matter less than their contemporaries. It, in part, takes up the challenge posed by Gayatri Spivak (1993) in her seminal essay titled "Can the Subaltern Speak?" The paper helps to illuminate disparate contexts in which communities are coming to know and represent themselves. This undertaking is not merely about presenting binary positions but rather accepts a research agenda to understand the role of education in community development and its contribution to decolonization. Decolonization in this light seeks to come to terms with the ways in which hegemonic forces of colonization insidiously pervade knowledge systems. Such forces seek to categorize and consolidate hierarchical systems and in the process re-arrange, re-present and re-distribute, materially and discursively, indigenous systems of knowing and being.

Construction of identities and ways of being are influenced by colonial relationships which on the one hand create groups of privileged knowledge based on adherence and implementation of the cannon, and on the other hand, disparate groups whose sense of rights and forms of agency are restricted to conformity, homogeneity, restraint, civility and silence. We define decolonization as the social imaginary poised in the presence of the policy and practice of community where "the subject splits, the signifier 'fades', the pedagogical and the performative are agonistically articulated". (Bhabha, 1994: 220). Community in this sense is a commitment to "enacting the impossibility of drawing an objective line between the private and the public, the civil and the familial" (Bhabha, 1994: 330).

SETTING RESEARCH AGENDAS

> Research is not an innocent or distant academic exercise but rather an
> activity that has something at stake and that occurs in a set of political
> and social conditions
>
> (Smith, 1999: 5).

Research does not occur in isolation but within the cultural contexts of communities. Such contexts are diverse and hold out the promise for creating dialogic spaces where the realities of lived experiences of those who have been marginalized and excluded struggle to be articulated. The chapters in this book represent the work of academics and intellectuals who, through a pursuit of critical self-reflection and deconstruction of their work as researchers and activists, make clear their commitment to researching issues of social justice. Their contributions provide contextual spaces which reveal and seek to unpack the complexities of cross-cultural perspectives, seeking to interrupt external representations of the communities in which they are involved, and exposing the experiences of "othering."

In Chapter 1 Antonia Darder and Zeus Yiamouyiannis contribute a Freirean reading of community. They argue for the development of political grace in the face of transformative engagements with communities. In the chapter they draw upon examples of how communities, subjected to environment dangers, struggled to reclaim their communities. Here, political grace is expressed as one, which acknowledges both the power of subordinated identities and the power of collective action. They claim that inherent to this decolonizing perspective are important questions for reflection that must hold as central such as: Who produces, analyzes and makes conclusions about the multiple and often divergent narratives or political needs of the community? Whose interests do the timetables and research agendas of political interventions serve? Who consumes the program or research and toward what end? What leadership and organizational structures, as well as communication styles, are being utilized to create a more solid grassroots political mobilization? What privileges and economic interests enable the production and consumption of education and research? How can these function in the interests of the residents' long-term, as well as short-term needs? These questions they argue, are key to the manner in which education, research and organizing are conducted, the analysis of research is developed, and the products of education, research and political organizing are utilized.

In Chapter 2 Jennifer Lavia progresses the idea of community as a political project through her postcolonial critique. She examines how constructions of community are complex and are shaped within the context of the diaspora of the Caribbean by the experience of colonialism and globalization. Lavia defines the decolonizing project as one that seeks to ask a fundamental question: How can cultural confidence be claimed in light of centuries of colonialism? Lavia draws on examples of a Caribbean intellectual tradition to interrogate community through lenses of: geopolitics, economics, cultural studies, feminism and educative derivatives such as grassroots pedagogies as a practice of community. She makes the case for decolonizing research agenda that engages from within and on its own terms and draws attention to the potentially transformative role of the public intellectual in this endeavor.

Barbara Comber brings to Chapter 3 an account of two projects in critical literacies in Australia. Drawing upon theories of social justice, critical literacy and place-based pedagogies, she examines how working with teachers to reassess their understanding of the community they teach helps create new insights about working "ethically and creatively towards sustainable and just society." The theme of literacy is continued in Chapter 4. "Changing Literacies: Schools, Communities and Homes" by Kate Pahl looks at research that has focused on honoring home literacy practices in order to listen to the voices of families and communities. The chapter takes the view that there are different literacy practices in different domains of life, and that home and community literacies are often not recognized in institutional contexts, such as schools and museums. The chapter outlines approaches to gathering data in homes and communities that listen to the voices of participants. The chapter describes how institutions such as schools and museums can become involved in this sort of work. Such projects include a community arts project, called "Capturing the Community" devised by a group of artists in South Yorkshire in Britain that engaged a group of parents and children in a school. Another project involved a group of families in curating an exhibition that aimed to transform understandings of migrant communities in South Yorkshire. Ways forward in engaging communities in projects are outlined and suggestions for further research into home and community literacies are proposed.

In Chapter 5 Lynn Mario de Souza and Vanessa Andreotti seek to understand and illustrate conflicts between local indigenous knowledges and global knowledges in official educational policy. The chapter describes the context of indigenous education in Brazil, where, in spite of the fact that present official policy purports to valorize and defend local knowledges against previous policies of assimilation and extermination, it encounters what appears to be resistance on the part of indigenous communities. The chapter proposes a means of understanding this resistance and the profound cultural conflicts and perceptions on which it is based, with important consequences for development education.

In Chapter 6 Jane Dodman chronicles an action research project in a unique preparatory school in an inner-city community in Kingston. This school is part of a community development organization. The school's stated objective is to offer the children a SLICE of life. Each letter of the SLICE stands for an important quality for children growing up in this context. The "C" in SLICE speaks to community and one of the teachers used an action research model to focus on community within the classroom in order to enable a sense of community to become a reality for the children within the different communities to which they belonged. A decolonizing approach is critical in addressing the negative self-esteem experienced by many people living in the inner city. This approach informed the classroom activities which are described and analyzed through the action research process.

In Chapter 7 Michele Moore develops a narrative about the unsettling, complex and yet uncharted field of integrating postcolonial studies and disabilities studies. She exemplified the precarious positioning of the research in light of histories of colonialism yet she perseveres with articulations that are decidedly provoked by a commitment to confronting barriers to inclusion and social justice agendas. Moore relates how her work with teachers in Trinidad and St. Lucia on a postgraduate education course has created a potent source for renegotiating old center/periphery relations and for constructing new ones on the basis of advancing a social model of disabilities for inclusive education.

The theme of disabled access and inclusion continues in Chapter 8. Tsitsi Chataika's chapter was born from her recently completed PhD study that focused on the personal experiences of disabled students in higher education in Zimbabwe. The chapter's main concern is that inclusion of communities of disabled students in higher education has been gathering momentum in various countries, but has not been seriously considered in Zimbabwe. Challenges facing disabled students in Zimbabwe are presented. Methodological resources that informed this study are brought to light; research findings are highlighted and conclusions are put forward. Practical recommendations to various stakeholders, including policy makers in the education of disabled students in higher education in Zimbabwe are also presented.

Chapter 9, by Evelyn Abram, Felicity Armstrong, Len Barton and Lynne Lye is a collaboration in writing which brings together experienced university researchers and research participants. This chapter explores issues of social justice, participation and representation through a study of school transformation in response to diversity. The social, demographic and economic life of cities in the UK has been radically changed as new communities arrive, often along circuitous routes, in response to war, persecution, poverty, and changing boundary structures and regulations. What are the issues raised for schools in terms of responding to new forms of diversity, and how can they draw on different cultures, perspectives and experiences in ways which are enriching and equitable? How can schools develop participatory democratic cultures and practices which reflect a commitment to the communities in which they serve and how are these reflected in learning, teaching and the curriculum? These questions are explored through the experience of an inner-city primary school which is involved in a process of change. The discussion includes an evaluation of the possible opportunities for school transformation presented by action research.

In Chapter 10 Sechaba Mahlomaholo locates community within the context of university teachers in South Africa and their struggle for academic freedom. Drawing upon Foucault's notion of genealogy, Mahlomaholo sites that the deeply embedded practices of the apartheid system in South Africa have not countered hegemonic policies and practice where unequal participation and representation remain central issue of interrogation and challenge. Mahlomaholo also makes reference to the privileging of knowledge of the dominant groups and notes that the voice of the academic teacher is silenced in light of course development. He wonders then to what extent are indigenous perspectives expressed through curriculum guides. He calls for participatory approaches to educational practice.

The issue of adult education is addressed in Chapter 11. Here, Anita Franklin draws upon her own experience working with widening participation agendas in the UK, where such agendas have made it possible for nontraditional groups to attend university. In this chapter Franklin looks back over twenty years of her work in adult education. Here she addresses concerns over current policy direction of adult education and its relationship to the connections between education, access and social justice. Drawing on her experience of adult education in a variety of settings, she discusses the opportunities and constraints met in combining adult education with community development, specifically in relation to women and black communities in Yorkshire. Within this context she outlines some of the key ideas associated with adult education and community development since the end of World War II, looking specifically at how and to what extent adult educators in the UK conceptualize social justice.

Patricia Ellis, also a pioneer in adult and education, uses her personal and professional experience of the Caribbean context to explore the issue of poverty alleviation programmes and community life in Chapter 12. In the Caribbean there is a concern about the increase in poverty and many governments are taking initiatives to improve living conditions in poor communities and the standard of living and quality of life of vulnerable groups. Consequently, in several countries Poverty Assessments are being carried out and special Poverty Reduction Units have been created. Historically Caribbean people have regarded education as a priority and as a mechanism for social mobility, and education is now also being seen as having an important role to play in helping people to "escape from poverty." The chapter draws on findings from several Poverty Assessments, and will identify and describe various poverty reduction initiatives. In addition, Ellis examines the extent to which, from the perspective of those who are experiencing poverty, these initiatives are achieving their goals.

In Chapter 13 entitled, "I Am a Certain Person When I Am Here, it is Not Who I Am: Refugees Voices Within Communities of Change" Judith Szenasi describes a small-scale ethnographic research project of refugees and draws on her experience of being a community development practitioner to narrate the lived experience of groups of migrant people when they first arrive in a small city based in the East Midlands in the UK. Szenasi explores the philosophical and methodological merits of proposing a refugee standpoint and interrogates what this might look like empirically. Such a standpoint, she argues, seeks to develop theories of refugee justice.

The thirteen chapters in this book provide a circulatory logic that serves to respond to questions of "othering," difference, marginalization, exclusion and communities of silence. They all reflect personal journeys in light of collective engagements and share a commitment to social justice. It is in the challenge of deconstruction and re-presentation that we are to find spaces for dialogue, knowledge reception and production, agency and re-imagining of community in its own terms. It is to the unfolding of such an exploration that we now turn.

REFERENCES

Appadurai, A. (2009). The shifting ground from which we speak, in J. Kenway and J. Fahey (Eds.) *Globalizing the Research Imagination*. New York: Routledge, pp. 41–52.

Appardurai, A. (2001). Grassroots globalization and the research imagination, in A. Appadurai (Ed.) *Globalization*. Durham, NC: Duke Universdity Press, pp. 1–20.

Bhabha, H. (1994). *Location of Culture*. London: Routledge.

Lingard, B. (2006). Globalisation, the research imagination and deparochialising the study of education, *Globalisation, Societies and Education*, 4 (2): 287–302.

Mutua, K. and Swadener, B. B. (Eds.) (2004). *Decolonizing Research in Cross-Cultural Contexts: Critical Personal Narratives*, Albany: State University of New York Press.

Rizvi, F. (2006). Epistemic Virtues and Cosmopolitan Learning. Radford lecture, University of Illinois at Urbana-Champaign, Adelaide Australia, November 27, 2006. Accessed December 27, 2008 at: http://www.aare.edu.au/aer/online/0801c.pdf.

Smith, L. (1999). *Decolonizing Methodologies: Research and Indigenous People*. London: Zed Books.

Spivak, G. (1993). Can the subaltern speak? In P. Williams and L. Chrisman (Eds.) *Colonial Discourse and Post-colonial Theory: A Reader*. New York: Harvester Wheatsheaf, pp. 66–111.

1 Political Grace and the Struggle to Decolonize Community Practice

Antonia Darder and Zeus Yiamouyiannis

INTRODUCTION

> *[Political grace] is an act of seeking not to participate in structures that profit one but not another, to not profit at the expense of others, but to be part of that which changes the structure, that is, to be redemptive, penitent, reconciliative, revolutionary.*
>
> (Wes Rehberg, 1995)

> Decolonization involves both engagement with the everyday issues in our own lives so that we can make sense of the world in relation to hegemonic power, and engagement with collectivities that are premised on ideas of autonomy and self-determination, in other words, democratic practice.
>
> (Chandra Talpade Mohanty, 2003)

In the midst of national and international economic malaise and its consequences, disenfranchised communities everywhere are forced to contend with conditions of political, economic and social alienation, as they struggle to survive the erasure of history, the erosion of dignity and obstructions to community self-determination. Unfortunately, even within the context of well-meaning community practice, there persists a tendency toward mechanistic approaches that render the poorest and most marginalized sectors of the population silent and passive in the face of their own historical and contemporary suffering. Experiences of debilitating democracy, and the manner in which these resonate with many of the problems experienced by poor and racialized working-class communities who seek greater horizontal relationships of self-determination, serve as the impetus for this reflection on the need for a decolonizing community practice—one that cultivates political grace among those who aspire to create both social and material change.

In the U.S. today, the negative consequences of globalized neoliberal policies are devastating. The concentration of wealth and power held by the international elite is staggering. The Bush administration alone spent over $650 billion on the war in Iraq. We face unparallel pollution of our waters and lands. Poor communities around the globe are forced to contend daily with the horrific impact of environmental destruction. Unprecedented surveillance of the population persists. An alarming consolidation of the mainstream media infuses new meaning to the old 'culture industry' thesis of the Frankfurt School. The U.S. incarceration rate—over two million—is the highest of any industrialized nation. Working-class populations across the country are experiencing the intensification of economic apartheid and resegregation of their communities. Economic safety nets for the poor are all but extinguished. Forty-five million are without health-care benefits. The disappearance of jobs in the last decade has left millions unemployed.

These conditions signal the urgent need for fundamental political change at both the structural and communal levels. But change in today's world seems especially difficult, given the manner in which corporations and public and private institutions remain entrenched in political processes of narcissistic proportions that obstruct democratic life. But all this is more that just about a bad president; it is about a bankrupt philosophy of power and its exercise within public life. This suggests pathology of power, with its elitism, arrogance and privilege that brazenly justifies and rationalizes both foreign and domestic policies of domination and exploitation, in the name of democracy and national security. And as such, its agents (whether astute or naïve) arbitrate dominance and aggression as worthy and legitimate strategies that, wittingly or unwittingly, preserve the status quo. The result is the perpetuation of social and material conditions that reproduce social estrangement, human suffering and wholesale abandonment of those who pay the greatest price for the excesses of capital. Even so, capitalism fails not only because of its morally wretched impact on the poor, but also its alienation of those it allegedly benefits.

Hence, it should be of no surprise that many of the ideas utilized to make sense of this phenomenon are inspired by Paulo Freire, the world-renowned Brazilian educator and the decolonizing reflections of Franz Fanon, whose efforts sought to address the impact and limitation of social dynamics between those with power, privilege and access and those who exist as disenfranchised subjects of history. Much has transpired since Freire (1971) first wrote his seminal text, *Pedagogy of the Oppressed*, or Fanon (1952) penned *Black Skin, White Masks*, yet what seems to remain constant are the structures and politics of inequality that breed poverty and human suffering. And, despite the recent election of Barack Obama to the presidency of the United States, impoverished populations, here and abroad, will continue to face the dreadful consequences of intensifying economic exclusion for years to come. Many of these communities are also subjected to the dehumanizing effects of serving as quasi-laboratories for the benefit of corporate experiments, university researchers and professional organizers. And, although some of these efforts may have positive outcomes, more times than not, the gains are short lived, as professional community organizers take on single issue campaigns in ways that paradoxically disempower those most in need. Given rising impoverishment around the globe, there is a serious need to nurture radical organizing strategies that embody the courageous power of political grace to support both acts of resistance and revolutionary transformation.

DISRUPTING COMMUNITY PRACTICE

> *It is on the assumption—that [humans] are sheep—that the Great Inquisitors and the dictators have built their systems. More than that, this very belief that [humans] are sheep and hence need leaders to make decisions for them, has often given leaders the sincere conviction that they were fulfilling a moral duty—even though a tragic one.*
>
> (Erich Fromm, 1964)

Despite an espoused rhetoric of social justice in community practice, many conflicts prevail that disrupt efforts to ameliorate symptoms of inequalities within disenfranchised communities. This phenomenon is often tied to the way both "dominance" and "empathetic" approaches (Yiamouyiannis, 1998) function to disrupt community dialogue, solidarity and grassroots actions to transform conditions of poverty and alienation. Recently, for example, a number of activists and organizers came together in a small mid-western university town to work on an environmental justice project that involved a historically marginalized black working-class community.

Twenty years earlier, a major power utility plant shut its doors, leaving behind a flimsy fenced-off contaminated toxic site in this community. Over the years, a growing number of what seemed to be toxic related cancers begun to erupt all along the perimeter of the toxic waste site. In response, an official campaign was initiated by a community coalition that included a non-profit organization, some university faculty and students, and members of a grassroots community group. Unfortunately, despite an expressed commitment to the community's welfare and empowerment, it did not take long before major conflicts erupted between community organizers, over conflicting views about the best approach to contend with the issue.

The leadership of the non-profit organization (an established professional change agency) favored attacking the problem from the standpoint of a human rights campaign. Several university students working with the organization proceeded to interview residents of the area, hoping to get them on board with their particular vision. In concert, the organization's leadership publicly focused on their past successes with other health related campaigns, whereby highlighting their extensive knowledge and expertise.

However, not all of the members of the coalition were necessarily impressed by the often-touted resumé of accomplishments. Instead, grass-roots community members advocated for a very different approach. That is, given the long history of problems faced by this community, there was a desire to create a community-centered and decolonizing approach to carrying out the work. Grassroots community organizers called for a dialogical or (de-objectifying) approach, anchored in the individual and collective histories of the residents. This would require greater time and space for the area residents to become involved in an *active* process of participation and decision making. The activists and organizers who held this perspective felt that, despite the blanket of urgency draped over the toxic waste issue by the non-profit organization, it was absolutely necessary to use this opportunity for community members to establish greater political confidence and collective empowerment among themselves.

The grassroots organizers expressed an unwavering desire to bring together community concerns related to toxic waste with other significant issues of environmental racism—namely, severe unemployment, police brutality, the miseducation of children, the instrumentalizing of community by academic researchers and historical government neglect of the area. Moreover, it was deemed vitally important to recover people's histories of struggle, from which to enhance community self-determination (Darder, 2002). The hope, of course, was that community members would become better armed not only to contend with the negative impact of the utility plant on the lives of the residents and their children, but to struggle together on community issues that would persist, once the toxic waste issue was mediated and rectified.

The deep fundamental differences in defining both the issue and organizing approach resulted in a major rupture in the relationship of the coalition's community practice. Distrust over unilateral decisions by the non-profit organization's leadership to define the campaign as a "rights" movement intensified the debate, creating an environment in which critical dialogue was almost non-existent. To make things worse, a racializing division also resulted, with the white leadership of the non-profit organization choosing to sever its organizing relationship with several key members of the grassroots community group, who all just happened to be of color.

OBJECTIFYING "RIGHTS"

I came into the world imbued with the will to find a meaning in things, my spirit filled with the desire to attain to the source of the world, and then I found that I was an object in the midst of other objects.

(Fanon, 1967)

The non-profit organization aggressively pushed for a "rights" approach, insisting this was the most effective strategy for contending with environmental issues. Their track record as an advocacy organization was used to legitimate their entitlement in directing (or controlling) the actions and decision-making of the coalition. There was no question that the non-profit organizational leadership and staff felt comfortable and safe in their grand task as advocates of the poor. Unfortunately, the power and privilege they wielded, through the control of organizational networks and non-profit resources, remained hugely unacknowledged even when grassroots community members objected to the disparities in power. Meanwhile, their universalizing attitudes towards human rights conveniently allowed them to "ignore the localities, particularities and daily manifestations of the oppression in their midst" (Rehberg, 1995: 85).

Another objection by grassroots organizers to an approach they saw as individualistic and objectifying, was that of legal actors being prematurely summoned to take on the case of the toxic site, without community residents ever having an opportunity to come together to consider their priorities and strategies for contending with the twenty-year-old problem. In this community, longtime residents knew that legal matters had seldom favored their needs or priorities; often signaling only greater discrimination in the application of legal decisions. Hence, grassroots organizers conveyed their objections to this decision, by explaining that a "rights" solution was actually foreign to the community; and the premature implementation of its requirements could easily function to thwart other creative and more empowering solutions that could be build upon the strengths of existing communal relationships. These sentiments are summarized by Jaime Martinez Luna (2006) in his reflections on Oaxacan indigenous communities, autonomy and self-determination. "One always reasons in terms of the individual right, one never thinks of the communal right; that is to say, one always reasons in term of the interests of an individual and it is understood that all positions derive from an individual interest. One never incorporates the possibility of understanding that the attitude is the result of a social fact, and better say communal fact, that thus merits a different treatment."

From a marginalized perspective, all "rights," including civil rights, must be social (collective) rights, since any individual right can be taken away and any individual singled out, without committed community support to protect that person. Therefore, it is the strength, acknowledgement, and dialogue of the community, which provides the protection, not abstract or legal guarantees. When, for example, a black community member is lynched by a white mob (despite laws to the contrary) and the perpetrators are exonerated by a jury of their peers, protection from further injustice and restitution of practical justice emerges from the black community's own organization, action and resistance, not external "expertise," sentiment or abstract principle. These things only have purchase when attached to a structure of power. If that power structure is embedded or invisible, as it is often with the dominant culture, it can lead its members to believe that they somehow enjoy "natural rights" or privileges. Those subordinated to the power structure know better and are in a far better position to construct rigorous, effective strategies of resistance and creativity, unclouded by liberal romanticism. This is so, because their concerns are born from a raw, more intimate, and less mediated or processed experience with the world.

From a dominant perspective and experience, "rights," even civil rights take on the character of individual rights, precisely because members are led to believe that their favored positions are a natural feature of the world. This sets up not only a discourse of "do-gooding" for liberal dominant members but one in which some kind of fault or deficiency must be imputed to the marginalized, so-called "underclass" of society. One sees this constantly in discourses in educational environments around "closing the achievement gap," whereby usually white enthusiastic young idealist try to bring hope, a joy of learning, and a prep school curriculum to transform and lift out the disadvantaged from their dire social, economic, or familial straits. If rights are an individual possession, then they become easily conflated with one's individual identity, fanning the prevalence of identity politics and single-issue voting, this further compartmentalizes and debilitates civic public action around shared concerns.

Given these concerns, insistence on a "rights" approach by the non-profit organizational leadership (more interested in accomplishing an "organizing product" than community empowerment and self-determination) served to disrupt the ability of the coalition to construct a "site of resistance" or a space of political grace (Rehberg, 1995). More specifically, this disrupted the necessary relational space for community organizers and residents to join together, across their differences, to co-create the transformation not only of the toxic site, but of the community they called home. This reinforces the notion that the meanings co-created within community practices are always partial and must be understood as contingent on the lived conditions that inform their production. What this example of interrupted solidarity clearly demonstrates is the unfortunate temptation to reinscribe dominance within community practice unto those who resist mainstream definitions and solutions.

Given this discussion, it should not be surprising that a politics of expediency, prone to expert quick-fix and task driven solutions, functions as one of the cornerstones of liberal strategies to community "intervention" (the word itself connotes a "platooning" in from the outside). Rather than to seek organic opportunities for voice, participation, and social action among community members themselves, the premature leap into a well-defined "rights" campaign leads to a "true-and-tried" solution. What cannot be ignored here is that mainstream solutions anchored in a "rights" approach are often much more compelling to mainstream (often "white") community organizers, since it allows them to feel far more secure, competent, and comfortable in leading the charge. This, despite their lack of lived knowledge about how generations of racism and poverty can disable community empowerment, through contradictions, conflicts, dependencies and despair (Darder, 2008). With this in mind, both Freire and Fanon's writings reinforce the need for establishing decolonizing dynamics that instill a sense of intimacy and openness or "authentic conversation," in grappling with class, cultural, gendered and racialized differences, within the context of community struggles.

In this light, our responsibility to a decolonizing practice must be connected to a consistent commitment to remain ever vigilant of self and the social and material conditions that challenge our privilege, entitlement and certainties of efficacy. This is particularly so where communities have been subjected to long-term abuses, predicated on historical legacies of genocide, slavery and colonization—with their lasting impact on both the oppressed and the oppressor. Given its emancipatory purpose, revolutionary community practice requires the exercise of an integral process—one in which the mind, heart, body and spirit are welcome in the active service of liberation. This integral dynamic generates the conditions for political grace to touch our communal exchanges. In its absence, our community practice can easily, albeit unwittingly, degenerate into acts of dominance and debilitating empathy that ultimately thwart dialogue, empowerment and social transformation.

SHATTERING OPPRESSIVE ECONOMIC NORMS

> The system we are fighting is not merely structural; it's also inside us, through the internalization of oppressive cultural norms that define our worldview. Our minds have been colonized to normalize deeply pathological assumptions.
>
> (Patrick Reinsborough, 2004)

The struggle to decolonizing community practice must unquestionably abandon mindless practices that adhere to the "American Dream." This begins with a critical interrogation of unexamined assumptions and commonsense notions about why people are poor, homeless, or unemployed, as well as challenging pre-packaged and recycled solutions to poverty based on ignorance. Such interrogations are important, given assumptions about poverty based on oppressive myths—myths which ascribe superiority, entitlement or privilege to those granted full subjecthood under norms that conserve racialized, patriarchal and capitalist desires. A decolonizing approach, on the other hand, requires that we confront misguided loyalties to economic values that normalize abject poverty, unprecedented incarceration, war policies and a host of other economically-instilled conditions of human suffering.

With this in mind, a political vision that can inform a decolonizing community practice must work to dismantle those values and assumptions that normalize colonizing dynamics. It is impossible to consider these norms effectively without attributing their stubborn persistence to the reproduction of class formation and the vastly unequal distribution of wealth. The growing gap between the rich and the poor, generated under neoliberal policies around the world, are consonant with the imperialist features of advanced capitalism.

In the U.S., we live with the overriding capitalist myth: "Free market is equal to democracy." Hence, any sort of regulation by the public sphere is considered in the current neoliberal climate as a detriment to democratic life. The reign of the marketplace is responsible for the commodification of almost every aspect of human life. Nothing that can be converted into exchange value is sacred, leaving all up for grabs to the highest bidder. Alongside, all welfare programs have been put on the chopping block, as they are shamelessly called "a drain on the economy." Over the last twenty years, Keynesian economics, with its belief in government responsibility for its most vulnerable, has systematically eroded, as neoliberal rule intensified both nationally and internationally. The abandonment of poor racialized communities is felt in a variety of ways—gross unemployment, absence of adequate healthcare, poor education, and environmental injustices that have left many communities living in the time-bombs of toxic waste and land erosion. And when, for example, neglect of the environment results in major disasters, such as Hurricane Katrina in New Orleans, corporate pirates immediately swoop down. Inspired by their narcissistic greed, they offer a fraction of land worth to area residents, still dazed from the shock of devastation (Klein, 2007).

Speculative economic pursuits coupled with deregulation of major corporations across the country have left millions of working people in dire straits—many who at another moment in history lived the "good life." Today, the myth of the "good life" tied to consumption still gains traction in the corporate media; but the promises of neoliberal speculative schemes fall flat for the majority who became prey to the "prosperity" glitz.

In *Decolonizing the Revolutionary Imagination*, Reinsborough (2004) argues that a "key to debunking the neoliberal myth of growing prosperity" is to understand through our community practice that,

> None of the money circulating in the speculative economy feeds anyone, clothes anyone, nor does it provide anyone with meaningful jobs. Rather, the speculative economy is mostly just a way for rich people—through their corporate institutional proxies—to use the money they already have to make more. Moreover, this massive speculative economy is a powerful destabilizing force that threatens local economies and ecosystems, since speculation is the opposite of sustainability and encourages a deeper disconnect between ecological realities.
>
> (p.213)

Characteristic norms of economic inequality are often enacted within community relationships that inadvertently affirm the very system they seek to challenge. The centralization of power is generally embraced at the expense of community autonomy and self-determination. People enamored by the "little kingdom" they establish become easily competitive and threatened by community people who challenge their arbitrary authority. The consequence here is that authoritarian views are preserved, reinforcing reliance on both physical and ideological relationships of dominance and control. Often media fabricated stereotypes of "the other," fuel distortions and delusions which seep into the organizing arena, potentiating false, racialized attitudes and beliefs that further fragment community relationships, rendering cultural knowledge as irrelevant.

The far-reaching web of capital has cleverly eclipsed the relational significance and relevance of subordinate cultures, by way of messages that reinforce materialism and blind consumption, as well as an unwarranted faith in the power of technology. There is no question that capitalism has effectively driven the planet closer to ecological collapse, as important support systems have been undermined by pathologies of power and hopelessly flawed values that seek to homogenize the very meaning of being human.

Most unfortunate here is the manner in which the "overconsuming class" fails to connect their affluence to the brutal poverty of three quarters of the world's population. In stark contrast, those who live in the shadows of monstrous affluence know only too well that the world remains in an economic vise (Reinsborough, 2004; Darder & Torres, 2004). By naturalizing the notion of life as toil and dreariness from which one must escape, rather than life as a blessing that inspires infinite creativity and connection, capitalist norms provide fodder for its structural and ideological machinery. If I cannot partake of political grace, deep relationships and authentic dialogues with others in community, then I am easily colonized by notions of dreariness, whose respite is fantasy and escape, either to a tropical island for vacation, or of "saving the world," or to a homogenous "American dream" peddling mechanistic formulas of consumption and work. How can I challenge the status quo if I depend upon it for my very identity, worth and sense of value? How can I say no to a system, which insists that I age and make decisions according to my exploitability—where my productivity and retirement are tied to my ability to generate quantitative profit?

There is little doubt that the Western mind is largely conditioned to enact dominion and mastery over all life, in its search to reach beyond human confusion, emotional anxieties and corporeal disruptions—including the sweaty, burping, farting, lusty body. This misguided yearning for transcendence from the earth into the heavens engenders mystifications and authoritarian fantasies of absolute control that alienate and interfere with organic relationships and ecological respect. In contrast, decolonizing approaches work to shatter social norms that displace the body and emotions in the act of knowing, in order to support communal relationships of embodied solidarity, trust and faith, shared responsibility for the welfare of the community and respect for the sacredness of all life. Within such a context, love as a vital revolutionary force infuses political grace into our community struggles, guiding us toward new possibilities for a more just world.

POLITICAL GRACE AND DECOLONIZING COMMUNITY PRACTICE

> *The human being, this vast and complex combination of pain and joy; solitary and forsaken, yet creator of all humanity; suffering, frustrated, and humiliated, and yet endless source of happiness for each one of us; this source of affection beyond compare, inspiring the most unexpected courage; this being called weak, but possessing untold ability to inspire us to take the road of honor; the being of flesh and blood and of spiritual conviction—this being is you!*
>
> (Thomas Sankara, 1990)

Paulo Freire consistently sought to ask, as should we, how those who enter oppressed communities can labor in ways that respect the wisdom, cultures and histories of the oppressed. This is particularly significant, given the mainstream culture of "expert" intervention, with its emphasis on profit, product or quick-fix solutions. Too often such efforts, inadvertently, splinter and uproot community self-determination (albeit unintentionally), as community members become colonized objects of study or organizing pawns to be instrumentalized for purposes beyond their own interests. Rather than supporting the creation of conditions for greater democratic life within oppressed communities, often practices and relationships utilized in grassroots political organizing only serve to further intensify subordination and harden inequalities. The outcome is mistrust and isolation—not just for disenfranchised communities, but also for those "experts" who in their unexamined ignorance miss precious opportunities to support collective transformation.

Hence, decolonization is necessary for all participants in a community, including those who occupy dominant or privileged social position. One cannot effectively exorcise damaging social beliefs and habits on the personal level without practically and theoretically identifying and challenging the collective structures that give rise to their production. In this process of decolonization, both oppressor and oppressed must reclaim and reassert the primal and central value of human life. This is made more difficult by privileging a rationality which has been narrowed to exclude "subjective" qualitative experience, as simply a luxury, a diversion or a matter of inconsequential taste. This subjectivity is counter-posed with an authoritative objectivity that pretends it exists only as natural law, without human roots. Again the alienation is evident.

The rationality that sustains such alienation is by necessity emotionless and spiritless. Those that would inscribe exploitation as human nature or as necessary means to desirable "profit" must find a way to deny that suffering or other qualitative states of being or experience have any value. Indeed, these attributes might otherwise be contemplated and weighed as costs, against the supposed benefits of exploitation. In the light of full examination, many, if not most, community members would judge the personal and social costs of exploitation too high and the systems that run on them (i.e., unrestrained capitalism) as invalid. So a kind of conceptual disciplining is enacted to exclude those costs from consideration. Love, for example, is made suspect, worthless or mere grist for fantasy; uncertainty an invitation to nihilism. Trespassing into subjective or uncertain realms are discouraged or prohibited (particularly for those seen as "other"), otherwise the larger claims to order, control, and predictability might be exposed as charades, along with the authority occupying "objective" structures. Fear of difference becomes the sentinel, denial a means of self-protection. Vulnerability becomes a kind of crime or, at the very least, an act of an irrational or naïve person. While, systematic cynicism reinforces hopelessness and despair.

The empowered community, embodied by political grace, threatens to undo all these pretensions. Hence, it is no wonder that systems of exploitation, including unrestrained capitalism, function to deny those collective practices which inspire political grace. Even assistance to the marginalized must reinforce dependency and resist challenges to this system—becoming a form of projection and fantasizing, whose aim is to fulfill individual narcissistic perceptions or identity about how the helper (i.e., organizer, teacher, community leader, etc.,) wishes to be regarded, rather than on changing the structural problems and conditions that give rise to voicelessness, suffering or exploitation.

Hence, what gives the concept of political grace its significance in decolonizing community practice is its relational power as a catalyst for resistance and transformation. To better reckon with what this means requires us to comprehend all people as full human beings. That is, an understanding of humanity as predicated on the intersections of physical, intellectual, emotional and spiritual life. Key to this perspective is an abandonment of Western scholarly traditions that relegate to inferior status or popular metaphysics anything that cannot be directly seen and measured. In its place, a decolonizing view of life embraces all aspects of our humanity, within the relational encounters that are essential to our participation as full subjects of history (Darder, 2002).

In fact, Rehberg (1995) in *Political Grace: the Gift of Resistance* affirms, "that the gift of political grace is the offer of full participation" (p. 26) and characterizes its presence and function as a decolonizing force in the following way:

It is an "other" which refuses categorization and systemization, ratio-nalization, yet which phenomenally appears to assemble in ways that privilege the unprivileged. This "other" offers itself as another dimension to the . . ."wretched of the earth." Though it defies naming, it discloses itself while its divine aspect remains partially unrecognizable . . . This is grace that definitively sides with the impoverished, that impels alternative possibility from its own radical alternative, that only has power of becoming material when people act in accordance with its gift. It infuses. It interrupts. It creates coincidence. It calls, yearns, struggles to be "visible," yet cannot entirely be so because of the limitations of the phenomenal realm.

(p. 22).

Political grace, then, can best be understood as an integral human experience that is the collective outgrowth of decolonizing dynamics. It constitutes an embodied force that is ever-present and exchanged freely, through relationships that embody respect and faith in the participants' capacity to name their world and, through this process, participate in transformative acts of co-creation. As a revolutionary force, shared political grace enables the establishment of "sites of resistance" where community members can reflect on their social and material conditions and grapple to find solutions, solidly anchored upon their histories, the priorities of their daily lives, and self-determined emancipatory dreams. It speaks to the enhancing power of communal experiences, which emerge freely through open, interconnected, and grounded relationships of decolonizing struggle, within the process of political transformation.

Within such an understanding of community practice, all lives are acknowledged as subjects to those who live them and, thus, have the potential of inspiring and transforming others. No one is expected to be side-lined, in order to assuage the narcissistic whims of another. Political grace in this context, is enhanced by collective heartfelt relations that promote more equitable distribution of time, attention, material resources—and the decision-making power attached to these—is among those most affected by the structures that reproduce injustice.

At this juncture, it is helpful to note that decolonizing relationships that inspire the exchange of political grace are not necessarily neat and orderly. They often are forged within radical moments of suffering that establish on-going contexts where affirmation, challenge, critique, resistance, dis-agreement, anger, joy, frustrations, confusion, confidence and other human expressions of naming the world are welcomed and expected, in the course of passionate engagement as responsible citizens of the world. Within the process of decolonizing community practice, both passive and active articulations of power are recognized as necessary parts of any dynamic that promotes democratic life. Unlike the "professional," "safe," comfortable, and carefully manicured rules of engagement of "group relations," a decolonizing dynamic supports a sacred place of convening, enlivened by passion, desire, activity, movement, fluidity, change, fears, tensions, rage, laugher, joy, noise and tears. Accordingly, participants find "breathing room" to be, to offer, to examine who they are—all from the authority of their lived experiences and their process of unearthing subjugated memories.

This encompasses a collective presence that coheres and transforms not by way of domination, but by way of political grace, generated freely within all present. In the absence of practices that humiliate and shame, freedom to exist flourishes, as participants accept greater responsibility for naming and renaming the world—a precious gift of life that we collectively nurture with humility and respect. In the presence of collectively inspired power, possibilities beyond our wildest imaginings emerge, to speak, to act, to be known; for also found in the experience of political grace is the radical courage necessary to risk the collective embrace of life-affirming love.

Political grace is, thus, generated within recognition of the comprehensive damage done to all members of a community when any participant is objectified. To objectify other persons in this space is to harm them, to reduce their subjectivity to an instrument for one's own pleasure or profit. However, objectification also precludes the humanity of the participant doing the objectifying, creating alienation and isolation. For in the process of eliminating the self-expressed subjectivity of the other and replacing it with one's own design, one eliminates relationship and the possibility of authentic dialogue. One is walled into one's own perceptions, desires, falsehoods acted out in a world of objects with no true human beings, merely projected representations of humans. Therefore one becomes an object of one's own gaze, driven by unexamined and unchallenged ideas, emanating from a preserving self-reference to one's own humanity, obligation, and contingencies, made void of the capacity to care or love that which resides outside the narcissistic realm (Fromm, 1964).

Through human connections bathed in political grace, a liberatory sense of love is generated, which is neither projection, domination, romanticism, or ideology, but rather more like the sustenance water, sun, and soil give a seed. This signals a sense of support that retains and honors the creative tension, as a precondition of human relationships. This kind of support, in both individual and communal relationships, respects and honors the presence of an organic space of "betweeness"—a generative gap, between our commonalities and differences—necessary for the emergence of transformative possibilities and collective co-creation to take root (Yiamouyiannis, 1998). In this light, our community accomplishments are collective works in the art of living, where the fuel for our co-creation is generated by the spiritual dialectic of our multiple encounters. Community practice from this vantage point is fundamentally decolonized when we acknowledge freely that no human endeavor is ever truly the product of a sole creator.

Last but not least, a decolonizing community practice must also be tied to our capacity to bare witness to life, not as passive spectator, neutral observer, or jaded critic, but as full participant in a revolutionary process to save ourselves and each other from the hellish conditions of alienation and greed. Herein, we bare witness to suffering and beauty, to war and peace, to anguish and joy, to the living and the dying. As such, political grace emerges and regenerates through the power of our connections to one another and to the earth; to life and our inner being. Ultimately, it is this powerful force that inspires our life commitment, beyond our alienated and fractured self-absorptions; to bare witness to the wonder of our sisters and brothers; and in solidarity with them, take back the dignity, freedom and self-determination that are our only birthrights as integral human beings.

YOUTH SPEAKS! DECOLONIZING
COMMUNITY PRACTICE IN ACTION

> *Even after a document was signed proclaim we were free*
> *You still raped our women and hung men from the trees*
> *And yes we were strange fruit*
> *But you'll never take our roots*
> *We will continue to create*
> *And maybe you will continue to hate*
> *But that too will end up on my pen and paper*
> *I let everyone know you are a hater*
>
> (Youth Speaks Poet)

> *The word speaks to culture, struggle, education, politics, Hip-Hop and*
> *community . . . informing potential . . . continuing our oral tradition.*
> (Youth Speaks website see: www.youthspeaks.org)

The communal tradition of spoken word summons the two-fold nature of resistance, which encompasses the communal embrace of political grace and new articulations of power as co-creations of new possibilities and transforming histories. First words become tools of resistance, which unmask the contradictory notions of law and justice—the gap between the legal and cultural image of justice and the practical lived reality of marginalized groups. Secondly it confirms a collaborative and horizontal empowerment, generated internally by the community and the lived experiences of its members. Radiating outward and onto the creative act, such resistance is *not* conferred by an orthodox hierarchical authority. Instead, it asserts its own kind of moral and historical authority to put "the system" itself on trial and under a microscope, to be probed and observed, subverting colonial dynamics of power.

The creator and cultural worker of the lyrics above, and many others like her, are part of a growing creative and collaborative movement known as *Youth Speaks*. The organization is a community, youth-inspired space (see:www.youthspeaks.org), that generates offerings of "slam poetry," a penetrating, incisive expression of lived perspectives, which challenge the gauzy fantasies peddled to youth by the commercial, economic, and political status quo. What makes this movement unique is its commitment to supporting the creative production of knowledge among its members, rather than simply the typical creative space of reception/rejection. *Youth Speaks* attempts to "shift perceptions of youth by combating illiteracy, alienation, and silence to create a global movement of brave new voices . . . [challenging] youth to find, develop, publicly present and apply their voices as creators of social change." What started as a community effort to involve youth has now evolved into established efforts to create a 'history department' in the Living Word Project, "using the model of performed ethnography to develop a consciousness around the social impact of historical elements that are somehow 'missing' from traditional educational texts."

The personal transformative effect this has on the *Youth Speaks* community, as well as the social effects it has for those who participates as witnesses of these co-creations is striking. Mateo, a twenty-seven year-old Filipino American, *Youth Speaks* participant, who was recently profiled in the *San Francisco Chronicle* (Vigil, 2008) (grew from a seventeen-year-old participant of the program to a mentor and director of one of the community programs. As he puts it: "It's hard to know where I would be without poetry, but I know where I am with it . . . Through words, poetry has the power to change the world. You make your parents laugh and cry by the words you share with them. You vote for your president by the words they speak."

Community members of all ages, who witness the spoken word events, gain a palpable understanding of the powerful ways in which the messages, habits, and philosophies of capitalist exploitation, in particular, are experienced and challenged by the courage of transgressive youth to speak the unspoken. Where capitalism accentuates ignorance and inspires insularity—for the purposes of maximizing profit—*Youth Speaks* brings together co-creating young poets in order to deepen their awareness of self and others. They find solidarity, not just from their camaraderie, but through the ways in which each is the other's witness. Through their communal relationships of affirmation and challenge, their shared passion and honesty helps participants to reach more deeply into the well of their integral humanity, so they can experience the fluidity of political grace among them, in order to create and express that which is most hidden and vulnerable, but often most meaningful.

Where capitalist norms engender emotional holes, deficits, doubts, insecurities, plastic pleasure, and fabricated needs to be filled by neurotic consumption, *Youth Speaks* participants explicitly challenge these manipulations, name the holes and deficits they create, and call into poetic account the personal and collective damage perpetrated upon the oppressed. For example, one poet expressed through his spoken word how body images in magazines assault his girlfriend; encouraging her to hold unhealthy attitudes about herself, and affecting his ability to form deeper connections with her. What makes these young people critically conscious is that beyond their individual concerns, they know that their struggles are collective and involve the well-being of their communities. It is a sense of community wellness and health that extends beyond individual concerns into the realm of collective empowerment.

Where capitalism requires a zero-sum, homogeneity of value—a fabricated "single scale scarcity"—*Youth Speaks* promotes heterogeneity and abundance as a necessary precondition of good spoken word. There is a sense of understanding that the word is born long before it is spoken (as Freire so rightly claimed) and encompasses the interconnectedness of communal distinctions. Different voices, different subjects, different ethnicities, different experiences, different sexualities, all express value as they are shaped and experienced coherently, through a free and ever-changing poetic medium of spoken word. No matter the source, a poem's ability to evoke and call into reality powerful truths that transcend the individual poet is not only what creates value and meaning, but what enhances the communal relationships that dialectically nurture political grace.

Inherent in capitalist relations is treatment of members from disenfranchised communities as mere recipients, hardened passive objects at the service of capital, rather than sentient and actively engaged citizens of the world. *Youth Speaks* supports youth as co-creators, as sensual subjects of history, through enacting their collective power and capacity for co-creation and collaboration within a dynamic process of community life. The *Youth Speak* community is composed of passionate initiators and active witnesses, in stark contrast to community projects that favor the passive spectators and referential servant.

The norms inspired by capitalism emphasize physical and/or quantitative material as holder and arbiter of value. *Youth Speaks* emphasizes the emotional as the holder and channel of value. Where capitalism feeds on fear, secrets, and privileged, surveilled access, the community of *Youth Speaks* poets and participants feed on courage and transparency, in the process of revealing their hidden truths, struggles, hopes and dreams within the human condition. Where capitalism promotes a splitting apart of the public and private, in its effort to privatize and shatter the public, *Youth Speaks* stridently encourages the sacred alliance of public and private, in its bold public offerings of searing and poignant insights, traumas and triumphs.

The spoken word of *Youth Speaks* poets shatters those myths of capital that deceptively promote leisure and untroubled neutrality as exemplars of the "good life." Instead, the *Youth Speaks* community offers troubled waters of nitty-gritty realities that bare witness to our complex humanity, incited by revolutionary imaginings inspired by passion and purpose. This is a courageous community of youth that seeks to remain vigilant, rather than to escape into fantasy and magical thinking as the "medium" for coping or deriving pleasure. They reject capitalism's relational investment in producing remoteness from Bourgeois assumptions about a cruel, dreary, or boring world. Decolonizing communities like *Youth Speaks* thrive on intimacy and presence; moving closer to the subject and one another, not farther. Inherent here is an intuitive impulse within this community of youth that sparks them to fend off their objectification and alienation, by delighting in the power of communal presence and the precious gift of being alive.

POLITICAL GRACE AND THE COURAGE TO LOVE

The Master's tools will never dismantle the Master's house.
(Audrey Lorde)

Youth Speaks, as a "site of resistance" exemplifies one of the most salient contemporary responses to Audrey Lorde's often recited dictum. Youth in these communities, along with those who witness and support their efforts, re-assert the communal power of oral tradition in their own cultures and, as such, the transformative potential of political grace, unavailable to the oppressed in the "Master's house." *Youth Speaks*, Oaxaca's indigenous people, independent media groups, and many other community-grounded communities and organizations around the world recognize that liberation is neither a process that can be guaranteed nor or an object that can be possessed. Instead, it demands our full presence and the collective courage of political grace born from resistance and struggle. Only in this way might we, together, forge the wisdom, faith, and strength of revolutionary consciousness to leap into the fire of human anguish and suffering, so that we might liberate ourselves and one another from the colonizing legacy of Western imperialism.

Just as young cultural workers of *Youth Speaks* reach out to one another, utilizing the tools of their own histories and lived experiences, we too must find the courage to struggle in solidarity to break with the alienating morass of capitalism that deadens our lives and betrays our revolutionary dreams. Our collective struggles to decolonize community practice are, intimately, tied to our personal struggles to liberate and awaken our minds, bodies, hearts, and spirits to the communal dance of life—a dance inspired by political grace and our renewed commitment to the power of love.

REFERENCES

Darder, A. (2002). *Reinventing Paulo Freire: A Pedagogy of Love*. Boulder, CO: Westview.

Darder, A. (2008). *Pedagogy of the Oppressed Revisited* in Public I Urbana, IL: CU Independent Media Center (11).

Darder, A., and Torres, R. D. (2004). *After Race: Racism After Multiculturalism.* New York: NYU Press.

Fanon, F. (1952). *Peau Noire, Masques Blancs.* Paris: Seuil.

Fanon, F. (1967). *Black Skin, White Masks.* New York: Grove.

Freire, P. (1971). *Pedagogy of the Oppressed.* New York: Seabury.

Fromm, E. (1964). *The Heart of Man.* New York: Harper & Row.

Klein, N. (2007). *The Shock Doctrine: The Rise of Disaster Capitalism.* New York: Metropolitan Books.

Martinez Luna, J. (2006). *Communality and Autonomy: A Compilation of Three Essays and Two Declarations by Indians of the Northern Sierra of Oaxaca.* (Translation by G. Salzman and N. Davies.) Available at : http://site.www.umb.edu/faculty/salzman_g/ Strate / Commu/index.htm.

Mohanty, C. T. (2003). *Feminism Without Borders: Decolonizing Theory, Practicing Solidarity.* Durham and London: Duke University Press.

Rehberg, W. (1995). Political grace: The gift of resistance. PhD dissertation, SUNY at Binghamton.

Reinsborough, P. (2004). Decolonizing the revolutionary imagination: Values crisis, the politics of reality, and why there's going to be a common-sense revolution in this generation, in D. Solnit (Ed.) *Globalize Liberation.* San Francisco: City Lights Book, pp. 161–211.

Sankara, T. (1990). *Women's Liberation and the African Freedom Struggle.* New-York: Pathfinder.

Vigil, D. (2008). Youth Speaks Encourages Young Poets in San Francisco Chronicle (March 30). Available at: http://www.sfgate.com/cgi-bin/article.cgi?f=/c/a/2008/03/30/PK4TVMO2S.DTL.

Yiamouyiannis, Z. (1998). Toward a philosophy of interpersonal self and self-esteem. Doctoral dissertation, Cultural Foundations of Education and Curriculum, Syracuse University (UMI No. 9842213).

2   Caribbean Thought and the Practice of Community

Jennifer Lavia

INTRODUCTION

Community is always deeply implicated historical and politically. Located in this way, community occurs within complex, contested and heterogeneous terrains, shaping and being shaped by cross cultural interactions, holding out the potential of being creative sites of dialogue, knowledge reception and knowledge production. This chapter concerns itself with constructions of community and the practice of community in a postcolonial context. It takes the Caribbean region as its site of inquiry as it seeks to explore how the effects of globalization occur in specific ways within specific local scenarios allowing forms of social action to emerge. These "vernacular discourses" (Appadurai, 2001) are decolonizing in intent and take on an agenda of social justice that seek to interrupt traditional, oppressive discourses of community on the one hand and on the other hand forge "strategies, visions and horizons" (Appadurai, 2001: 3) that promote the centrality of the poor and oppressed and the communities which have given birth to them. It is in this pursuit of democracy, full human development and capabilities and social justice that a practice of community becomes a decolonizing project.

This chapter shares, with other chapters in this book (see Darder and Yiamouyiannis; De Souza and Andreotti; Ellis; and Moore for example) a deep concern for the location of community in relation to colonial histories. Such histories have fashioned and continue to fashion centre/periphery relations and yet despite centuries of enslavement, indentureship and discursive and material evisceration subaltern communities have struggled to regain and reclaim their cultural confidence. The chapter therefore also seeks to offer insights into the problem of defining community within a postcolonial context.

Existing debates about community often tend to be portrayed from a position of marginalization and difference. Often silenced, ignored and unrecognized, constituent members of identified communities are perceived as mere recipients of aid and expertise. Represented in this way, ideas about human development are usually framed within binaries of donor-recipient relations and these images become even more vivid when they are considered in geo-political terms of development involving north-south interactions. Very rarely is any recognition paid to the contribution to knowledge that is evidenced by the work of marginalized communities; more so cultural expressions of indigenous organisation are often regarded as exotic practices that are culturally curious. In this way, the chapter offers to current debates about the politics of representation, a critical, postcolonial analysis of the experience of community (re-) constructed philosophically and methodologically through "epistemic virtues" of postcolonial theory, feminist theory and poststructuralism (Rizvi, 2009: 109).

In this chapter I contend that these philosophical and methodological endeavors, made visible through Caribbean thought embrace "issues of historicity, reflexivity, relationality, positionality and criticality" (Rizvi, 2009: 109) to navigate issues of identity and community. My understanding of community has been shaped by a vantage point of being a Caribbean woman, educator, researcher and activist. The assertion of such an epistemic location is not accidental but a choice to privilege a perspective of the colonized about how internal effects of colonialism and new forms of globalization are felt and experienced within every day Caribbean life. A commitment to a decolonizing agenda leads me to explore the centrality of Caribbean thought and to show how conceptions of community have been influenced by political, economic, cultural and feminist analyses that have unapologetically focused on transformational practice that confront the regimes of power.

This chapter is divided into four sets of narratives. The first reflects on dilemmas and opportunities for researching communities. The second presents the Caribbean problematic of defining community in light of culture and identity. The third presents an example of grassroots pedagogies. The fourth segment deliberates the issue of cultural confidence.

RESEARCHING COMMUNITY

Researching community is unsettling! That is if common assumptions are to be confronted and interrogated. In the previous chapter Darder and Yiamouyiannis discuss the necessity for developing political grace as a central philosophical and methodological strategy for decolonization within community contexts. Moving through grassroots pedagogies, they underscore affects of political engagement by the community, for the community, that articulate the courage to transgress in the face of social injustice.

I refer here to the concern with decolonization in light of how practice can be transformative. However, I am mindful that the intent of practice may not necessarily lead to outcomes that are transformative. As such the (postcolonial) researcher may be precariously perched within the field of inquiry having to negotiate states of in-betweeness that require deconstruction of self in relation to the local and the global. My intention here is to propose how a postcolonial reading of community can broaden understandings of the ways in which people struggle to make sense of the world from their vantage points.

Appadurai (2001) describes vantage points as social imaginaries that struggle to be articulated through place, space, method, language and media. Here, the epistemological conundrum is unpacked through processes of inquiry intended at 'catching that circulatory logic' constitutive of cultural engagements and flows. Positionality is shaped in this sense through 'cultural motion' through the uncertainty of shifting terrains and through re-interrogation of relationships of "history to the present" (Appadurai, 2009: 48).

Rizvi has underscored the importance of finding vantage points and locates this philosophical and methodological process within a set of dispositions which he calls "epistemic virtues" (Rizvi, 2009: 109). These include "issues of historicity, reflexivity, relationality, positionality and criticality [which] have become central to the research approach" (Rizvi, 2009: 109). Given that virtually all communities are globally networked, Rizvi has argued for an examination of the field in light of the globalizing effects on the day-to-day experiences of the community. Further, he has argued that the field is determined by the location of the researcher, and this location in turn determines the configuration of engagements that circulate through cultural exchange.

The issue of vantage point is also profoundly posed by Linda Tuhiwai Smith when she declares "from the vantage point of the colonized, a position from which I write, and choose to privilege, the term 'research' is inextricably linked to European imperialism and colonialism" (Smith, 1999: 1). Smith deconstructs research in light of its representation as a 'collective memory of imperialism' that allowed a research process which intervened in the day-to-day lives of indigenous communities, shaping and reframing these communities as objects of inquiry. Borrowing from Edward Said, Tuhiwai Smith emphasises that the intent of this collective memory as manifest through dehumanising research processes was foundational to establishing positional superiority of Western knowledge in which "knowledge and culture were as much part of imperialism as raw materials and military strength. Knowledge was also there to be discovered, extracted, appropriated and distributed" (Smith, 2006: 557).

My concern with the issue of researcher location is that it is critical to the quality of questions that ought to emerge in researching community. In this sense I return to the notion of how complex and unsettling rules of engagement can be. Here I am referring to the deeply-rooted connection between colonialism as a specific form of imperialism with ways of being, thinking and living of communities that have been othered, through epistemic regimes that are normatively positioned. Here postcolonial theories become useful theoretically and methodologically.

Speaking of the "postcolonial" in the context from which I write, is an acknowledgement that the term conveys ambiguity, and occurs within a contested terrain; this "affirmation of ambiguity, porosity and translations" (Dimitriadis & McCarthy, 2001: 3) presents opportunities and possibilities for interrogating the complexity of the conditions of postcoloniality and more specifically for unearthing the "complicated interrelations" (Dimitriadis & McCarthy, 2001: 3) occurring within transnational encounters. In these terms, postcolonial theories offer a language of critique and a language of possibility (Freire, 1970). It is in this sense that I speak of the postcolonial where an aspirational disposition is adopted through the agency of everyday life.

Consequently, developing a politics of hope is central to the process of decolonization. With such a process lies a deeply educative function which according to bell hooks "enables us to confront feelings of loss and restore our sense of connection. It teaches us how to create community" (hooks, 2003: xv). Here, Appadurai has proposed a case for strengthening a capacity to aspire "which argues that aspiration, the capability to hope, is itself a maldistributed capacity whose maldistribution properly understood might arguably be even more salient a feature of poverty or even a definitional feature than income inequality or other material deficits" (Appadurai, 2009: 46). Thus, Appadurai speaks of the urgent tasks of strengthening agency through representation and developing "voices as a cultural capacity." In this sense communities "will need to find those levers of metaphor, rhetoric, organization, and public performance that will work well in their cultural worlds" (2004: 67).

As I end this first narrative I highlight the epistemic conundrum that interferes with building capabilities of hope within the Caribbean region. Nettleford has written that "Caribbean society is in dire need of a sense of community and of integration of personal awareness with collective consciousness" (2003: 144). What hope of cultural confidence then can our communities have given the conflictual, violent and contrived historical circumstances of our people in the region? What is the role of the public intellectual in reclaiming community in the region's own terms? According to Nettleford "great systems of thought spawned by indigenous Caribbean Experience and a developed intellectual capability are still not seen as possibilities that can emerge from the archipelago" (2003: 145). It is to these epistemic, cultural and political concerns that I turn to in the second narrative of this chapter.

HISTORICAL MOMENTS ON IDENTITY AND CULTURE

According to Girvan (2001) "at the close of the nineteenth century the Caribbean had not yet been invented. The nation state was very much a privilege of the imperial powers" (p.18). Notions of community within the context of the Caribbean may be viewed from different vantage points. Girvan has stated that "the definition of the Caribbean might be based on language, identity, geography, history and culture, geopolitics, geoeconomics, or organization" (Girvan, 2001: 4). Whatever the traditional academic fractures might be, each disciplinary stance begins to coalesce around understandings of globalization and its affects for more than 500 years upon the region. Girvan continues, "both the name itself and its later application to a geographical zone were inventions of imperial powers" (2001: 4).

Community in this multi-disciplinary sense therefore comprises a range of political arrangements mainly based on historical configurations but also based on the requirements of the Caribbean to give account of itself globally. The Caribbean Community (CARICOM) is a case in point.

CARICOM, which today comprises fifteen territories within the Caribbean, has positioned itself as a means by which regional integration can be realized through a pursuit of economic integration and cooperation among its members. The motivation for such an economic cooperative resides in the several failed attempts at regional integration and rapid economic, political and technological changes internationally as well as the desire for a common Caribbean identity. In that light, in the 1980s CARICOM established a West Indian Commission to investigate the requirements for forging a common Caribbean identity and to redefine the region in its own terms. It engaged in what Best (2000) referred to as "a diagnostic," to re-position the Caribbean as region and peoples in light of its own understanding of itself; its inner vision and its capabilities. In this sense "the notion of Caribbean has been and is being continuously redefined and reinterpreted in response to external influences and to internal currents. The Caribbean is not only multilingual, it has also become transnational" (Girvan, 2001: 6).

> Despite the dilemmas and vicissitudes of identity through which Caribbean people have passed and continue to pass, we have a tiny but important message for the world about how to negotiate identity.
>
> (Hall, 2001: 25)

According to Stuart Hall, what constitutes a Caribbean cultural identity has become a central concern in light of a diverse range of effects of globalization in particular the insights to be gained in understanding "important movements of decolonization, of independence, of nationalist consciousness in the region" (Hall, 2001: 26). These same sentiments are echoed by Nettleford who has claimed:

> The entire world is gone "creole"—in the Caribbean sense of forging from the disparate elements of a "village-world" new expressions which are challenging Caribbean peoples to a new sense of being, a new worldview and by implication, new ways of knowing.
>
> (2003: xv)

Globalization is not new to the Caribbean. Indeed, interpretations of the Caribbean have been shaped by the way the region has endured and survived over 500 years of European colonialism. Notions of community at macro, meso and micro levels of policy and practice are impacted subtly and overtly by the ways in which Europe disrupted well-established civilizations, uprooted them and transplanted many of them in the global space called the Caribbean. In this sense community was forced and forged out of contrived means on the one hand and survival on the other and as Stuart Hall's claims "everybody from the Caribbean comes from somewhere else" (2001: 27).

Both Hall (2001) and Nettleford (2003) have noted that common ground of community is therefore problematic especially in relation to issues of identity and how the Caribbean comes to know itself. According to Nettleford (2003) "We continue to speak of this region of some 30 million people as *Hispanic* or *Ibero* Caribbean, the *Anglophone* Caribbean, the *Francophone* Caribbean, the *Dutch-speaking* Caribbean and so on. Such hyphenated fragmentation emphasises the legacy of a heritage of separation and shattered identities" (xiii). Yet the common experience for the peoples of the Caribbean is that we were all dislocated, transplanted and translated and then educated to live within actual and virtual realities of the plantation.

George Beckford (1972) in a critique of Caribbean political economy has written, "The plantation was an instrument of colonization" (p. 30). He extends his argument to relate that contemporary Caribbean societies continue to evidence the structures and practices of the plantation. According to Beckford, the plantation was an economic unit designed for wealth accumulation. Seen as "institutions of international dimensions" (p. 37), the plantation became the apotheosis of social, political and economical relations, where expatriate voices were made legitimate by virtue of their economic right to rule. On the plantation the slave had no voice.

Beckford (1972) extends his thesis to examine the development of the plantation community. He states "we find that the plantation community is one with an inherently rigid system of social stratification" (p. 54). Thus life on the plantation for those who work on the plantation is about survival and "regardless of cultural or ethnic differences, the plantation is a binding of force that welds people on it together" (p. 54). In this regard, the Caribbean community is made up of peoples and societies "crafted through the cross-fertilization of disparate elements. The Caribbean itself the expression of such diversity as well as survival and beyond, has struggled for all of five centuries with the task of mastering the management of the complexity of such diversity"(Nettleford, 2003: xi–xii).

It is Frantz Fanon who aptly expressed the deep-rootedness of the colonial imagination. Just as the plantation was the unit of social and economic organisation, it was also the psychic space of acculturation. Colonial attitudes and values reproduced through education systems ensured the imperial schooling of young colonials; a mechanism designed to ensure the thorough internalization of a hatred of self and preference for the contrived self. It is in the effort to decolonize the mind that contribution of Caribbean thought to self-determination can be interrogated.

INDEPENDENT THOUGHT

Prior to 1960s and 1970s, Caribbean intellectuals such as C.L.R James, Eric Williams and Sir Arthur Lewis had already signaled an interdisciplinary epistemic authority about the conditions of the Caribbean in relation to itself and to the rest of the world. Dimitriadis & McCarthy (2001) in deconstructing James' work have written:

> For James, the intellectual is not simply an academic or an expert ensconced in the safety of the ivory tower; the intellectual is a transformative social subject committed to a particular articulation of the classed, raced and gendered interests, the needs, desires and aspirations of embattled social groups. The intellectual straddles the contradiction of the world of the private, solitary practice of scholarship and the public world of embattled masses, their popular imagination and their popular will.
>
> (p. 42)

Eric Williams led the nationalism movement in Trinidad and Tobago. Williams' seminal work *Capitalism and Slavery* provided original scholarship on the issue on the Trans-Atlantic trade in slaves. Williams' thesis located the Caribbean within the context of the world economy as opposed to previous colonial interpretations where the Caribbean was represented as tangential to economic development of Europe. The text was the first of its kind to consider the Caribbean as a colony of exploitation and acknowledge the Caribbean as the subject of its research. In other words what Williams did was to speak from the voice of the colonized to provide an historical account of the relationship between the Caribbean and globalization.

Sir Arthur Lewis' intellectual contribution was awarded a Noble Peace Prize in 1979 for it influence on development economics. Lewis, like James and Williams located his theory of development within the lived colonial experience of the Caribbean and this "grounded *development economics* in a model which assisted in establishing the subject as a distinct area of economics" (Levitt, 2005: 336). According to Levitt, Lewis's contribution can be seen in the intent

> that developing countries have to engage the world economy on their own terms, not on terms set by global markets or international institutions. His emphasis on the internal and domestic wellspring of development and the primacy of domestic food production, directly

challenges currently prevailing economic doctrine which holds that countries which do not adjust domestic policies to global markets will be marginalized.

(2005: 336)

The significance of drawing upon the example of these public intellectuals is two-fold. In the first instance, if we are to talk about community in relation to the Caribbean it is necessary to refer to the epistemic references which lead us into different interpretations of community. I return here to Rizvi's argument about the location of the researcher and the necessity for such a location to be guided by ethical practice including historicity, positionality, rationality, criticality and reflexivity. These three contributions interrupted and challenged the cannon by setting agendas on the Caribbean's own terms. The second point of significance resides in the unapologetic and strident acknowledgment of the link between the globalization and development as distinct conditions of a colonial experience. The colonial question therefore was recognized an invasive of all social systems of the Caribbean and the right to development had to be reclaimed in light of global imagination.

In the 1960s and 1970s there was an upsurge in intellectual activity in the Caribbean. Stimulated by international radical movements of the time, and disenchantment over the promised project of decolonization that had not been realized, young Caribbean intellectuals, influenced by theories of structural economics and critical theories, led a wave of innovative intellectual projects about Caribbean life and development.

Lloyd Best, one of the main proponents of the notion of "independent thought" co-founded the New World Group in 1960. This group drew together creative intellectual capabilities from within the Caribbean into philosophical and dialogic endeavors to rethink economic, social and political development and systems in light of postcolonial aspirations of the Caribbean. In other words, the task of developing "epistemic sovereignty" is one which begins a commitment to examine the Caribbean from inside the Caribbean. According to Best (2004) to recognize community is to acknowledge the three problems requiring constant interrogation:

The first problem is the population is introduced and transplanted. The second problem is that the population is introduced from many different cultures and institutions and they have to make it anew in a anew place. And third thing is that they were colonized. So in addition to the adaptation to each other, to one another, they also had to adapt to the straightjacket in which they we put by the colonizer.

(p. 5)

Best (2000) insists that Caribbean as community would be forged through "a diagnostic" that will make sense of the complexity of the Caribbean;

establish epistemologies and ontologies about the Caribbean; [and] engage in critical policy studies that would lift the debate and practice "above local peculiarities and individuals" to the level of discourse (p. 283). This stance calls for "articulation of a moral philosophy—in the old sense—starting from history as well as social, cultural and physical geography, to arrive at an ontology, and epistemology and a hermeneutic" (p. 284). Further he conceded that "a theory of action" is critical to "survival and viability" of the region. In the final analysis, Best is strident in advocating that the Caribbean learn the lessons of the ancestors rather than beginning from metropolitan pronouncements. Best's conclusion that "in the end there is nothing so practical or compelling for finding creative composure as reverting to being, knowing and the reinterpretation self, with the aid of both myth and reasoned history" (p. 284) seeks to overcome Walcott's constant reminder of one of the barriers to community when he says, "But we are all strangers here" (Walcott, 1998: 10).

CARIBBEAN FEMINIST THOUGHT

Conceptions of community within the Caribbean context have also being shaped by feminist Caribbean thought. Here, the epistemological and practical project of confronting power (Barriteau, 2003) has been pursued in ongoing dialogic spaces and processes "of confrontations, resolution, contradictions, and contestation" (Antrobus, 2004: 35). Contemporary Caribbean thought is made richer by the critiques of Caribbean feminist (Antrobus, 2004; Barriteau, 2003; Baksh-Soodeen, 1998; Mohammed, 1998, 2002; Reddock, 1998, 2004 for example) who in the course of interrogating regimes of power set themselves the task of constructing a practice of community that "continues to develop a politics of epistemological and activist engagement with societal institutions and practices" (Barriteau, 2003: 9). In this way, the epistemic journey has produced narratives of a different kind, ones that repel pathologies of *othering* by asserting agency and ones that draw us closer to understanding the contextual complexities of everyday lives of Caribbean women.

   According to Antrobus constructions of understandings about communities of women are to be found in "the assertion of women's agency" (Antrobus, 2004: 39). Two texts provide the central concern in this regard. The first is that of context. It is the context that shapes constructions of feminism where, in the case of the Caribbean, circulatory logic impacting the feminism movement is to be found within struggles against colonialism, for nationalism and in sympathy with international actions and movements for social justice. The second, more fundamental case for agency according to Antrobus is "the internal process of feminist conscientization" (2004: 39). Antrobus elaborates that the process of coming to feminist consciousness for many Caribbean feminists has been in the course of "discovering their own marginalization *as women*" (2004: 39) where there has been a blurring of the lines between the personal, professional and political. Caribbean feminism has also kept close to a decolonizing agenda in which the transformative function of social action and political movements have been the creative sites for unearthing an inner vision of self as *woman* and *woman* as community. In the Caribbean to speak of *woman* as opposed to *women* signifies a profound and powerful imaginary of resilience and survival that is meant to enjoin a collective consciousness.

Caribbean feminist scholarship has largely been responsible for drawing the region's attention to spaces of inequality, marginalization, impoverishment and exclusion. In tracing the historical development of the women's movement in the Caribbean, several writers have acknowledged the strategic role of agency where women have acted on behalf of and through their communities. Antrobus (2004: 41) makes the case that during the period 1940–1960 "although they did not name themselves 'feminist' the women who worked to promote changes as part of nationalist struggles, acted out of consciousness of themselves as women within societies that sought to circumscribe their lives, and they acted in solidarity with other women to challenge male privilege and power where this was present."

One of the most significant developments with regard to women's participation in Caribbean development was the establishment of the Women and Development Unit (WAND; and subsequently the Centre for Gender and Development within the University of the West Indies). According to Antrobus (2004) "regarding the work of WAND, the establishment of the unit within the then Extra-Mural Department, a space within the university with a tradition of being responsive to the needs of the communities serves, was intended to give it the autonomy and freedom to allow women across the region to define its programme" (p. 45). The women's movement was able to mobilize communities of women to set agendas for change through multi-level, interdisciplinary networks that encouraged grassroots participation in local, national, regional and international activities.

The WAND programme brought to bear the lessons learned from communities of women in the 1940s and 1950s where as Joycelin Massiah notes "one of the characteristics of the Caribbean women's movement is its inclusiveness allowing for a wide variety of views, styles, concepts and approaches" (Messiah, 1998: 9 quoted in Antrobus, 2004: 42). The education agenda of the programme was central to the aim of developing feminist concientization and this, coupled with materials production and dissemination created a range of grassroots pedagogies for community development, agricultural extension and participatory research.

Reddock (1998) in recounting the history of the women's organizations in the Commonwealth Caribbean details the work of the Caribbean Association for Feminist Research and Action (CAFRA). Reddock has noted:

The significance of CAFRA lay in its decision to challenge head-on the prejudice and negative assumptions traditionally associated with the concept of "feminism." In so doing it sought to define a Caribbean feminism which links women's subordination with other systems of subordination—race, class and nation- and sought to go beyond traditional boundaries of language and culture.

(p. 63)

In this second narrative I drew upon some examples of indigenous intellectual histories within the Caribbean to show how the problem of subaltern consciousness struggles to be articulated within a politics of representation and recognition. The public intellectual in the Caribbean has no choice but to don multiple role of intellectual and activist where practice is regarded more in terms of praxis and poised to seize and create opportunities for transformation, revolution and change that are culturally relevant and intent on developing capabilities of hope.

I turn now to the third narrative where I describe the work of a grassroots organization which has taken up a practice of hope.

HOW CAN WE HELP? GRASSROOTS PEDAGOGIES AND THE CONTEXT OF COMMUNITY

Fazal Rizvi (2009) has placed emphasis on the inextricable link between globalization and postcolonialism. He has argued that "colonialism does not cease to have salience just because a country has become independent. It affects all aspects of life in one form or another" (p. 104). Consequently the legacies of colonialism perpetuate and in the course of development hybrid forms of responses and reconstruction to the normative strategies of oppression struggle to be articulated within new spaces and possibilities. It is in this light that SERVOL emerged.

SERVOL (Service Volunteered for All) is a non-governmental, community-based organization that stands as an expression of the imagination of a community that works for its self-determination. According to its philosophy, SERVOL "is an organisation of weak, frail, ordinary, imperfect yet hope-filled and committed people seeking to help weak, frail, ordinary, imperfect hope-drained people become agents of attitudinal and social change in a journey which leads to total human development" (Pantin, 1992: 1).

The architects of the SERVOL (a Catholic priest and a well-known West Indian cricketer), took the simple step of walking through one of the most deprived communities of Port of Spain, the capital city in Trinidad and asked the simple question to the huge number so unemployed youth who were hanging out in the streets: "How can we help?" The selection of the community of Laventille was itself very significant and worthy of further inquiry. It is in this community during the period of slavery, that some of the Africans, who were enslaved and brought to Trinidad, escaped the brutality of the plantation and set up spaces of freedom. Laventille then developed on the basis of the physical defiance of a transplanted and traumatized people, refusing to be subject of enslavement. It is also in this community that the steel pan (the only musical instrument to be invented in the twentieth century) was born. Best (2000) has reminded us that a significant part of our creative consciousness created by a historical need to survive or perish is through our various art forms, for example, making space where is none (i.e., the limbo) and creating something to give to the world out of nothing (i.e., the steel pan).

Derek Walcott, poet and cultural critic expresses the settings that could very well be a community like Laventille in this way:

> To set out for rehearsals in that quivering quarter-hour is to engage conclusions not beginnings, for one walks past the gilded hallucinations of poverty with a corrupt resignation touched by details, as if the destitute, in their orange-tinted back yards, under their dusty trees, or climbing to their favelas, were all natural scene designers and poverty were not a condition but an art. Deprivation is made lyrical and twilight with the patience of alchemy almost transmutes despair into virtue. In the tropics nothing is lovelier than the allotments of the poor, no theatre is as vivid, voluble and cheap.
>
> (1998: 3–4)

The theatre of the street was metaphorically played out when Gerard Pantin and Wes Hall walked into the community of Laventille. Pantin who was a teacher at a high school at the time reflects:

> All teachers are born ignorant. I have had the unusual, experience of having ignorance thrust upon me at the age of forty-two! Imagine what it is like to have and Honours Degree in Science, a Diploma in Education and a Licence to teach Theology, and to walk into the ghetto world of switchblades, guns and sudden violence in an attempt to "help" the community. Suddenly, I was a child again, stripped of all pretensions and illusions, confronted by naked hostility and suspicion and having no idea where to begin. There and then under the inspiration of sheer panic I discovered my philosophy of ignorance.
>
> (1983: xx)

Pantin emphasizes that we must assume that we know nothing about the community than run the risk of displaying "cultural arrogance". By this he means that too often engagement with communities is often based on a drop-in syndrome where the community is an object of charitable offerings. This point is also made aptly by Darder and Yiamouyiannis in the previous chapter. Smith (1999) also recoils at this practice in respect of indigenous communities in New Zealand. This is an epistemic problem that disregards the value of indigenous knowledge and imposes upon communities, representations and practices that may be inimical to their development.

The SERVOL philosophy is also expressed through a practice of attentive listening, dialogue and negotiated access to the voices of the community. In this regard, it adopts a stance of respectful intervention in which there is sensitivity and high regard for the organic nature of the community that it knows what it wants. SERVOL's philosophy also accepts the community as a communicative space in which disparate formulations of the notion of family converge and find confidence in an organized way through a collaborative education.

The SERVOL model, which has been celebrated as exemplary by the United Nations and other global institutions, has been able to internationalize itself through the adoption of its model in other territories in the Caribbean, in South Africa and in parts of Europe, each adapting the framework to suit their cultural contexts. What is significant in this example of community is the all embracing use of grassroots pedagogies positioned on pillars of hope that touch the daily lives of members of communities from early years to the elderly. SERVOL has established life centers and life development programmes in early childhood education, adolescent development, parent out research programme, disability programme and elderly care programmes along with matching the employment needs through vocational skills training and the development of advance technology centers. Additionally, the programmes offer second opportunities to a range of peoples in a range of difficult circumstances.

The example of SERVOL offers us a practice of community that can be clearly associated within the "epistemic virtues" as outlined by Rizvi as discussed earlier. SERVOL offers five pedagogical projects that are couched within integrated themes of "cultural survival, self-determination, healing, restoration and social justice" (Smith, 1999: 142).

CONCLUSION: CULTURAL CONFIDENCE AS ASPIRATION AND THEORIES OF HOPE

I conclude with a final narrative of the chapter; this is the issue of cultural confidence. I posed the question earlier of what hope of cultural confidence can there be for Caribbean community given the fractured histories. Cultural confidence can be found to reside in the development of a collective consciousness which according to Spivak "is *the* ground that makes all disclosures possible" (Spivak,1988: 2002). She specifies that consciousness in the context of subalternity is decidedly historicized and political.

In his fictional narrative Lamming describes the Caribbean community in terms of the collective consciousness of the village. He has written:

> It is the collective human substance of the Village, you might say, which is the central character. When we see the Village as collective character, we perceive another dimension to the individual wretchedness of daily living. It is the dimension of energy, force, a quickening capacity for survival. The village sings; the village dances; and since the word is their only rescue, all the resources of a vital oral folk tradition are summoned to bear witness to the essential humanity which rebukes the wretchedness of their predicament.
>
> (Drayton & Andaiye, 1992: 47)

In this chapter I have advanced some ideas about how understandings of community can be constructed and understood within the context of the Caribbean. These are tentative disclosures of an ongoing search in my own practice, to unearth the inner vision of a creative diasporic space and a belief in the enduring optimism of creatively colorful peoples whose traumas and healings are displayed as public performances of community life. Arguably, these interrogations will suffice a desire for "the education of feeling [which] must be at the heart of any struggle for liberation." I do hold out hope that such a decolonizing intent will serve to warn, to provoke, to question, to reposition and to re-imagine.

REFERENCES

Antrobus, P. (2004). Feminist activism: The CARICOM experience, in B. Bailey and E. Leo-Rhynie (Eds.) *Gender in the 21ˢᵗ Century: Caribbean Perspectives, Visions and Possibilities*. Kingston: Ian Randle Publishers, pp. 35–58.

Appadurai, A. (2001). Grassroots globalization and the research imagination, in A. Appadurai (Ed.) *Globalization* Durham, NC: Duke University Press, pp. 1–20.

Appadurai, A. (2004). The capacity to aspire, in V. Rao and M. Walton (Eds.) *Culture and Public Action*. Stanford, CA: Stanford University Press.

Appadurai, A. (2009). The shifting ground from which we speak, in J. Kenway and J. Fahey (Eds.) *Globalizing the Research Imagination*. New York: Routledge, pp. 41–52.

Baksh-Soodeen, R. (1998/Summer) Issues of difference in contemporary Caribbean feminism. *Feminist Review, Special Issue: Rethinking Caribbean Difference*, 59: 74–85.

Barriteau, E. (Ed.) (2003). *Confronting Power, Theorizing Gender: Interdisciplinary Perspectives in the Caribbean*. Mona, Kingston: University of the West Indies Press.

Beckford, G. (1972). *Persistent Poverty: Underdevelopment in Plantation Economies of the Third World*. Kingston: The University of the West Indies Press.

Best, L. (2000). Independent thought, policy process, in K. Hall and D.Benn (Eds.) *Contending with Destiny: The Caribbean in the 21ˢᵗ Century*. Kingston: Ian Randle Publishers, pp.274–285.

Best, L. (2004). Race, class and ethnicity: A Caribbean interpretation. Paper presented on March 3, 2001 at York University, Toronto, The Third Annual Cheddi Jagan Lecture. CERLAC Colloquial Paper.

Dimitriadis, G. and Mccarthy, C. (2001). *Reading & Teaching the Postcolonial: From Balswin to Basquiat and Beyond*. New York: Teachers College Press.

Drayton, R. and Andaiye. (Eds.) (1992). *Conversations: George Lamming— Essays, Addresses and Interviews 1953–1990*. London: Karia Press.

Freire, P. (1970). *Pedagogy of the Oppressed*. New York: Continuum.

Girvan, N. (2001) Reinterpreting the Caribbean, in B. Meeks and F. Lindahl (Eds.) *New Caribbean Thought: A Reader*. Mona, Kingston: The University of the West Indies Press, pp. 3–23.

Hall, S. (2001). Negotiating Caribbean identities, in B. Meeks and F. Lindahl (Eds.) *New Caribbean Thought: A Reader*. Mona, Kingston: The University of the West Indies Press, pp. 24–39.

hooks, b. (2003). *Teaching Community: A Pedagogy of Hope*. New York: Routledge.

Levitt, K. (2005). *Reclaiming Development: Independent Thought and Caribbean Community*. Kingston: Ian Randle Publishers.

Messiah, J. (1998). On the brink of the new millennium: Are Caribbean women prepared? The 1998 Inaugural Lucille Mathurin Mair Lecture, Mona: University of the West Indies Press.

Mohammed, P. (1998/Summer). Toward indigenous feminist theorizing in the Caribbean. *Feminist Review, Special Issue: Rethinking Caribbean Difference*, 59: 7–33.

Mohammed, P. (Ed.) (2002). *Gendered Realities: Essays in Caribbean Feminist Thought*. Mona, Kingston: University of the West Indies Press and Centre for Gender and Development Studies.

Nettleford, R. (2003). *Caribbean Cultural Identity: The Case of Jamaica: An Essay in Cultural Dynamics*. Kingston: Ian Randle Publishers.

Pantin, G. (1992). *SERVOL Through the Years—1970–1993*. Report. Port of Spain: SERVOL Ltd.

Reddock, R. (1998/Summer). Women's organizations and movements in the commonwealth Caribbean: The response to global economic crisis in the 1980s. *Feminist Review, Special Issue: Rethinking Caribbean Difference*, 59: 57–73.

Reddock, R. (2004). Caribbean masculinities and femininities: The impact of globalization on cultural representations, in B. Bailey and E Leo-Rhynie (Eds.) *Gender in the 21st Century: Caribbean Perspectives, Visions and Possibilities*. Kingston: Ian Randle Publishers, pp. 179–216.

Rizvi, F. (2009). Mobile minds, in J. Kenway and J. Fahey (Eds.) *Globalizing the Research Imagination*. New York: Routledge, pp. 101–114.

Smith, L. (1999). *Decolonizing Methodologies: Research and Indigenous Peoples*. London: Zed Books.

Smith, L. (2006). Colonizing knowledges, in H. Lauder, P. Brown, J. Dillabough, and A. H. Halsey (Eds.) *Education, Globalization & Social Change*, Oxford: Oxford University Press, pp.557–569.

Spivak, G. (1988). *In Other Worlds: Essays in Cultural Politics*. New York: Routledge.

Walcott, D. (1998). *What the Twilight Says: Essays*. London: Faber and Faber Ltd.

3 Critical Literacies in *Place*
Teachers Who Work for Just and Sustainable Communities

Barbara Comber

INTRODUCTION

L: Well if we didn't learn about this, later on, if no one learnt and no one did anything about it, the earth could like be destroyed like in 100 years.

G: It's sort of good because then you learn, then you go back and tell your parents, and then they'll tell somebody else, and they'll tell somebody else. Not everybody will do something, but . . .

L: But the great majority probably will. . . .

M: Yeah, because if we start polluting here, then it will go into Lake Sambell, into the . . . into the Murray, and that will go all the way up to Adelaide.

The young people quoted above are growing up in a bio-region facing social and economic effects of climate change in rural Australia. The conversation gives some sense of their understandings of the need to do things differently and how their learning about the environment at school filters through to family conversations and, they hope, beyond into the wider community. As a counter-balance to the students' optimism, today's teachers face complex and demanding sets of expectations that they will achieve higher academic standards, contribute to children's health and well-being, and innovate by incorporating new technologies into the curriculum; and all this in the face of global and local change of mammoth scale—populations, climate change, economic chaos, violence and unemployment.

How do teachers committed to social justice tackle such challenges as they work with increasingly culturally and linguistically diverse groups? How can teachers ethically and appropriately customize their curricula and pedagogy to challenge and recognize community "funds of knowledge" (Moll et al., 1992)? Such work is not easy to imagine and sustain in the face of increasing "audit cultures" (Comber, 1997; Wong, 2008) in education which insist on one-size-fits-all approaches and the standardization of assessment. In this chapter I draw upon theories of social justice, critical literacy and place-based pedagogies and two research projects to discuss how teachers are working ethically and creatively towards a sustainable and just society in their place(s).

In tackling these questions I am concerned with the impact of poverty on teachers' work and students' learning in particular places. The relationships between poverty (and more broadly, class) and education have been explored by numerous theorists (Bourdieu, 1991; Connell, 1993; Freire, 1970; Walkerdine et al., 2001). Our literacy studies have been especially influenced by scholars who recognize that educators can contest the usual patterns of literacy and educational achievement which relate strongly to social background (Moll et al., 1992). In other words when teachers have high expectations for young people and work with families to design meaningful curriculum, students located in high poverty and working class communities can achieve against the odds and develop positive aspirations for ongoing education (Comber et al., 2006). Such a curriculum starts from the perspectives of the most disadvantaged (Connell, 1993).

We have developed our collaborative literacy studies with teachers within the broad tradition of critical literacy, which offers teachers and learners possibilities for interrogating dominant discourses and practices which reproduce unequal power relations through language. Critical literacy is informed by a range of approaches including the work of Freire, that of anti-racist and feminist scholars, and also from the field of critical linguistics, most notably critical discourse analysis (Fairclough, 1995; Janks, 2005; Luke, 2000). Critical literacy is also informed by literacy anthropologists (Barton, Hamilton & Ivanic, 2002) who have shown how literate practices are social, cultural and ideological rather than autonomous practices (Street, 1993). Critical literacy not only involves questioning practices of privilege and injustice, but people using language to exercise power to enhance everyday life. Yet, it is also important to acknowledge the limits of literacy, and indeed pedagogy, in making tangible differences in people's immediate lives. However there may be under-explored approaches which bring together key dimensions of critical pedagogy, place-based pedagogies and critical literacy, that are sustainable for educators and communities.

Gruenewald (2003) argues that critical and place-based pedagogies have important synergies, plus important productive differences from which each stands to be enriched. As he explains:

> If place-based education emphasizes ecological and rural contexts, critical pedagogy—in a near mirror image—emphasizes social and urban contexts and often neglects the ecological and rural scene entirely.
>
> (p. 3)

As he goes on to point out the silences in both critical pedagogy (around ecology and rurality), and place-based education (around urban poverty, multiculturalism, and racism) have led to "missed opportunities to strengthen each respective tradition by borrowing from each other" (Gruenewald, 2003: 4). In revisiting Freire's work he notes that the emphasis is *both* on reading the *world* and the *word*. Gruenewald takes Freire's work as an example of critical pedagogy more broadly in his detailed analyses of the emphases and the silences in critical pedagogy and place-based education. Here I shift the focus to critical literacy. I believe critical literacy and place-based pedagogies have in common a respect for cultural and linguistic differences and an awareness of the interlinked nature of language, power, economy and place. To some degree in what follows, I attempt to take up Gruenewald's challenge in merging the two traditions of pedagogy— critical and place-based. The projects referred to in this chapter exemplify the ways teachers in urban and rural school communities work through literacy for an eco-social justice—what Gruenewald would call *a critical pedagogy of place.*

Whilst applauding the insights derived from several decades of research on literacy in communities, Moje (2000) points out that there are risks in the way in which the term "communities" is used in the context of literacy studies.

> The need for research in communities of practices outside the classroom seems clear. However, my exploration of issues surrounding community-based literacy research suggests that well intentioned though our work may be, literacy researchers risk overdetermining, essentializing, and romanticizing what it means to engage in community-based literacy if we do not define what we mean by community and explicitly acknowledge the complex nature of communities, especially the ways communities overlap, converge, and conflict . . .
>
> (Moje, 2000: 82).

Moje's warning is timely. In considering school communities, I am particularly concerned with the ways in which schools have the potential to become positive nodal points for the students, families and wider populations they serve, which are often, but not always "local." Communities are complex and changing, contested and contradictory. The very heterogeneous nature of communities—even when the common shared factor may be poverty—is what makes teaching simultaneously so demanding and potentially so rewarding. Recent housing and educational policy solutions which attempt to engineer "mixed communities" (Smith & Lupton, 2008) or "mixed-income communities" (Lipman, 2008) are based on problematic assumptions that assume deficits in the poor. The work I discuss here starts from the perspective that all communities have funds of knowledge that schools can recognize, mobilize and add to.

PEDAGOGIES IN PLACE: RESEARCHING SPACES OF "BELONGING" AND REPRESENTATION

In many senses it is hard to contain these two projects within the limits of a chapter, because the highlighted themes—change, community, justice—defy the usual boundaries of research projects. For this reason I have employed two different rhetorical strategies. In one case I give a sense of the complex long-term critical literacy curriculum around the negotiation and construction of a garden, and in the other, I have taken more of snap-shot approach by discussing a field trip to one rural school community.

*Urban Renewal from the inside out*grew out of a long-term relationship between University of South Australia (UniSA) researchers and educators in a northwestern school in suburban Adelaide. The research team worked to design and build a garden in the barren space between the preschool and the primary school and to involve university architecture, journalism and education undergraduate students and academics in the process. We already shared a common language concerned with education for social justice and a common agenda working against deficit discourses and practices to achieve significant learning for socioeconomically disadvantaged young people. With the added leadership of architect and scholar, Stephen Loo, we were introduced to the vocabularies of spatial literacies, belonging and community consultation (see Comber et al., 2006; Comber & Nixon, 2008). In terms of "community," the school is located in one of the most culturally and linguistically diverse areas of Adelaide, with the majority of families on low incomes. Many of the families are refugees from countries which have been ravaged by violence. The school is located in an area of "urban renewal" where existing post-World War II low-rent housing is gradually being replaced by housing designed for first home buyers, at a cost beyond which most of the current occupants will be able to afford.

The *River Literacies* project grew out of a long-term professional development and publication program called *Special Forever* conducted annually by the Primary English Teaching Association (PETA) since 1993 and funded by the Murray-Darling Basin (MDB) Commission. The program has produced integrated work plans across curriculum areas and engaged students in producing artistic and print-based responses to the environment. Annually it involves approximately 400 schools from across the region and approximately 20,000 primary school students engage in environmental communications work. The project gives children opportunities to publish their writing and art and showcase the talent of young people in their place.

As researchers who had worked with critical and digital literacies, our team was invited by PETA to investigate how primary teachers designed curriculum and pedagogies which engaged students in developing critical knowledge about the environment and the skills for communicating this knowledge in multi-media and multimodal texts. The research involved two main elements—a critical discourse analysis of the archive of fifteen anthologies and collaborative practitioner inquiry with eight of the *Special Forever* coordinators. The coordinators investigated their practice in terms of an eco-social justice approach and an expanded range of literacies, media and modes of communication through which young people would represent their growing knowledge and concerns about the environment. In terms of "communities," the schools were located throughout the MBD region which crosses four states of Australia and Australia's largest river system. The population includes a mix of long-term farm owners and irrigators, townsfolk providing a range of services, and more recently, people looking for low-cost housing or seasonal work. A series of droughts has gripped the region resulting in a severe and ongoing shortage of water which is increasingly recognized as "climate change." This has impacted significantly, but unevenly on the economic prosperity of the region. Some farmers are leaving the land; others are selling their water allocations; and some services are shutting down in the smaller townships.

Both studies, the *Urban Renewal* and *River Literacies* projects, involved working with complex "communities" at a time of considerable hardship and change—with many facing the prospect of uncertain economic futures and livelihoods, and unpredictable locales in which to dwell and work. During a period where globalization appears to have captured the imagination of many educational theorists, we have been looking increasingly at the impact at the local level through schools as key sites within communities and the potential of change (good and bad) for young people's learning. Schools may become central sites for people, across generations, places and cultures, to connect and form new alliances. Even in searching for the vocabulary that does a better job of describing heterogeneous local populations, it is clear that schools are located in material places catering for different families who come via different pathways, histories and trajectories. I argue that an engagement with place as curricular can afford significant opportunities for critically literate practices and the development of an eco-social justice disposition. Young people are positioned as researchers, communicators and designers and as apprentice problem-solvers of problematic places.

GROVE GARDENS

The *Urban Renewal* project, which led to the design and development of the Grove Gardens, grew from conversations between school principal Frank Cairns and teacher Marg Wells. They wanted to connect the curriculum more overtly with the neighboring community and wished for an outside place where staff, parents and students might meet, work and socialize—a garden with shade and seating. Wells and her class had already been involved with the urban developers who were designing and building new community gardens nearby. Added to this she and the principal had visited a school in South Africa where a very poor school had developed a vegetable garden to feed its students. Two of the research team, Nixon and Comber, had developed long-term relationships with the principal and teachers and won funding which allowed them to work with the children to re-make a section of the school grounds into a garden jointly designed, made and researched by the school community, university researchers and students.

The key pedagogical idea was to position the school students as researchers and designers, rather than passive observers of urban renewal. It was to make them agents of change, rather than victims of gentrification. Using the multi-disciplinary approaches of architecture, journalism and education, our aim was to make available to the students and teachers additional discursive resources for imagining change, re-designing spaces as belonging and sustainable places, and for representing relationships with place. We hoped that the university students in architecture, journalism and education, would better learn how to consult with, listen to, and teach primary school students. Hence we were concerned to shake up the usual power relationships that may exist between those who are "clients," "interviewees," students and those in the professions. The architecture students were required to engage in community consultation not only with teachers, parents and neighbors; their main "community" in this project was school children. The journalism students were involved in various ways in working with young people to document their views about the changes within the school and the wider area in terms of 'urban renewal'. Rather than making media programs about the children's experience, they were to make media accounts of various kinds with the children as co-producers. The university education students were invited to develop a transdisciplinary curriculum and co-research children's participation and literacy development.

The school students produced a vast range of texts of various genres and in different media across in the time of the project:

- Mindmaps and writing about buildings and structures
- Color and pencil drawings of the school, buildings and houses
- Drawing and writing about Central Business District structures
- "Building shapes": Computer-generated images of shapes combined to make images of interesting buildings
- Design of interiors and exteriors of buildings and favorite places
- Windows book based on the one by Jeannie Baker (1991)
- Written reflections and drawings of design elements in the parks
- Labels of objects and design elements on pegged-out to-scale designs
- Notes, drawings, paintings, 2D plans and 3D models of designs for the area
- Illustrated belonging poems
- Ideal pet environments
- Eggs as spaces and environments
- Consultation books: illustrated writing about what children would like to see and do in the area (Comber & Nixon, 2008).

Importantly work on the "word" in this project was connected integrally with work on "place," namely the Grove Gardens or other significant local places or conceptual spaces, such as the egg or the window. Children were engaged in a range of practices from measuring and pegging out their designs, to researching and planting local flora. As researchers we observed a high level of commitment, motivation and determination from the children which was sustained over several years. They learnt that they would have to negotiate and compromise on design, that it would take a very long time for the garden structures to be designed, built and available for their use; they learnt that the water feature and other things they had wished for were modified in terms of risk management and cost limitations, they learnt about the kinds of vegetation that would be sustainable.

These lessons are fundamental to learning about the world—its people and its places. At the same time they were assembling more complex spatial literacies and ways with words that could be tested in the context of an authentic "place-making" project.

Over a two year period two key teachers, Marg Wells and Ruth Trimboli designed a significant amount of their literacy curriculum around the design, making and recording of the garden and other significant places and spaces—both real and imagined. Before the garden was ready children researched which indigenous plants could survive Australia's hot summers with little water. Architect and academic, Stephen Loo worked with his students to consult with the children, teachers, parents and the community to design, build and install the shade structures, paved pathways, garden spaces and seating. There is no space here to elaborate the richness of the curriculum, nor the aesthetics of the final garden. Rather I turn briefly to the ways in which this pedagogy involved critical literacy and place-based education and in the process and over time evolved into a critical pedagogy of place.

The project invoked key principles of critical literacy in that it repositioned young people as researchers of language practices. They examined the ways in which architects, children's authors and developers represented people, places and structures. They developed a range of spatial and multiliteracies to design and argue for their preferred garden spaces. They understood that places, like language, are constructed. They began to realize the decisions people make about places and environments have long-term effects and whether people feel a sense of belonging there. A number of the young people, though only in their third and fourth year, began to voice aspirations to go to university and pursue careers in design and architecture.

Yet for all this, the project did not always meet its ambitious goals. Shortly before the garden was completed the children's artwork was vandalized by a former school pupil. The school students were resilient enough to reproduce their designs and the architecture students identified materials which would resist such attacks. In interview, some children continued to express fears about further possible damage. There were race-related references in their statements which indicated that the neighborhood beyond the school was still demarcated in various ways around culture and ethnicity. In closing with these revelations, my intention is not to under-value what was accomplished through the project, simply to note that developing a critical pedagogy of place entails grappling with the ongoing everyday politics of identity and relationships beyond the school.

DETOX SCHOOLING

In this section I refer to excerpts from field notes made during visits to schools in the Murray-Darling Basin. Approaching the writing in this way may give readers some sense of the unfolding revelations made possible by our extended field trips and discussions with educators and young people.

> We arrive in Beechworth on the Sunday afternoon before we are due to visit the school. Wendy Renshaw, the *Special Forever* Coordinator and Year 5/6 teacher, other staff and community members are at the school getting ready for the following week; we meet them there for a quick school tour. It's freezing and the school has high ceilings and big, cold corridors. Over dinner at the local hotel we appreciate more fully that this is a school "on the move" with multiple ongoing projects. We hear briefly about *Learnscapes*. The school, as an environment, is the object of study and planning; that is, children, teachers, parents and various community members participate in planning and action to make the school an environmentally sustainable institution; the curriculum is designed around the school as a series of learning scapes.
>
> Our itinerary for the next two days is outlined. Meet at Wendy's class at 9 o'clock; go to whole school assembly; observe students in Wendy's class; meet Betty a community volunteer now working part-time on *Learnscapes*; interview the principal, Jill. The next day we will interview Wendy and volunteer students before heading back via Swan Hill.
>
> The next morning we walk through the historic town of Beechworth to the school. In the light of day, we can see how Beechworth is set up for tourists—bed & breakfasts, nice restaurants, a great bakery and so on. When we arrive at the school we realize just how impressive the buildings and the grounds are. The central school building is a classic style brick building with a slate roof, built in 1875, with three portable classrooms set on five acres of land. The school, as well as many of the trees in its grounds, has National Trust Heritage listing. As we look for Wendy's classroom, a transportable building, we hear popular music broadcast through school's public address system, as the children gather. When it is turned off, it is then time for students to be lined up outside their classrooms. Wendy has a year 5/6 composite class of thirty-one students.

Wendy is an experienced teacher of twenty-six years. Her interests include environmental education, multiliteracies, information and communications technologies and visual arts. As the children enter the classroom and find their places (by finding where their sketch books are located), Wendy takes the roll informally and asks about how the weekend sports went for various students. The students are quiet, friendly, relaxed and respectful. They know the routines and things just seem to happen. Then it is time for the whole school assembly in a double classroom which functions as a hall. There are many news items, including the announcement that the school has a won a government grant to improve its grounds and develop an outside classroom; least week's winners of the golden wheelie-bin award for the class with the most litter-free lunches are also announced. The school choir sings. It's a long assembly and an autistic child makes loud noises throughout the first half. The children don't appear distracted. There is a jovial atmosphere with repartee between principal, teachers and children.

Back in the classroom, Wendy explains our visit and the options for the day's work—either finish their science report on an Indigo native or write a script and/or storyboard for a three minute animated film, radio segment or a community service announcement. Their theme is "reducing our environmental impact"; their brief, "design and create a short animated film with a clear message that demonstrates and encourages behaviours that reduce environmental impact to ensure the survival of your researched Indigo Shire bird or plant species." Small groups of students rush off to begin this task with great enthusiasm. The two groups of students I observe begin role-playing immediately. One pair of boys go straight to a computer and get head-phones.

G: Call 1800 and talk to us about how you have been doing what the . . .
L: Interview six people. What should our radio station be?
G: Is it going to be AM or FM?
Both: Stop annoying us—We're getting down to business [to other students who approach them].
L: What should our first question be? *What have you been doing on the environment lately?*

Callie and her group decide to work on an animation called "the litterer," forgetting they will have to weave in what they know about the native bird they have studied. Many forget they are meant to base their work on the research they have done around Indigo's native plants and birds. Initially the medium and genre seems to be all engrossing as they imagine themselves as talk-back hosts or various characters in a short scenario or start to make the plasticine figures for their animation. There is an explosion of clichés and stereotypical character improvisations in the first thirty minutes as they try various possibilities for their stories. Later in reviewing their drafts, Wendy demands again that they think through how to build in their in-depth knowledge into their media message. As observers we are struck by just how challenging this curriculum is and how invested these students seem to be. As lunch-time approaches, two boys from her class offer to show us a bird hide they're building near a huge wood-pile. They are clearly possessive of this space and there are other children who love the huge wood-pile there also.

After lunch, we meet Betty, a community volunteer who has been appointed part-time to help teachers and students with *Learnscapes*. She has been involved with the school for over five years and has files and records of various environmental projects they have been involved in during that time. This particular year they are seeking a WasteWise accreditation. Late on that afternoon we interview Jill the principal about the emergence of the environmental curriculum at Beechworth Primary School. We begin to understand that the school's commitment to sustainability did not just happen and that maintaining it and growing it is contingent upon more than one passionate teacher. In the interview, the principal explains how thinking about the school site as a series of learning scapes has re-oriented and re-connected a fragmented staff and alienated clientele:

> *Over the past six years we have grown from disenchantment, having little concern for each other and the environment, a lack of trust and cooperation, lack of student engagement in their learning and student learning outcomes, lack of staff morale, to a school who is proudly achieving success in all of these areas.*

She describes her initial impressions upon her appointment to the school:

> *the community was in distress, and that's all that needs to be said, and the kids didn't have much value in their own school, they didn't, it was very messy, very untidy, a lot of . . . litter. They didn't have much pride in themselves because there were quite a few discipline concerns, especially with the boys, and I don't believe the parent community had much pride in their school. So therefore we found, I found, a neutral, a neutral thing that wasn't as emotive as . . . the three Rs . . . , so we started on a project to enhance supposedly our environment, but in all of the other ways we addressed all of the other issues that we had to do.*

So they had begun to develop a vision for the school, addressing the broad question: 'What do you want from the school?' The *Learnscapes* blueprint was achieved with the assistance of a facilitator and had been developed over an extended period of time and involved the school leadership team, all teachers, community members, parents and children. Interestingly, in beginning with a shared focus on the physical environment, the principal avoids what she sees as the more emotive "three Rs." In tackling a broader malaise reported in the school community, through mobilizing the collective to enhance the school as an environment, the principal and her colleagues shift attention from less tangible matters and re-focus on doable projects with visible material outcomes, designed to enhance the health and well-being of students, staff, parents, the community, the school environment and its wider ecology.

The next day Wendy explains to us how she demonstrates sourcing reliable information about the environment from local experts, written resources and materials available on the Internet. The class has produced a rubric to critically evaluate science reports according to specified criteria. Students have chosen one species of local indigenous plant or bird to research more closely with the initial goal of preparing a report to present to their peers. Giving students significant time and strategies to build a knowledge base is crucial in enabling the communication and action that will follow. Later their illustrated reports will be mounted on the walls of the outdoor classroom for other students to read. Further, their research will guide the regeneration of a habitat within the school's own grounds in order to attract indigenous flora and fauna.

Building frameworks for understanding and action takes serious investment of time and cannot be rushed. When we invite students to come and tell us about their learning, we are overwhelmed with volunteers:

C: Well *Learnscapes* would be like just looking after our school, like planting some vegetables in our garden and stuff, and picking up the pine cones and picking up some rubbish, and yeah, and weeding the gardens and everything.

S: And there's this wet . . . there's an underground spring down the back of our school, and we're trying to make the spring come up again, and we're trying to make the water rise, so we keep putting things in there and stuff.

C: Yeah, put it back to its natural, how it was.

L: In *Learnscapes* we're cleaning up the school, and down at the basketball court there's a whole lot of weeds, bracken, that is supposed to be a little garden, and five/sixes are going to fix that garden up, and even perhaps help with *Learnscapes* and they're going around carrying wheelbarrows and pick up leaves and plant little trees.

Talking with group after group of young people indicates to us that they are conscious of the school's commitment to environmental sustainability and ethical eco-social justice. We see that this school community is conscious of its history, its situatedness within a micro-environment and the larger Basin ecology, and a sense of its responsibilities for future lives and landscapes.

The environmental communications curriculum and pedagogy at Beechworth Primary piques our interest as literacy researchers with long-term commitments to critical literacy and social justice. In attending to place and non-human inhabitants and phenomena, potentially it may address a missing element in the field of critical pedagogy (Gruenewald, 2003; Martusewicz & Edmundson, 2005). What might these goals and aspirations mean for young people's understandings of the environment, their emerging dispositions with respect to water, flora and fauna, their capacities to communicate, and their literacy repertoires? What might this mean for redesigning literacy curricula?

The projects at Beechworth were long-term, collaborative and cumulative. The school stood for something in its community and modelled ethical practices towards the environment starting with its own institutional practices regarding waste and sustainability. In terms of the students' literacy accomplishments, we could see that the serious commitment to learning and action was mirrored in the high quality work students produced. Time was devoted to students building significant content knowledge and communicative repertoires in the interests of the bigger shared project. The learning had visible and material outcomes.

The research and text production contributed to ongoing pedagogical resources available to other students, staff and community members. This approach educates young people to accomplish shared goals, as it educates them in science, new media and civic responsibility. Interestingly this school has many non-school like features, the chook shed, the trading table, the outside classroom, the half-made bird hide, the wood-pile, the gallery of student work on outdoor surfaces and fences, ribbons keeping people out of a natural scrub area under regeneration. In Gruenewald's terms (2005: 3):

> Place-based pedagogies are needed so that the education of citizens might have some direct bearing on the well-being of the social and ecological places people actually inhabit.

There are material signs of Beechworth Primary School becoming a different kind of learning place. We were increasingly struck by just how aware and active these young people and their teachers are in the MDB about global ecological challenges.

We have coined the term, "*detox* schooling," to explain this approach. As they come together to work on the school site and its surrounds, to remove rubbish, to remake specific gardens, to rebuild habitats, the school community rebuilds positive and productive educative relationships. The environmental sustainability curriculum here begins with the materiality of school—its spaces and practices—as the object of study and renewal. In "improving the school" the Beechworth educators initiate a broad re-culturing, reinvigorating, renovation and re-planting project. A whole school shared vision and a deliberate plan is important to go beyond pockets of good practice.

As we visited other schools involved in the *River Literacies* project we witnessed many instances of teachers involving local community members in redesigning an environmental communications curriculum. We saw indigenous elders, bird-watchers, weavers, rangers and many other community members find places for themselves in the school world. The school communities did not shy away from difficult issues—such as balancing the demands of tourism with damage to the river's edge; lack of access to favorite places during habitat regeneration programs, irrigators' need for water versus that of the river ecology. The teachers were actively fostering engaged citizenship and positive identity work in young people. The literacy programs were embedded in real research and action.

CONCLUSIONS

Teachers who work for justice and sustainability have a vision for their curriculum that transcends lessons, terms and school years. They work from an informed critical analysis of what it will take to make places fairer, safer, healthier and happier. Making place the object of study—with its human and non-human inhabitants—can provide a wealth of material through which young people can assemble rich literacy repertoires in representing how things might be and negotiating to make things better. When young people are involved in "changing places" for the better and contributing to the reconceptualization of space there is significant potential to alleviate the alienation and depression that can otherwise arise from the abstract study of problems such as pollution, climate change, migration, regional economic decline. I do not mean to suggest that such work is a panacea for all ills; indeed this is hard work and likely to bring to the surface contradictions and conflicts that some may wish to protect children from. However these hyper-mediated times relentlessly inform the next generation about the woes we have created; they need to have access to educative community responses both within the school and in the wider community.

It is not justice to pretend to young people that life can be sustained without changing. It is not justice to ignore the inequities that result in new houses being built for other people's children. Environmental damage, extinction of species, and urban regeneration are proper topics for a critical pedagogy of place, one that incorporates insights from research and theorizing in critical multiliteracies.

NOTES

1. The project was conducted by Comber, Nixon and Ashmore—Centre for Studies in Literacy, Policy and Learning Cultures; Loo—Louis Laybourne School of Architecture and Design; and Cook—School of Information, Communication and New Media (UniSA), with teachers, Marg Wells and Ruth Trimboli and young people from Ridley Grove R-7 School. The project was funded by the Myer Foundation http://www.myerfoundation.org.au/main. asp. The views expressed in this paper are those of the author only, and do not necessarily represent those of the Myer Foundation.
2. River Literacies is the plain language title for "Literacy and the Environment: A Situated Study of Multi-Mediated Literacy, Sustainability, Local Knowledges and Educational Change," an Australian Research Council (ARC) Linkage project (No. LP0455537), between academic researchers at UniSA and Charles Sturt University, and PETA. Chief Investigators were Comber, Cormack, Green, Nixon and Reid. The views expressed here are those of the author.
3 The Sustainability Victoria Waste Wise Schools Program assists schools to minimize waste, reduce litter and save money through meaningful integrated learning opportunities. Some schools have reduced the amount of waste going to landfill by up to 99% and have saved thousands of dollars. http:// www.gould.edu.au/html/WasteWiseSchools.asp.

REFERENCES

Baker, J. (1991). *Window*. London: Julia MacRae.
Barton, D., Hamilton, M. and Ivanic, R. (Eds.) (2002). *Situated Literacies: Reading and Writing in Context*. London: Routledge.
Bourdieu, P. (1991). *Language and Symbolic Power*. J. Thompson (Ed. and Trans.). Cambridge: Harvard University Press.
Comber, B. (1997). Managerialist discourses: Local effects on teachers' and students' work in literacy lessons. *Discourse*, 18(3): 389–407.
Comber, B. and Nixon, H. (2008). Spatial literacies, design texts and emergent pedagogies in purposeful literacy curriculum. *Pedagogies*, 3(2), 1–20.
Comber, B., Nixon, H., Ashmore, L., Loo, S. and Cook, J. (2006). Urban renewal from the inside out: Spatial and critical literacies in a low socioeconomic school community. *Mind, Culture and Activity*, 13(3), 228–246.
Connell, R. (1993). *Schools and Social Justice*. Toronto: Our Schools/Our Selves Education Foundation.
Fairclough, N. (1995). *Critical Discourse Analysis*. London: Longman.
Freire, P. (1970). *Pedagogy of the Oppressed*. New York: Herder & Herder.
Gruenewald, D. (2003). The best of both worlds: A critical pedagogy of place. *Educational Researcher*, 32(4), 3–12.
Janks, H. (2005). Deconstruction and reconstruction: Diversity as a productive resource. *Discourse*, 26(1), 31–43.
Lipman, P. (2008). Mixed-income schools and housing: Advancing the neoliberal urban agenda. *Journal of Educational Policy*, 23(2), 119–134.
Luke, A. (2000). Critical literacy in Australia: A matter of context and standpoint. *Journal of Adolescent and Adult Literacy*, 43(5), 448–461.
Martusewicz, R. and Edmundson, J. (2005). Social foundations as pedagogies of responsibility and eco-ethical commitment. In D. Butin (Ed.) *Teaching Social*

Foundations of Education: Contexts, Theories and Issues. Mahwah, NJ: Lawrence Erlbaum Associates, pp. 71–91.

Moje, E. (2000). Critical issues: Circles of kinship, position and power: Examining the community in community-based literacy research. *Journal of Literacy Research*, 32(1), 77–112.

Moll, L., Amanti, C., Neff, D., and Gonzalez, N. (1992). Funds of knowledge for teaching: Using a qualitative approach to connect homes and classrooms. *Theory Into Practice*, 31(2): 132–141.

Smith, J. and Lupton, R. (2008). Mixed communities: Challenges for urban education policy. [Editorial]. *Journal of Education Policy*, 23(2), 99–103.

Street, B. (Ed.) (1993). *Cross-cultural approaches to literacy.* Cambridge: Cambridge University Press.

Walkerdine, V., Lucey, H. and Melody, J. (2001). *Growing Up Girl: Psychosocial Explorations of Gender and Class.* New York: New York Press.

Wong, J. (2008). How does the new emphasis on managerialism in education redefine teacher professionalism?: A case study in Guangdong Province of China. *Educational Review*, 60(3): 267–282.

4 Changing Literacies
Schools, Communities and Homes

Kate Pahl

INTRODUCTION

In this chapter I look at literacy from the inside out, that is, I describe how literacy practices are constructed and understood from the perspective of homes and communities and how these visions can inform practices in other settings such as museums and educational contexts. I explore what we can learn from these family and community literacies that then can be carried over into more formal school settings. I take a "strength" perspective to families, recognizing that those literacies that are within homes are valuable and can be used as "funds of knowledge" (Gonzalez, Moll & Amanti, 2005) for literacy learning in schools. This perspective aims to foreground those missing perspectives that are often marginalized, silenced, ignored or denied. I focus on ways of hearing local knowledge of spaces, listening to narratives within communities and how it is possible to use public spaces to provide listening opportunities. I describe two case studies of practice in which narratives from homes and communities were placed in a wider public space. The first was a project involving a group of artists working with a school to place children's representations in an art gallery. The second involved a group of British Asian families who represented their family stories and artifacts in a community exhibition.

In this chapter, I recognize that relationships of power and domination are inscribed in material spaces (Gruenewald, 2003: 5) and that these places are social constructions filled with ideologies (Comber, this volume). I focus on,

> the importance of people telling their own stories (reading the world) in a place where people may be both affirmed and challenged to see how individual stories are connected in communities to larger patterns of domination and resistance in a multicultural, global society.
> (Gruenewald, 2003: 5)

I look at two examples in which communities were able to place their narratives and representations in public spaces and thereby change the way the communities were heard and represented. I argue for the importance of creating, "public spaces where communities can analyze, envision and construct the meaning of development for themselves." (Gruenewald, 2003: 5). In this chapter, I consider how identities are instantiated or realized within artifacts and how these artifacts themselves realize identity narratives. I argue that,

> the cultural materials out of which identities are fashioned are the rhetorical, poetic and visual devices through which people understand their world.
>
> (Karp & Kratz, 2000: 195)

In this chapter I look at how children and families communicate these identities through their literacy practices, and through representations in public spaces. These representations were visual as well as oral, and deployed in linguistic as well as visual and artifactual means.

I begin by arguing that literacy can be understood as a *social practice*, and is subject to power relations, and ideologies connected to control and dominant discourses (Street, 1993; 2000). Rather than focusing on the literacy that is taught in schools, that is print associated with books, and certain kinds of assessment exercises, in this chapter I am concerned with literacy in lived lives, as letters, in text messages, on screen, tangled up in drawings and images, on bodies as tattoos, as notes, as poems and as diaries (Barton & Hamilton, 1998). In this chapter I take the social and the everyday to be central to my understanding of literacy. I consider literacy to be part of a much wider communicational landscape that includes oral storytelling, visual cultures and phenomena such as dance, drama and art experiences. Everyday experience provides a rich tapestry of communication, in which print is embedded. I conceptualize literacy as young children see it, which is connected to drawing, and can be understood as multimodal that is, it is tied to meaning making that includes gesture, image and model making (Kress, 1997). I see literacy as something that is encountered in different forms, and different modes. When we go about our daily lives literacy is embedded in many other ways of communicating and being (Gee, 1999; Moje, 2000). The communities we inhabit are saturated with print, with messages, on walls, and on clothing and artifacts, intertwined with meanings that are created and found. Literacy can also be understood as spatial, that is linked to the neighborhoods where children grow up, and their sense of space and place informs their literacy lives (Comber, this volume).

In this chapter I argue for literacy research that fosters social justice through listening to local voices and concerns. I argue for a community-focused approach that recognizes the complexity of literacy when understood from the perspective of communities. I offer a research methodology that draws in the voices of marginalized communities and describe the risks of working in this way. I try and engage with local realities in concrete ways. Many communities live with racism and with the struggle for their children's voices to be heard and their visions explored. I then advocate creating new forms of knowledge that can be transferred into learning. I therefore suggest an approach that starts with *listening* to communities, translates this in to a tangible community outcome, and then creates learning resources from this that can be used in the wider context from which this project may have been a small part.

In doing so I draw on recent research that argues that considers "local literacies" to be worth listening to and honoring in literacy research (Barton & Hamilton 1998). Barton and Hamilton (1998) argued that there are many literacies connected to the many domains of life. This presupposes that literacies are plural and reside in different domains of practice. For example, Qur'ranic literacies are one kind of literacy practices (Rosowsky, 2008). Children attend school, but they also attend after-school provision for learning Arabic in Qu'ranic schools centered upon the recitation of the holy Qu'ran. Teachers in these Qu'ranic schools might teach literacy differently from the way it is taught in mainstream schools, but both are pathways through literacy. Texting and digital literacies might not be allowed in schools, but are the communicative medium of many teenagers. Young children might draw and narrate their worlds, and families might tell stories, these are all useful communicative practices that people engage within in out of school settings. Digital literacies are increasingly powerful outside school but are rarely recognized within school (Marsh, 2005). Many young people use artifacts, such as mobile phones, to accompany their social networks, in which literacy is embedded. Families have important artifacts connected to storytelling and narratives (Pahl, 2004). I focus particularly on the ways in which artifacts draw in identities and practices that can then be used in storytelling and family learning contexts, building on the heritage of elders in the community, and acknowledging the experience of migrations and transformations of identities across diasporas.

LITERACY LEARNING THROUGH ARTIFACTS

The focus of both studies was on using material artifacts, both as a way of articulating meaning, in the first study and as a way of honoring family meanings, in the second study. All families hold cultural resources within them. These cultural resources may be a family bible, or Qu'ran, a sewing machine, or a teddy bear that speak to and represent the identities of the people who use them and engage with them. When working with migrant communities it is important to hear stories of migration and listen to these stories. Many stories come with artifacts and these artifacts trigger and accompany family stories. By placing home objects in communities and museum exhibitions, it is possible to recognize different cultural identities.

Museums can offer "third spaces" where new kinds of identities can be recognized and upheld (Macdonald, 2003; Bennett, 2005). Within homes and museums are important artifacts that stretch back over generations. These artifacts can be identified with memories, with varying importance for families. In this chapter, I explore how home narratives nurture inter-generational literacies. By placing these home narratives in public spaces, I argue that it is possible to create new spaces for change. This kind of work can open up a critical space in which struggles for local knowledge within a community context are articulated, valued, heard and responded to. One of the key reasons for doing the Ferham Families exhibition was because of the artist and web designer involved with the project: Zahir Rafiq's articu-lation that he wanted to create an exhibition that reflected his reality. Faced with the threat by a racist party, the British National Party, campaigning at his children's school gates, he told the project team:

> As an Asian person myself I thought it was a good idea to get positive messages across to the general public in Rotherham, to show that, you know, immigrants contribute to this town and work really hard and to this day, the present day, they still contribute in certain ways, posi-tive images of Asians, in today's political climate, there is a stereotype of how Asian families, they just think about arranged marriages. I'm not saying that doesn't go on but the majority of people are just nor-mal, law abiding, not boring, but to just get that normal view of Asian families, common view of Asian families, common something that the white population can relate to, because at the moment they can't relate to Asian families, at the moment, but there is so much that they can, and I hope that will come out of this project, that's why I wanted to do it, it's a great cause.
>
> (Zahir Rafiq Interview, 07/19/06)

The Ferham Families exhibition, described below, was an attempt by the project team (Zahir Rafiq, Andy Pollard and Kate Pahl) to answer and challenge those stereotypes, in ways that could create new kinds of spaces and enable the families' voices to be heard.

THE CASE STUDIES

In this chapter, I draw on two case studies from two local communities that offer ways of working that can be applied to wider contexts. One was a study of a community art project and the other was a museum exhibition. I draw connections between these two cases, and focus on the crossings that take place from home to school and from home to community contexts (Hull & Schultz, 2002). In that sense, the cases themselves are bridges to help medi-ate practice and I hope they are useful for other practitioners to read.

The first is an account of how a group of artists worked in one school in a small town in South Yorkshire, in order to engage the school more closely with its community. Like the work of Comber and colleagues in Australia (Comber, this volume) and Janks and Comber in South African and Australian contexts (Janks & Comber, 2006) this project worked in a spatially oriented way to encourage children to describe and map their community through use of photography and drawings. Literacy was threaded through the project but the project's aims were wider than that, and centered around the need to link parents, school and the community, and to listen respectfully to the voices and concerns of the young children in the school.

In the second case study I describe how I worked in a community context, with a web artist and a museum curator, with a group of families, to curate an exhibition of objects and narratives of migration from families originally of Pakistani heritage called "Ferham Families." This was then placed on a website and then subsequently, material from the website was used to develop a family learning resource, for museum educators and family learning educators, called "Every Object Tells a Story." (www.everyobjecttellsastory.org.uk). The project originated from a particular community, Ferham, which is in Rotherham, South Yorkshire, and developed in conjunction with a community artist, a local museum, a local school and a family learning co-ordinator, together with a community museum curator and a university researcher. The focus was on finding out what artifacts were special to a group of families of Pakistani heritage, and how these connected to migration narratives. This research project was originally funded by the Arts and Humanities Research Council Diasporas, Identities and Migration research fund. The aim was to develop a data set and to put on a museum exhibition as well as a website to describe the families' stories. The project team found the process of collecting narratives, artifacts and putting these into an exhibition very exciting but also challenging. The challenge in that project was to represent the narratives of migration and artifacts from the homes of the families that represented their identities in the way that they wanted. The project "Every Object Tells a Story" drawing on the exhibition, created a learning resource that has been used in national and international contexts.

LOCAL LITERACIES AND GLOBAL CONCERNS

Within this chapter, I present an argument about how the local can be tied to global concerns and policies. Brandt and Clinton (2002) argued that by focusing only on local contexts, ethnographers of literacy missed the way in which some literacy practices had a "thing-like" status, such as banking practices. When we use literacy in local contexts, it is possible to trace a thread across from those local projects to more globalized forms of literacy. Street later argued that it was possible to trace these practices from local to global contexts, and to account for their embedding and disembedding beyond the local (Street, 2003). Kell (2006) in her study of women's house building practices within South African contexts argued that, "we cannot ever definitively say what is global but that we can perhaps say what is 'not-local' when we understand and make explicit the point of view of 'local'" (p. 166). Kell stresses the importance of gaining understandings from the local, and from there, she argued that it is possible to "layer up" understandings of what texts mean to participants within the contexts from which they arose. This approach was taken up more recently by Blackburn and Clark (2007) who focus on the use of literacy as a tool for social justice and change. They argue for a thorough understanding of the local and, like Kell suggest that it is important to, "examine the relationship between the local and global from the perspective of the local" (p. 19). It is this perspective that this chapter has drawn on in making connections between situated, local literacies, in local contexts, and wider, more "global" forms of knowledge that develop its own trajectories, narratives and histories.

LISTENING METHODOLOGIES

Ethnography was originally used in the context of social anthropology to build up an understanding of cultures, through, "thick description" (Geertz, 1993). In research, I find that it is a way in which through participant observations, repeated interviews, visual methods and collection of texts and artifacts, to build up a deep cultural understanding of people's meanings. Ethnography requires a reflective understanding of processes and practices (Coffey, 1999). It also requires time in the field (Jeffrey & Troman, 2004). It can be messy and complex and exhausting (Lareau & Schultz, 1996). It can involve photography and video data as well as linguistic data (Pink, 2001). It is also crucially concerned with uncovering the everyday, and paying attention to issues of power, control and ideology (Willis, 2000). In both projects, detailed ethnographic work helped build up understanding about the meanings of what was being voiced. Doing ethnography allows the making of culture, culture "as a verb" (Street, 1993) to be uncovered, as the ethnographer spends time in the field, establishing categories and beginning to make connections across the data. In ethnography there is a constant discussion between the voices of the informants, the people who might otherwise become "othered" through the research process, and the researcher (Hallam and Street, 2000). This dialogic process is constant, and recursive. In the case of the projects, interpretations were taken back to the participants in the studies to check and reflect on. The children in the first study took pictures to reflect their vision of the project. The families were involved in coding and deliberating upon the meanings created by the exhibition. Ethnographic interpretation is "dialogic between existing explanations and judgements . . . and ongoing data collection and analysis" (Heath & Street, 2008: 57). It involves recursive work, entering a field and remaining within it for a time, in this case about two years of time was spent in each community, working alongside the artists and community development workers to create a jointly developed outcome, that everyone had a stake within. Many times interpretations were carried back to the families, for them to say, well yes, but also this happened, and for further illumination to occur within the data set.

The research methods for the first project, which involved watching the impact of a group of artists who worked in an infants' school for over four years, included detailed interviews with all the staff, plus the artists. In addition, children were given cameras to record their images of the school. Children's text-making was recorded and tracked, and children were interviewed about their work. In many cases, children were keen to be heard and to tell the story of the things they were doing. Part of my work as an ethnographer was to connect up the children's visions with those of the architect and artists. Ethnographies are shaped by the timescales that construct them (Jeffery & Troman, 2004; Pahl, 2007a) and these timescales also need to adjust to both entering the field, being in the field, withdrawing from the field and then writing up the data and responding to this experience. Ethnography involves attending to everyday practice, the "taken for granted" within the field, and listening to local voices and concerns. It involves a stance that has been described as being "the familiar stranger" (Agar, 1996). In some cases data gathering followed a very intensive pattern, of going in on a very regular basis, and then returning some time later to check interpretations and feed back ways of presenting the data. In the case of the families, the families themselves helped write labels, pieces of text for the website and placed objects within glass cabinets themselves, helping co-curate the resulting exhibition.

The studies described here had the aim of making a change. In both cases the change was instigated by the community members, children and families who wanted to create new kinds of spaces. In the case of the "Capturing the Community" project, the result was a printed magazine and an exhibition of the children's images in the local art gallery. In the case of Ferham Families, the result was an exhibition and a learning resource pack together with a website. The process of doing the research was tied to a wider goal—that of social change and transformation. In that sense, 'doing ethnography' was only one part of a much wider project.

CAPTURING THE COMMUNITY

The project I discuss here was a photography project called "Capturing the Community" where children, parents, teachers and artists went out into their local community and their homes and took photographs of what they observed and then created learning resources from their images and artwork. The project was initiated by a group of community artists called Heads Together. Each child in a class of five and six-year olds was given a disposable camera to take home. They were asked to take pictures of their favorite objects in their home. The children then turned the images they created into pictures, by photocopying their chosen photographs and coloring them in, using paint. They then developed these into abstract pictures and large collaborative pictures, following the threads of their images. The parents also created images of the children's images in abstract forms. These images were then mounted and displayed at the local art gallery. A magazine created by the children and parents was printed using the children's images and stories.

I conducted a series of ethnographic-style interviews with children who participated in the project after they had taken part, and recorded their accounts of the project. I also interviewed parents, teachers and teaching assistants about the project and obtained a rich data set that reflected on the project and evoked it in language. I asked the children to talk to me about the images they took.

Here is Lucy talking about her image:

Lucy: Yeah. I took one of me dog.

Kate: (laughing) You didn't!

Lucy: It wouldn't sit still though. It just kept moving. Me dad's sat him down and put lead on him and hooked him to door and he got stuck so I took photo quick so and then when I took it back to school we had picture and we got to copy it on a piece of paper and then we got to color it in.

(Interview, March 2006)

The children did not just bring images into the classroom. The images they created conjured up stories from home—sometimes radically different from the stories that they heard at school. Some of these stories were embedded in the children's everyday worlds of pets and dolls and babies,

Katie: I took a picture of my brother when he was a baby with my two guinea pigs and I took a picture of my favourite food that I like eating and I took a few pictures of the dolls on my bed.

(Interview, March 2006)

As I heard the stories from the children, they revealed other aspects of their lives,

Chloe: I took a picture of my cat and my dad when he was in hospital.

Kate: Oh right!

Chloe: It's in the Cooper gallery.

Kate: You have told me about this.

Chloe: And me rabbits.
Kate: Are they still around?
Chloe: One of them died on January.

(Interview, March 2006)

Here, Chloe is telling her stories in the context of her pet dying and also her father being in hospital. The image of her cat and her dad was then made public in a local exhibition in the Cooper Gallery to which many parents and members of her community went. Her home stories are therefore made public in a way that children do not often experience. In the interviews about the pictures, I noticed how stories from home, some more painful than others, were evoked by the pictures they took. Here, Katie and Chloe are talking about the guinea pigs,

Katie: We've got three because my sister she used to live with me but now, and when . . .
Chloe: . . . she doesn't . . .
Katie: Her mum and dad split up, she used to live with me all the time she had a guinea pig but now (unclear) we've got two guinea pigs and hers died on um my and my sister's birthday, on the same day, so it died on both of our birthdays.
Kate: So many people have rabbits and guinea pigs who died.
Chloe: Mine bashed its head on the, it was really really schizo and he was being so schizo, he banged his head into a cage, and they were both brothers.

(Interview, March 2006)

Recent work (Scanlan, 2008) that has looked at children's stories from home, and the process of these stories coming into school has commented on how stories of loss and danger are more readily voiced if the origin is home. These stories evoke worlds outside school. The work initiated by Heads Together created something new and different—a community book with stories from the children within it.

Kate: So that's, so you took a picture of a guinea pig and you turned them into the book and you kept that. Did you keep that? (they nod) Did you turn them into a picture?
Chloe: Yes, we took a picture and then with Katy from Heads Together we coloured it in with some pastels. With some tracing paper.
Katie: She came in and we got to pick one of our pictures and I had another one and I did that one and I think it was of my dolls on my bed and she photocopied this big picture of it
Chloe: and she photocopied it in black and we went over it in colour and I picked on of my dolls on a pillow and I did that.

Katie: We had to think really well because it took quite a long time to photocopy them it took about half a day.

Chloe: it took about all morning and then we did it in the afternoon.

Kate: So quite a long day.

(Interview, March 2006)

The children described how a piece of home experience, the picture of the guinea pig, was turned into a book. The image of the dolls on the bed was also photocopied and turned into artwork. This artwork was then made public by exhibiting it in the local art gallery. The themes in these artworks came from the home domain, the artifacts of identity, the doll that Chloe identified as being her favorite object. These girls are drawing on home identities, of their life as little girls growing up. In her book about working-class girls' narratives, Steadman (1982) talks of the invisibility of working-class girls' narratives and how they are intertwined with loss and also drama of babies wanted and lost and found. The small town where this research was set had a background of former mining activity and also farming, with many families living on a small housing estate local to the school, between the town and the countryside. These voices are sometimes missed in mainstream education. The girls in Maybin's *Children's Voices* (2006) where working-class girls were given tape recorders as they went around school describe worlds outside the classroom that hinge on different kinds of narratives, connected to everyday life and loss.

In the course of watching the children and artists work together I gathered evidence that this way of working was very powerful in listening to children's voices. I have written elsewhere (Pahl, 2007b) about how a child, May, drew her home environment as part of a project in which children re-designed the school playground and mapped their play environment. As Comber (this volume) argues, children grow up in specific spaces and places that can be utilized when they compose texts, as sources of specific knowledge and understanding. Their understanding of their spaces and places of outside play, local shops, community networks and relationships can be rich sources of knowledge within the classroom. Mapping that knowledge and 'Capturing the Community' enables this knowledge to be realized and shared.

FERHAM FAMILIES

In the second project the focus was on families of Pakistani origin and the narratives and stories that could be presented in a community exhibition. As part of the project, extended interviews with key family members explored themes that were important to the family. Here I focus on one family. There was a grandfather, now passed away, and a grandmother, who originated from the Pathan regions of Pakistan. The grandfather came to Rotherham in the 1950s and made it his home. His wife accompanied him in the 1960s and it was her stories of hardship that dominated the narratives of her four children. They in turn raised families in Rotherham. Their stories were of their parents' experiences but also of who they were and what their family values were. This quotation from a longer interview with one of the family members was placed in a prominent situation within the Ferham Families exhibition:

> I talk to my sister about this from time to time, and I said to her, I said last time, everything, you know, up everything in the stars the sky, the atmosphere, the air, imagination, everything interesting right above, you get from my dad and then if you look down, everything in the soil, the grit, dirt, sweat, you know plant something foundational hard work, you get all that from my mum, do you know what I mean, and we are in the middle here hovering really, in the strange world.
>
> (Son, Interview, November 2006)

In this excerpt, as part of the interview, the youngest son of the family reflects on who he was and how his values derive from his parents. His identity is a mix of the two. This complex identity work was enabled through the project, whereby through repeated interviews, participants discussed how they themselves were situated within and across diasporic contexts.

Many of the narratives collected by the project team talked of the hardships the families experienced when they first came to Rotherham in the 1960s. While the men initially came over, the women followed, and had to adjust to the cold and the Victorian housing. The elder grandmother in the family experienced this, as told by her daughter:

> Right mum was saying in the evening we'd clear out the fire and then we'd have the firelighters, wood and the coal ready for the first person that got up in the morning would light the fire. Because she often tells us stories about how difficult it was.
>
> (Daughter, Interview August 2006)

This story was handed down the family, and became shaped and re-shaped over time, as the families told and re-told their stories to us. Hymes (1996) that this way of telling stories, of narrative as a fund for life, is something often ignored by mainstream education. Artifacts such as sewing machines evoked the ways in which the families survived and were able to provide food and clothing for themselves. For example, the daughter of the family described how

> . . . mum sewed herself. She used to make dresses for me and everything, she'd crochet, embroider and sew, learnt everything at school.
>
> (Interview, June 2006).

She described it as being

> a Singer one and it was bought when my brother . . . when he was
> born dad bought mum the sewing machine as a present. We still have
> it somewhere.
>
> (Interview, June 2006).

In the resulting exhibition, the case that was put together represented the sewing machine (not the original, which was never found) together with an example of the daughter's sewing, her wedding outfit, as well as a wad of cotton, which the family used to grow on their farm in Pakistan and used to line the duvets they used to keep themselves warm in the cold winters in Rotherham.

The case represented both the experiences of the people who told us their stories but also the material reality of their experiences. In the fore-front of the case, the daughter included images of her wedding, as well as other weddings she herself had designed. Her own interest in sewing and decoration had come from her mother, as well as her father, who had redecorated the house with her every year. Again, both parents' identities had been passed down to the grown-up children, who articulated this to us in interviews. Both the stories of the sewing machine and the wedding stories were then used in family literacy contexts within the local area as part of the "every object tells a story" family learning project. This resource is now on the web (www.everyobjecttellsastory.org.uk) and has been used in international contexts as a resource for literacy and language work in communities.

CONCLUSION

In these two projects, the important focus was on hearing the voices of the participants and placing them fully at the heart of the process. In the first example, the children presented their work at the local art gallery, as well as in a published magazine. In the second project a community exhibition and subsequent website meant that the families' words and artifacts were visible to the wider community as well as being used for family learning within schools and museums. This way of working, in which the voices of families, and the intergenerational stories within families, is radically different from the way schools operate. Schools take children of one age group and focus on particular tasks that are related to testing regimes. By contrast, in these projects stories and literacy practices in homes are embedded in a wider web of communication that involves identities, creates change and addresses local and global concerns. It is important to listen for the ephemeral, to the unheard stories from the past for things that might be missing and hear them. These projects focus on stories that lie at the heart of communities. These projects show that "Context matters. Contexts help to shape people and people shape contexts" (Lee, 2008: 268) and that by hearing these contexts, communities can be transformed.

REFERENCES

Agar, M. (1996). *The Professional Stranger: An Informal Introduction to Ethnography* (2nd edition). New York: Academic Press.

Barton, D. and Hamilton, M. (1998). *Local Literacies: Reading and Writing in One Community*. London: Routledge.

Bennett, T. (2005). Civic laboratories: Museums, cultural objecthood and the governance of the social. *Cultural Studies*, 19 (5): 521–547.

Blackburn, M. V. and Clark, C. (Eds.) (2007). *Literacy Research for Political Action and Social Change*. New York: Peter Lang.

Brandt, D. and Clinton, K. (2002). The limits of the local: Expanding perspectives of literacy as a social practice. *Journal of Literacy Research* 34(3): 337–356.

Coffey, A. (1999). *The Ethnographic Self: Fieldwork and the Representation of Identity*. London: Sage.

Gee, J.P. (1999). *An Introduction to Discourse Analysis: Theory and Method*. London: Routledge.

Geertz, C. (1993). (Fontana edition, first published 1973). *The Interpretation of Cultures*. London: Fontana.

Gonzalez, N., Moll, L. and Amanti, C. (Eds.) (2005). *Funds of Knowledge: Theorizing Practices in Households, Communities and Classrooms*. Mahwah, NJ: Lawrence Erlbaum Associates.

Gruenewald, D. A. (2003). The best of both worlds: A critical pedagogy of place. *Educational Researcher* 32(3): 3–12.

Hallam, E. and Street, B. V. (Eds.) (2000). *Cultural Encounters: Representing 'Otherness'*. London: Routledge.

Heath, S. B. and Street, B. V. with Mills, M. (2008). *Ethnography: Approaches to Language and Literacy Research: National Conference on Research in Language and Literacy*. New York and London: Teachers' College Press.

Hull, G. and Schultz, K. (2002). *School's Out: Bridging Out of School Literacies with Classroom Practice*. New York and London: Teachers College Press.

Hymes, D. (Ed.) (1996). *Ethnography, Linguistics, Narrative Inequality: Towards an Understanding of Voice*. London: Routledge.

Janks, H. and Comber, B. (2006). Critical literacy across continents, in K. Pahl and J. Rowsell (Eds.) *Travel Notes from the New Literacy Studies: Instances of Practice*. Clevedon: Multilingual Matters Ltd., pp. 95–117.

Jeffrey, B., and Troman, G. (2004). Time for ethnography. *British Educational Research Journal* 30 (4): 535–548.

Karp, I. and Kratz, C. (2000). Reflections on the fate of Tippoo's tiger: Defining cultures through public display, in E. Hallam and B.V. Street (Eds.) *Cultural Encounters: Representing 'Otherness.'* London: Routledge, pp. 184–228.

Kell, C. (2006). Crossing the margins: Literacy, semiotics and the recontextualization of meanings, in K. Pahl and J. Rowsell (Eds.) *Travel Notes from the New Literacy Studies: Instances of Practice*. Clevedon: Multilingual Matters Ltd., pp. 147–172.

Kress. G. (1997). *Before Writing: Rethinking the Paths to Literacy*. London: Routledge.

Lareau, A. and Schultz, J. (1996). *Journeys Through Ethnography: Realistic Accounts of Fieldwork*. Boulder: Westview Press.

Lee, C. (2008). "2008 Wallace Foundation Distinguished Lecture: The centrality of culture to the scientific study of learning and development: How an ecological framework in education research facilitates civic responsibility. *Educational Researcher 2008:* 37(5): 267–279.

Macdonald, S. (2003). Museums, national, postnational and transcultural identities. *Museum and Society* 1(1): 1–16.

Marsh, J. (Ed.) (2005). *Popular Culture, New Media and Digital Literacy in Early Childhood.* London: Routledge/Falmer.

Maybin, J. (2006). *Children's Voices: Talk, Knowledge and Identity.* Hampshire: Palgrave Macmillan.

Moje, E.B. (2000). To be part of the story: The literacy practices of gangsta adolescents. *Teachers College Record,* 102 (3): 651–690.

Pahl, K. (2004). Narratives, artifacts and cultural identities: An ethnographic study of communicative practices in homes. *Linguistics and Education.* 15 (4): 339–358.

Pahl, K. (2007a). Timescales and Ethnography: Understanding a child's meaning-making across three sites, a home, a classroom and a family literacy class. *Ethnography and Education.* 2 (2) pp 175–190.

Pahl, K. (2007b). Creativity in events and practices: A lens for understanding children's multimodal texts. *Literacy* 41(2): 86–92.

Pink, S. (2001). *Doing Visual Ethnography.* London: Sage.

Rosowksy, A. (2008). *Heavenly Readings: Liturgical Literacy in a Multilingual Context.* Clevedon: Multilingual Matters.

Scanlan, M. (2008). My story in a box. Unpublished PhD thesis, University of Bristol.

Steadman, C. (1982). *The Tidy House: Little Girls Writing.* London: Virago Press.

Street, B. V. (1993). Culture is a verb: Anthropological aspects of language and cultural process, in D. L. Gradoll etal. (Eds.) *Language and Culture.* Clevedon: BAAL and Multilingual Matters, pp. 24–44.

Street, B. V. (2000) Literacy events and literacy practices: Theory and practice in the New Literacy Studies in M. Martin-Jones and K. Jones (Eds.) *Multilingual Literacies: Reading and Writing Different Worlds.* John Benjamins Publishing Company: Amsterdam/Philadelphia, pp. 17–29.

Street, B. V. (2003). What's "new" in New Literacy Studies? Critical approaches to literacy in theory and practice. *Current Issues in Comparative Education 5(2).* Available at: http://www.tc.columbia.edu/cice/articles/bs152.htm.

Willis, P. (2000). *The Ethnographic Imagination.* Cambridge: Polity Press.

5 Culturalism, Difference and Pedagogy

Lessons from Indigenous Education in Brazil

Lynn Mario T. Menezes de Souza and Vanessa Andreotti

INTRODUCTION

This chapter seeks to understand and illustrate conflicts between local indigenous knowledges and global knowledges in educational policy and pedagogical practices. It is divided into three sections. The first section offers a brief overview of the theoretical debate around culturalism. The second section takes as an example the context of indigenous education in Brazil, where, in spite of the fact that present official policy purports to valorize and defend local knowledges against previous policies of assimilation and extermination, it encounters what appears to be resistance on the part of indigenous communities. This section proposes a means of understanding this resistance and the profound cultural conflicts and perceptions on which it is based. The last section outlines the implications of the theoretical debates and example of indigenous education in Brazil to educational agendas based on social justice. This section presents the conceptual framework of the educational project "Through Other Eyes" (TOE) as an example of an attempt to address the issues and challenges identified in this chapter.

CULTURALISM

Krishnaswamy (2002) speaks of the "unprecedented valorisation of the cultural" and the "culturalist turn" in recent social, post-colonial and globalization theories. Krishnaswamy analyzes the work of non-Western theorists such as Said, Bhabha and Spivak and criticizes the socio-constructionist "culturalist" manifestations of these theories for fore-fronting "internal" and "semiotic" as opposed to "external" and "material" aspects such as the economic and the political in struggles for social justice:

Culturalism has not always been content to "complement" traditional modes of analysis of the political and economic systems; rather it has sought to displace or even subsume the economic and the political with(in) the cultural by claiming a certain theoretical priority and critical prerogative for cultural analysis. If the explanatory value of a theoretical category derives from its ability to rigorously demarcate and distinguish, the indiscriminate and promiscuous invocations of culture in contemporary theoretical discourses of globalization should, I believe, prompt us to take a more critical look at the category itself [. . .] We may need to radically refashion the category of culture before we can reclaim its true subversive potential and produce knowledges that are truly transformative.

(123)

Wendy Brown (2006) in contrast, focuses on mainstream Western, Eurocentric discourse but also recognizes the recent valorization of the cultural. In her analysis of this discourse, Brown considers that the culturalization of conflict and difference has the effect of depoliticizing both of these terms; like Krishnaswamy, she sees the need to problematise the concept of culture. However, for Brown, this time from the point of view of Western discourse, the culturalization of conflict and difference ideologically produces an opposition between culture and individual moral autonomy in which liberal democratic culture promotes the vanquishing of culture and the emergence of the individual moral subject as critical, possessor of will, reason and independence of choice. For this liberalized individual, culture becomes a background or a context for moral and ethical action and not a restraint on such action. This belief, according to Brown, produces an us–them opposition between Western liberal, democratic cultures and non-Western, non-liberal cultures which, emphasizing a collectivity, do not permit the emergence of an autonomous moral individual; for such societies, it is believed that rather than a background or context for action, culture is a restriction, dictates values to its members and only permits undemocratic collective action, with no individuation, no rationality, no will and no choice: "[. . .] 'we' have culture while they 'are' a culture. Or, we are a democracy, while they are a culture" (150–151).

Brown goes on to show how the logic derived from this culturalist opposition between non-liberalized culture and moral autonomy articulates a series of oppositions in terms of equality, justice and freedom: "liberalism considers itself unique in its capacity to be culturally neutral and culturally tolerant, and conceives nonliberal "cultures" as disposed towards barbarism" (150–151). Ironically, Brown's suggestion to overcome these culturalist dichotomies is by way of culture itself, by critically exposing the cultural and religious origins of these beliefs. However, rather than depoliticizing conflict and difference as "cultural," Brown's strategy is to *politicize* the cultural.

The Canadian indigenous educator Marie Battiste (2004) defines culturalism as an academic and pedagogical posture, inherited from colonialism, based on the assumption that mainstream (i.e., "Western," "colonial," "Eurocentric") culture and knowledges are the global and universal norm to which indigenous, local knowledges and cultures deviate from. A culturalist perspective, according to Battiste, homogenises both Western and indigenous knowledges and defines indigenous cultures as deficient and lacking. Battiste proposes a reconceptualization of "mainstream" non-indigenous culture as heterogeneous and changing and suggests that as a stand against culturalism, all cultures should be seen in terms of their constitutive internal complexity, heterogeneity and diversity. For Battiste this heterogeneity is a result of the intercultural contact that occurs between indigenous cultures and non-indigenous cultures. In spite of this contact, for Battiste, each culture maintains a certain degree of specificity and difference on the basis of which the cultural identity of each community is constituted. Battiste clearly rejects the notion that these differences be seen in terms of the cultural superiority of any one culture.

Also defending the focus on the internal complexity and heterogeneity of cultures, Benhabib (2002) calls for a politicization of cross-cultural discussions of difference. She states that "understanding the other is not just a cognitive act. It is a moral and political deed" (p. 31) and suggests a heuristic distinction between a "social observer" and a "social agent":

> The social observer—whether an eighteenth-century narrator or chronicler; a nineteenth-century general, linguist or educational reformer; or a twentieth-century anthropologist, secret agent or development worker—is the one who imposes, together with local elites, unity and coherence on cultures as observed entities.
>
> (p. 31)

In contrast to the position of the "social observer" the position of the "social agent" is that of a participant in a culture, experiencing its traditions, stories, rituals, myths and material conditions through shared, contested and contestable accounts. For Benhabib (2002), the point of view of the "social observer" does not take into account the observer's own social, historical and ideological positioning in relation to the other culture being engaged with. The position of the "social observer" of cultural difference reveals "a view from the outside that generates coherence for the purposes of understanding and control" (p. 30). Benhabib suggests that a problematization of culturalism requires seeing critically the interrelationships of the self and the other, understanding the implications of the differences and perspectives of the two positions of the social observer and the social agent, avoiding a simple relativism and moving toward a critical constructivism. For Benhabib, this critical constructivism cannot accept the relativistic stance that "anything goes" nor can it fall into a trap of universalistic normativism; she suggests that "democratic equality", a product of politicized appreciations of cultural interconnectedness and asymmetries and of the varying positionalities of "self" and "other" in intercultural engagements, should be based on a notion of "weak universalism." This "weak universalism" assumes that shared norms can exist, but need to also be contingent in the sense that they may need constant adjustment when taking into account the cultural backgrounds and the varying degrees of interrelatedness and its implications between participants in actual intercultural engagements.

In a similar spirit attempting to "politicize" culturalism and situate cross-cultural encounters and engagements within a context of established asymmetries of power, Peterson (2001) calls for a critical awareness of the symmetries, benefits and dangers involved:

> In response to challenges of increasing cultural diversity, [. . .] we can have important relationships and common ground with people who are very different from us. These connections, however, do not come easily. They require conversation [. . .] but conversation alone is not enough. Emancipatory conversations are the fruit of work together, the result of alterations in relationships between groups. [. . .] In order to create community with people from different backgrounds, in order even to hold meaningful conversations with them, we need to work together [. . .] we need not merely to accept their differences.
>
> (pp. 236–237).

Peterson, citing Welch (1999: 63–64), emphasizes the insufficiency of this need to go beyond merely accepting difference and plurality—patronizingly "tolerating" the difference of others as *them*—in order to perceive how these engagements can change *us*:

> [W]e can see foundational flaws in systems of ethics only from the outside, from the perspective of another system of defining and implementing that which is valued [. . .] Enlarging our moral vision [demands] a process of learning to see the world through multiple lenses.
>
> (pp. 63–64)

The consideration of culturalism as discussed in this section helps to explain and contextualize the valorization of cultural over political aspects in our analysis in the next section of this chapter where we examine the apparent resistance to empowerment in indigenous education in Brazil.

THE BRAZILIAN CONTEXT AND THE CULTURAL LOGIC OF PREDATION

Unlike most of the other South American nations, the indigenous population of Brazil represents less than 1% of the national total; however, the political significance of this part of the population may lie in the fact that it occupies, or lays claim to 11% of the land. In terms of the definition of "indigenous," Allen (2002) criticizes the standing UN definition of an indigenous person as an "existing descendant" of an ancient people rather than of "existing nations"; for Allen, this "individuation" of the indigenous permits the incorporation of indigenous individuals and groups into existing First World social, political and economic structures. By failing to challenge the claims to homogenous national unity and nationhood made by the UN's powerful First World settler nations, the term "indigenous populations" potentially undermines all levels of indigenous self determination and permits that groups such as the English druids or the English working class may also be considered by some to be "indigenous" (p. 214).

Referring to the indigenous of New Zealand and North America, Allen describes the self-definition of the indigenous in terms of identity (*blood*) and narratives (*memory*) of connection to specific *lands*; indigenous activists in these regions have created an interdependent and inseparable triad out of blood/land/memory. A similarity with this triad may also be perceived in Brazil in the indigenous cultural "logic of predation" as we shall see. These issues of blood/land/memory are the bases of proposals for formal indigenous education which seek to valorize the indigenous in opposition to processes of cultural assimilation to a supposed national unity or homogeneity.

Formal indigenous education has existed in Brazil for centuries; non-formal, traditional, out-of-school education has always existed in indigenous communities and even where formal schooling exists, it persists parallel to the latter. The latest Brazilian Constitution of 1988 officially recognized the existence of indigenous cultures and languages within the nation and made formal indigenous education an issue of official national policy and interest. Having previously—since the sixteenth century taken, with few exceptions, the form of religious, cultural and linguistic assimilation, the recent official policies for indigenous education in Brazil aim at a "differential, bilingual and intercultural" education.

Official policy now proposes the "preservation" of indigenous cultures, languages and knowledges and recognizes that these were threatened by previous policies of assimilation. The Indigenous Education Act of 1998, informed by anti-colonial, anti-eurocentric, Freirean-oriented members of Brazilian civil society (NGOs, educators, linguists and anthropologists) clearly aims at the empowerment of indigenous communities. This empowerment takes the form of the concept of "differential education" where, different to what occurs in the non-indigenous national school system, indigenous communities have the power of decision over the knowledges to be taught, the language of instruction, the selection of teachers, the time schedule and the authorship of the teaching materials of the community indigenous school. This policy of "differential bilingual and intercultural" education assumes that, in the name of "cultural preservation," the indigenous communities will opt for schools which teach their indigenous languages, knowledges and cultures. However, the situation is not as straightforward as it may seem, and many indigenous communities prefer to use the indigenous school to learn *non*-indigenous knowledges, to learn the *national* and not the indigenous language, to use the school *occasionally* for ceremonial purposes or complex variations of these possibilities (Baniwa, 2006; Cavalcanti, 1999; Ferreira Netto, 1997; Freitas, 2003; Maher, 2007; Silva & Ferreira, 2001a; 2001b).

Considering that the official policy for the "differential" indigenous school arose from a movement originating mainly in non-indigenous civil society (Monte, 2000), to *resist* previous official policies of cultural assimilation and thus *empowering* indigenous communities, how is one to understand this apparent indigenous *resistance* to what key non-indigenous agents in the process see as *empowerment?* This section proposes a means of understanding this resistance and the profound and complex cultural conflicts and perceptions on which it is based. As such, a good place to begin may be with the *logic of predation.*

The Brazilian anthropologist Carlos Fausto (2000) describes what he calls the "cultural logic of predation" which lies at the basis of several Brazilian indigenous cultures. This logic, as the basis of a form of knowledge construction (an epistemology) is itself based on a concept of nature and existence (an ontology) which is non-humanist in the sense that it sees all forms of nature, human and non-human, as being inter-related; nature is not seen as a set of resources or "objects" at the disposal of human beings or "subjects." On the contrary, it is seen as a complex of equal, interrelated living beings, all of whom are equally "subjects"; this "equality" between beings is seen in terms of quality and not quantity. Thus different groups of living beings are considered to de "different" in *qualitative* terms, but *quantitatively* "equal" (they are not deemed superior or inferior to each other).

An important aspect of this cultural logic is the dire need for newness and difference in which each being can only survive if it acquires a quality that it does not already have. When confronted for example by qualitatively "different" beings, seen as more capable of survival than oneself, this Other being is considered to be desirable and needs to be captured and consumed in order that its perceived greater capacity may be acquired. In this process of "predation" of a perceived desirable quality, the motive is not to eliminate the difference of the Other being, but to accede to or take possession of this difference, thus transforming oneself into the other, having acquired ("predated," "consumed") the quality deemed to be desirable for sustained vitality and survival. In figurative, cultural terms this "logic of predation" is based on the perception that one is not a homogeneous stable and self-same being; one is constituted heterogeneously by differences one acquires from others. It is a cultural logic that, instead of valuing purity and the preservation of sameness, values hybridity as the basis of identity.

Given this indigenous cultural logic, how would members of such cultures see the concept of "preservation"? The answer is that "preservation" is seen paradoxically not as "the maintenance of the same" but as the constant need to acquire difference and newness in order to remain the "same." In terms of the proposals for cultural "preservation" for indigenous education and the "differential" school, whereas *officially* (i.e., from a state, non-indigenous perspective) "preservation" means maintaining the (indigenous) language and culture of the community in the school, from the perspective of the "logic of predation," it means to guarantee survival by constant change through the acquisition of newness, of difference—through the acquisition of what does not yet exist in the culture and the community; hence the varying configurations of the elements of the indigenous school (use of indigenous or non-indigenous language; use of indigenous or non-indigenous knowledge and culture) according to the specific needs of each community.

What then is being resisted and who is being empowered? If resistance is understood as resistance to domination—of a more powerful Other (Hoy, 2005)—then the cultural logic of predation, whereby one seeks to take possession of a more powerful (because it may guarantee better chances of survival) and hence desirable quality, may be seen itself as a logic of resistance. Thus, what may be seen by the non-indigenous as an apparent refusal of the empowerment supposedly implicit in the recent educational policies for "differential" indigenous education, may in fact already be an implementation of resistance and empowerment; resistance in *indigenous* cultural terms and not in the terms of non-indigenous, Western cultural logic. In other words, whereas current official policy proposes the *maintenance* and *preservation* of indigenous cultures, languages and knowledges, the indigenous reaction is to see these very policies as threats to their cultural logic of constant change and adaptation through the "predation" of more powerful newness and difference. In concrete terms, when given the option of choosing between the national non-indigenous language and the indigenous language for use in the community school, the non-indigenous national language is perceived as "different," as "more powerful" or more capable of survival, and hence as more desirable; as such, it becomes a quality of "predation" to be acquired and taken possession of; the same process of "predation" occurs in relation to the choice between indigenous and non-indigenous knowledges to be taught in the community school.

The official policy of "preservation" and the promotion of indigenous empowerment, on the other hand, may be perceived by the indigenous population as a persisting policy of domination as it hinders the cultural logic of predation and its implicit desire for the acquisition of newness and difference in the production of indigenous identity. The logic of predation may be seen to have close connections with what Allen (2002) called the triad of blood/land/memory as the basis of indigenous self-identity. Consider, for example the words of the then leader of the recently created indigenous teachers' association of the Amazonian state of Acre in north Western Brazil, Isak Pinhatã:

We believe it is time for us to discuss among ourselves and develop a proposal for [indigenous] university education. We don't accept that the [non-indigenous] institutions develop these for us, we ourselves have to be the agents of the process as we want to continue with the education of teachers in a process which we have already begun a long time ago [. . .] The indigenous teacher will act as mediator between his culture and the other culture, he will reflect upon his own and the other society. He will know what to put together in order to build a society of indigenous peoples without [outside] interference into his own ways of learning; on the contrary, he will do this in order to become stronger. Even if one masters the world of the technology of writing, one has to respect the traditional forms of learning. We have to respect the set of knowledges that goes from one's family to the elders of the community.

(Pinhatã, 2008)

The creation of the teachers' association was stimulated by, and is still housed by a non-indigenous NGO, with a long and continuing history of civil society participation in indigenous education in the region. The logic of predation may be said to be at play here in the appropriation of the non-indigenous political concept and form of a regional teacher's association that considers itself to be "authentically" indigenous.

A similar posture is echoed in the words of Gersem Baniwa, another indigenous teacher and activist from another region of the Amazon:

In order to attain self-determination, we have to also occupy the positions of authority in the (indigenous) schools. We cannot permit that other people impose things on us; we have long been dependent on others. And only now we are succeeding in attaining self-determination in the (indigenous) school.

(Cited in Ferreira, 2001: 107)

The very concept of self-determination is non-indigenous in origin and acquired through "predation" as suggested by Ailton Krenak, another indigenous activist from west-central Brazil:

[T]he idea of self-determination is very vague. Each indigenous person may understand it in a different way. And each (non-indigenous) ally of the cause imagines a different form of self-determination for the indigenous. There are models which are closer to indigenous aspirations and others which are very distant. There are indigenous communities which don't even dream of self-determination. What we are talking about is not a concept of the whole of the indigenous population, but only of a part of it, which through a process of struggle and resistance, began to understand certain forms of organization and started to assimilate forms of organization which are not indigenous. The very word ("self-determination") is strange to us.

(Cited in Ferreira, 2006: 101)

In spite of the apparent essentialism of the triad blood/land/memory, this complex cultural logic of predation paradoxically sees hybridity and change as part of the maintenance of sameness, and hence an intrinsic part of cultural "preservation." The preservation of this logic as an indigenous cultural logic may curiously and paradoxically also be understood as cultural essentialism in the sense that even though change is seen as necessary and vital, it is culturally not perceived as change but as maintenance by its members.

In spite of the valorization of heterogeneity and hybridity resulting from intercultural contact between the indigenous and the non-indigenous in settler nations such as Canada, New Zealand, the U.S. and Brazil, the risk of assimilation to the nation that these contacts seem to encourage is counterbalanced politically and culturally by cultural logics such as that of "predation" in Brazil and "blood/land/memory" elsewhere. These logics acquire a complex political dimension of resistance to the dominant logics of assimilation to the nation.

As Turner (2006) and Allen (2002) both show, in a long history of treaties and losses of land/memory/blood, indigenous communities in settler nations politically demand to be treated on an equal footing with the dominant non-indigenous community, as "nation-to-nation":

This process begins with a first stage of essentialist markers of indigenous identity and progresses toward some form of anti-essentialism. That trajectory will not exist so long as indigenous minorities insist on fighting not only for "civil" or "equal" rights within multicultural First World settler nations, but also for the re-recognition of political identities based on a treaty paradigm of nation to nation status. [. . .] the treaty paradigm requires a level of essentialism, a clear border between one nation and its treaty partner. It is the idea of that clear border, described in the shifting emphases of the blood/land/memory complex, that has made it both compelling and possible for politically, economically and militarily weak indigenous minorities [. . .] to continue to claim their distinct identities in the contemporary era.

(Allen, 2002: 220)

In relation to this *political* use of the cultural, Nandy (2003) draws attention to the concept of the modern state and its nation-building tendency to homogenize existing cultural diversity into a supposedly single national culture and national language. For Nandy, defenders of such a view see *culture at the service of the state* in the sense that cultural elements, which in their heterogeneity do not contribute effectively to the project of the singular nation, are considered defective and must be eliminated. On the other hand, in what Nandy calls a "culture-oriented" view, the state is seen as the protector of cultural diversity, and *at the service of culture*. In the case of indigenous education policies in Brazil, in the shift from a policy of assimilation to one of differential intercultural and bilingual education, the indigenous school becomes an instrument at the service of indigenous culture; if it was the contrary and culture was perceived as the instrument of the state, indigenous schools would perhaps not exist.

Therefore, it can be argued that it is in this manner—the school and the state at the service of culture—that indigenous communities perceive the role of the indigenous school. Seeking to relate to the non-indigenous state in an egalitarian state-to-state relationship, and perceiving how the state officially dictates the use of the school, indigenous communities also proceed, state-like, to dictate the use of the indigenous school, turning the school into a politically and culturally contested site of intercultural encounters and engagements. However, to their surprise and chagrin at how the indigenous communities actually use the indigenous school in officially unexpected and unprecedented manners, to serve the cultural purposes of their communities, the presupposition seems to persist—on the part of the non-indigenous actors in indigenous education—that the culture is at the service of the state and can be moulded by official state policies.

PEDAGOGICAL IMPLICATIONS FOR EDUCATION FOR SOCIAL JUSTICE

This analysis of the context of indigenous education in Brazil illustrates some of the tensions and conflicts that may arise in the interface between local and global knowledge systems. These tensions and conflicts point to the need for a different educational agenda that will equip potential "social agents," using Benhabib's terms, to understand and address the complexity of the asymmetries and interrelatedness of global and local processes and to create responsible and ethical engagements with peoples and communities who have been marginalized, silenced, ignored or denied voices.

This new educational agenda should take account of the lessons from culturalist conflicts and restrictions and move beyond a mere acceptance and preservation of difference, in order to connect the "internal" and the "external," in Krishnaswamy's terms, *and* to politicize the meaning-making, "semiotic," "culturalist" aspects of intercultural engagements, as Brown (2006) proposes. In order to achieve these aims, this agenda should support learners to acquire new tools of analysis and "new lenses," as called for by Welch (1999) and Peterson (2001).

This final section offers an outline of four pedagogical implications for this new educational agenda, emerging from the culturalist tensions illustrated in the theoretical discussions and the example of indigenous education in Brazil. In an attempt to illustrate the pedagogical process "in practice," these four implications are also mapped against the educational agenda of the UK-based Through Other Eyes educational project on indigenous perceptions of issues related to international development.

The first pedagogical implication is the need for a strategic relativisation of one's own parameters of analysis and idealized future projections. This relativization will point to the heterogeneity, partiality and context dependency of its own construction, as suggested by Benhabib (2002). This will work as a safeguard against unexamined interventions and analyses that project one body of knowledge as universal and that reinforce the position of the "social observer" who does not take account of her own positioning, as described by Benhabib (2002).

The second implication is the need for better informed and more nuanced tools of analysis that take account of power relations, the complexity of the process of construction of culture and identity, as indicated by Battiste (2004), as well as the cultural situatedness of the analyst, bridging the position of the "social observer" with that of the "social agent." These new analytical tools should transform the "objects" of analysis into "subjects," who are also carrying situated analyses and "looking back" from a different standpoint.

The third implication is the need to foreground difference and conflict as sources of learning and to learn to sit comfortably in the discomfort that this creates. This requires a reconceptualization of learning itself based on the notion of contextual negotiation and away from ideas of transmission or consensus. In this sense the logic of predation of difference of the Amazonian cultures discussed in this chapter may offer a useful pointer of where a more productive focus could be.

The last implication is the need for a different idea of relationality that opens the agenda for social justice to negotiation and to the risks and uncertainty that come with that, in an attempt to move the debate beyond the dichotomy of cultural assimilation or preservation, which homogenizes cultural difference either way. This would require the "social agent" who wants to work in solidarity with marginalized communities to engage in dialogue with these communities and to have a critical awareness of asymmetries of power and the benefits and dangers of her interventions, as Peterson (2001) advocates. This dialogue should also support Peterson's call for moving beyond merely accepting difference and plurality towards a pedagogical process focused on how these engagements can change the social agent herself. This pedagogical process politicizes difference, as Brown (2006) suggests, but also takes account of Krishnaswamy's (2002) concerns around the material and external circumstances in this encounter by emphasizing dialogue, critical awareness and mutual learning.

THE EDUCATIONAL PROJECT THROUGH OTHER EYES

These four implications are reflected in the conceptual framework of the project "Through Other Eyes" (TOE) which was based on indigenous perceptions of the agenda for international development. TOE is an international initiative that aims to support educators to develop a set of tools to reflect on their own knowledge systems and to engage with other knowledge systems in different ways, in their own learning and in their classrooms. This set of tools was designed to enable educators

- To develop an understanding of how language and systems of belief, values and representation affect the way people interpret the world
- To identify how different groups understand issues related to development and their implications for the development agenda
- To critically examine these interpretations—both "Western" and "indigenous"—looking at origins and potential implications of assumptions
- To identify an ethics for improved dialogue, engagement and mutual learning (Andreotti & Souza, 2007: 2)

The conceptual framework of Through Other Eyes consists of four types of learning which can be mapped against the implications identified above: learning to unlearn (strategic relativization of perspectives), learning to listen (taking account of complexity, power and situatedness), learning to learn (reconceptualizing difference, conflict and learning) and learning to reach out (emphasizing relationality and opening the agenda for negotiation). These concepts are expanded in the TOE publications (reproduced with permission below).

****

Learning to unlearn is defined as learning to perceive that what we consider "good and ideal" is **only one** perspective and this perspective is related to where we come from socially, historically and culturally. It also involves perceiving that we carry a "cultural baggage" filled with ideas and concepts produced in our contexts and that this affects who we are and what we see and that although we are different from others in our own contexts, we share much in common with them. Thus, learning to unlearn is about making the connections between social-historical processes and encounters that have shaped our contexts and cultures and the construction of our knowledges and identities. It is also about becoming aware that all social groups contain internal differences and conflicts and that culture is a dynamic and conflictual production of meaning in a specific context.

Learning to listen is defined as learning to recognize the effects and limits of our perspective, and to be receptive to new understandings of the world. It involves learning to perceive how our ability to engage with and relate to difference is affected by our cultural "baggage"— the ideas we learn from our social groups. Hence, learning to listen is about learning to keep our perceptions constantly under scrutiny (tracing the origins and implications of our assumptions) in order to open up to different possibilities of understanding and becoming aware that our interpretations of what we hear (or see) say more about ourselves than about what is actually being said or shown. This process also involves understanding how identities are constructed in the process of interaction between self and other. This interaction between self and other occurs not only in the communities in which we belong, but also between these communities and others.

Learning to learn is defined as learning to receive new perspectives, to re-arrange and expand our own and to deepen our understanding— going into the uncomfortable space of "what we do not know we do not know." It involves creating different possibilities of reasoning, engaging with different "logics," trying to see through other eyes by transforming our own eyes and avoiding the tendency to want to turn the other into the self or the self into the other. Therefore, learning to learn is about learning to feel comfortable about crossing the boundaries of the comfort zone within ourselves and engaging new concepts to rearrange our "cultural baggage," our understandings, relationships and desires in dialogue with "others." This process requires the understanding that conflict is a productive component of learning and that difference is what makes dialogue and learning relevant and necessary.

Learning to reach out is defined as learning to apply this learning to our own contexts and in our relationships with others continuing to reflect and explore new ways of being, thinking, doing, knowing and relating. It involves understanding that one needs to be open to the unpredictable outcomes of mutual uncoersive learning and perceiving that in making contact with others, one exposes oneself and exposes others to difference and newness, and this often results in mutual teaching and learning (although this learning may be different for each party involved). Learning to reach out is about learning to engage, to learn and to teach with respect and accountability in the complex and uncomfortable intercultural space where identities, power and ideas are negotiated, and that the process itself is cyclical: Once one has learned to reach out in one context, one is ready to start a new cycle of unlearning, listening, learning and reaching out again at another level.

(Andreotti & Souza, 2008: 28–29)

****

This conceptual framework was designed to assist educational agendas of "global knowledge systems" engaging with local-indigenous knowledge systems in order to promote more ethical and responsive mutual learning. Though this framework does not address strategies that might be necessary in political struggles between indigenous communities and Nation-states, we hope it may contribute towards an understanding of at least some of the issues involved. Through Other Eyes is currently being piloted in universities in the UK, Brazil and New Zealand in the area of teacher education.

In conclusion, a different kind of educational engagement with indigenous knowledges might offer the necessary tools for global knowledges to move beyond ethnocentric conceptualizations of culture, knowledge, reasoning and learning. This involves understanding the constitutive heterogeneity at work in the indigenous cultural logic of predation and its outer, political, appearance as essentialism whereby it perceives internal *change* as a strategy of essential and vital *maintenance*. The pedagogical implications that emerge from this discussion point to a new agenda for education for social justice where reflexivity, complexity, heterogeneity, contingency, dialogue and mutual learning become central to the learning process.

REFERENCES

Allen, C. (2002). *Blood Narrative: Indigenous Identity in American Indian and Maori Literary and Activist Texts*. Durham: Duke University Press.

Andreotti, V., and Souza, L. (2008). Translating theory into practice and walking minefileds: lessons from the project "Through Other Eyes." *International Journal of Development Education and Global Learning*, 1(1): 23—36.

Andreotti, V., and Souza, L. (2007). *Learning to Read the World Through Other Eyes*. Derby: Global Education.

Baniwa, G. (2006). *Desafios da Escolarização Diferenciada, Povos Indígenas no Brasil 2001–2005*. São Paulo: Instituto Socioambiental.

Battiste, M. (2004). Bringing Aboriginal education into the contemporary education: Narratives of cognitive imperialism reconciling with decolonization, in J.Collard and C. Reynolds (Eds.), *Leadership, Gender and Culture. Male and Female Perspectives*. Maidenhead, Berkshire: Open University Press, pp. 142–148.

Benhabib, S. (2002). *The Claims of Culture: Equality and Diversity in the Global Era*. Princeton: Princeton University Press.

Brown, W. (2006). *Regulating Aversion: Tolerance in the Age of Identity and Empire*. Princeton: Princeton University Press.

Cavalcanti, R. (1999). Presente de branco, presente de grego? Escola e escrita em comunidades indígenas do Brasil Central. Unpublished MA dissertation. Rio De Janeiro : Museu Nacional.

Fausto, C. (2000). Of enemies and pets: warfare and shamanism in Amazonia. *American Ethnologist* 26(4): 933–956.

Ferreira Netto, W. (1997). O ensino da língua portuguesa como língua estrangeira em comunidades indígenas. *Ensino de Português Língua Estrangeira* 1(1): 108–113.

Freitas, D. (2003). Escola makuxi: Identidades em construção. Doctoral thesis. Campinas: Universidade de Campinas.

Hoy, D. (2005). *Critical Resistance: From Poststructuralism to Post-Critique.* Cambridge: MIT Press.

Krishnaswamy, R. (2002). The criticism of culture and the culture of criticism: At the intersection of postcolonialism and globalization theory. *Diacritics* 32(2): 106–126.

Maher, T. (2007). Do casulo ao movimento: A suspensão das certezas na educação bilíngüe e intercultural,, em M. Cavalcantie S. Bortoni (Orgs.) *Transculturalidade, Linguagem e Educação.* Campinas: Mercado de Letras.

Monte, N. (2000). Os outros, quem somos? Formação de professores indígenas e identidades inter-culturais. *Cadernos de Pesquisa* 111: 7—29.

Nandy, A. (2003). *The Romance of the State: And the fate of Dissent in the Tropics.* New Delhi: Oxford University Press.

Peterson, A. (2001). *Being Human: Ethics, Environment and Our Place in the World.* Berkeley: University of California Press.

Pinhatã, I. (2008). [Online interview.] Accessed 12/28/2008 at http://www2.uol.com.br/pagina20/4abril2003/site/15042003/entrevista.htm.

Silva, A.L. and Ferreira, M.K.L. (Eds.) (2001a). *Antropologia, Historia e Educação.* São Paulo: Global.

Silva, A. and Ferreira, M. (Eds) (2001b). *Práticas Pedagógicas na Escola Indígena.* São Paulo: Global.

Turner, D. (2006). *This is Not a Peace Pipe: Towards a Critical Indigenous Philosophy.* Toronto: University of Toronto Press.

Welch, S. (1999). *Sweet Dreams in America: Making Ethics and Spirituality Work.* New York: Routledge.

6 A SLICE of Life
Changing Perceptions of Community amongst Children and Teachers in Kingston, Jamaica

Jane Dodman

INTRODUCTION

During a visit to the Stan Amos Preparatory School, in inner-city Kingston, I met and spoke with a woman who had three grandchildren attending the school. She said, "We must give our children love, food and education." This grandmother represents the many parents and grandparents of children in the school and throughout Jamaica who think that education is so important that they are prepared to make sacrifices so that their children can have opportunities which were not available to them. Her wisdom expresses the feelings of many Jamaicans who see education as the way out of poverty and the means of upward mobility.

The Stan Amos Preparatory School, a primary school in Beth Town in downtown Kingston, is the only school of its kind in the inner-city. The aim of this chapter is to describe and analyse an action research project undertaken by the Grade 1 teacher, as she sought to reposition her children's perceptions of community. Inner-city residents are deeply conscious of the stigma attached to their communities and the ways in which it excludes them from the wider society. Some employers reject applicants by stating "You come from a bad area where only robbers and gunmen and their families live" (Levy, 2001: 24). The Grade 1 teacher attempted to help the children to appreciate the people and the place in which they lived and attended school.

The research sought to hear the teacher's voice, as she utilized indigenous knowledge as a means of challenging the children's taken for granted assumptions and affirming the positive aspects of their community. She promoted an agenda for social justice as she encouraged the children to think and behave in ways that would make a positive difference in their community. The self-reflective process of the research also encouraged the teacher to change her own perceptions of community.

The school, as an integral part of the Stan Amos Institute, a community development agency, shares the agency's mandate that "human development is the key to community and national development." This motto is taken from the tenth-anniversary commemorative magazine prepared in 1988 by the non-governmental organization that later founded the Stan Amos Preparatory School. The relationship between the institute and the school is recognition that it is only when people have a sense of their own purpose in life that they will have the potential to work with others to become agents of change in their local community and the wider society. Accordingly, the school is not only committed to providing educational opportunities for individual children, but also to finding ways in which the process of change in the school can contribute to social justice and inclusion in a community that functions on the margins of society.

My personal involvement with inner-city residents has been shaped and enabled by my work with the Stan Amos Institute for over twenty-five years. A short-term appointment in the early 1980s has led to a lifetime commitment to Jamaica and in particular to educational institutions that work with persons who would easily drop out of the formal education system, were it not for the intervention of such institutions.

OVERVIEW OF THE ACTION RESEARCH—
OFFERING THE CHILDREN A SLICE OF LIFE

What does it mean to offer a SLICE of life to the children in the Stan Amos Preparatory School? This is the school's stated objective and each letter of the SLICE stands for an important quality for children growing up in this context—Self-esteem, Love, Industry, Community and Excellence. All six of the classroom teachers in the school sought to effect change in the children's understanding and practice of the SLICE through an action research project on one aspect of the SLICE during the course of one academic year. I functioned as the research coordinator and facilitator and in this chapter I will focus on the action research on community, undertaken by the Grade 1 teacher.

Before describing and analyzing the action research project I will provide a brief overview of life in the inner-city and the educational issues relevant for the research.

THE JAMAICAN CONTEXT: COMMUNITY
LIFE IN THE INNER-CITY

Although Jamaica is classified as a middle-income country with medium levels of human development (UNDP, 2004), it still struggles with its colonial legacy, the negative impact of structural adjustment policies, large debt repayments and high inequality. The legacy of Jamaica's history and the struggles facing Jamaicans today find form and content in inner-city communities like Beth Town and educational institutions like the Stan Amos Preparatory School.

The action research project took into consideration the contending realities of life in the inner-city. Negative images of inner-city communities dominate the literature and media representations (Chevannes, 2001; Levy, 2001). These communities are characterized by various forms of social deprivation including poverty, high levels of unemployment and overcrowding. Sometimes residents are seen as being dependent, as the recipients of food, other handouts and kindly deeds by middle class people from uptown communities. All these elements contribute to the sense of social injustice and exclusion experienced by people who live in the inner-city.

However, the literature also shows some of the positive elements of life in the inner-city. For example, Chevannes (2001) emphasizes the positive impact of culture which emanates from inner-city communities, describing downtown as the location for the "cutting edge in Jamaica's music culture, where dance-hall fashion statements originate, the Jamaican patois acquires new words and expressions" (p. 152).

Other positive definitions of community focus on relationships. A constant refrain of the people in *They Cry "Respect!"* (Levy, 2001), was that in earlier times "people lived good" (p. 10), referring to relationships of kindness and mutual help. They identified positive facets of present day community life, which brought people together in educational and parenting programmes, community organizations and youth clubs.

Respect speaks to one way in which people experience social justice and inclusion. Dodman and Dodman (2006) contend that the concerns of citizen action and issues of class, power, sexual/gender relationships and culture tend, in Jamaica, "to be subsumed under the discourse of 'respect' and 'justice'" (p. 94). They cite as examples, *They Cry Respect!,* (Levy, 1996), the national anthem, which requests "true respect for all" and the explanation of Nettleford (2003) that "the word 'respec' (for respect) is frequently intoned in the argot of Jamaican urban inner city and rural life" (p. xix).

THE JAMAICAN EDUCATIONAL SYSTEM AND THE STAN AMOS PREPARATORY SCHOOL

The Jamaican educational system has its origins in the English educational system. This system resulted in cultural alienation as children were taught British and European history; local music was seen as demeaning and they were not allowed to talk patois, which was considered "bad English." Patois is a language with its own structure and vocabulary, which includes African and English words. Educational initiatives in the past forty years have sought to respond to the needs of Jamaicans and for human resource development to take place:

Against the background of recent transfer of power from imperial metro-pole to colonial periphery, and in the context of an on-going engagement with the imperatives of social transformation and dynamic change, as well as of an increasing consciousness of the need to grapple realistically with problems and possibilities of identity (personal and socio-cultural).

(Nettleford, 1991: 15)

Private preparatory schools, for children aged six through twelve, offer smaller classes, a wider range of extracurricular activities and greater mate-rial resources than government primary schools. More children achieve the necessary grades in the national Grade Six Achievement Test (GSAT) to be awarded places in traditional high (grammar) schools, the most successful schools academically.

The Stan Amos Preparatory School, with an enrolment of 200 children, is a unique school as it caters to children whose parents cannot afford the school fees charged by the traditional preparatory schools. It opened in 1994 with a commitment to addressing some of the inequalities within the educational system by offering education to children who would otherwise be excluded from such schools. The school is supported through donations and fundraising events and parents are encouraged to make a small finan-cial contribution. The action research project provided an opportunity to explore the ways in which the school was offering the kind of education envisioned at its inception.

FRAMEWORK FOR THE ACTION RESEARCH

The theoretical framework for the action research draws on an eclectic range of literature from several contexts that speaks to the postcolonial experience, issues of social justice and the awakening of crucial conscious-ness. I wanted to place the research within a theoretical framework that related to education in Jamaican. Issues of social justice were critical to the objectives of the research, which focused on effecting positive change in the lives of children who experienced exclusion and social stigma. Paulo Freire's work has been very influential in my personal journey as both an educator and a community practitioner, with his focus the role of education in effecting personal and community transformation.

Cultural Studies and a Postcolonial Approach

Evans (2001), in her examination of Jamaican schools, provides a help-ful framework for the context and the research. She favors combining the cultural studies approach with a postcolonial perspective as this recognizes the inequalities that exist because of the colonial experience. She contends that "Cultural studies, when applied to education in a postcolonial context, turns the gaze on the experiences of those who are marginalized—students from poor or working-class homes—and the ways in which color, class and gender influence these experiences" (p. 19).

Evans (2001) notes that some people value more highly what is British, American and white. Some still regard Jamaican patois as "bad" English, which must not be spoken if people wish to become educated. These tensions and dualities are a legacy from the colonial period and from a dual educational system for whites and blacks and it becomes very difficult for students "to establish an identity and a firm sense of will" (p. 20).

Similarly, Smith (1999) acknowledges the role of schools in "assimilating colonized peoples, and in the systemic, frequently brutal, forms of denial of indigenous languages, knowledges and cultures" (p. 64).

Social Justice

A central concern of this book is the way in which the process of change can bridge the gap between social justice and exclusion. Griffiths (2003) provides an appropriate definition of social justice as a "dynamic state of affairs that is good for the common interest, where that is taken to include both the good of each and the good of all, in an acknowledgement that one depends on the other" (p. 54).

Evans (2006), drawing on Austin-Broos's research, recognizes that "the notion of 'heritable identity' which places an individual in Jamaica's social hierarchy . . . goes beyond class and race and includes education" (p. 40). One of Austin-Broos's (2001) informants said, "'Yu caan tek a chil' from below Torrington Bridge put 'im in a school and mek 'im 'educated'" (p. 259). Translated, this means "you can't take a child from below Torrington Bridge, put him in a school and make him educated." The Stan Amos Preparatory School is below Torrington Bridge, one of the perceived boundaries of inner-city Kingston.

Critical Consciousness

Under-resourced schools and large classes, as well as the colonial legacy, resulted in the continuation of an educational system that has been elitist and exclusionary and reliant on rote learning. Freire (1996) describes this as "banking education," whereby students are turned into "'containers,' into 'receptacles' to be 'filled' by the teacher" (p. 53). Freire's vision of critical consciousness as the overall objective of a problem-posing educational process was particularly influential to this research. Central to this process is the way in which an awakening to critical consciousness and a problem-posing approach to education can create a climate for personal and community transformation. The research provided an opportunity for the teacher to draw on the experiences of children and teacher in an environment that was more student-centered.

Action Research

The main emphasis of action research is on effecting change in a particular context through the research process. Reason and Bradbury (2001) provide the following working definition:

> Action research is a participatory, democratic process concerned with developing practical knowledge in the pursuit of worthwhile human purposes . . . It seeks to bring together action and reflection, theory and practice, in participation with others, in the pursuit of practical solutions to issues of pressing concern to people, and more generally the flourishing of individual people and their communities.
>
> (p. 1)

Other writers concur with these definitions (Berge & Ve, 2000; Burns, 2007; Carr & Kemmis, 1986; Elliott, 1991; Griffiths & Davies, 1993; Zeichner, 2001) and the following constitute the main concerns of action research:

- The importance of the context and the examination of a single situation;
- A desire amongst practitioners to improve practice and effect change through planned action;
- The production of and contribution to knowledge through a process whereby each participant's contribution is taken seriously;
- Learning comes from action;
- The validation of theories through practice;
- The critical role of self-reflective inquiry;
- Greater equity and social justice.

THE ACTION RESEARCH—OFFERING
THE CHILDREN A SLICE OF LIFE

Access and Positionality

As a staff member at the Stan Amos institute, I had been involved with the school since its conception. The school was an expression of the Stan Amos Institute's commitment to children growing up in the inner-city. I had worked at the institute in Beth Town for ten years until the early 1990s when the administrative office moved to another location. I still had responsibilities in Beth Town and had access to the school at any time. I participated in institute, school and community events. I had taught other members of the children's families when I had been a teacher in the Institute's Early Childhood programme and was well known by community residents, staff and children.

The action research project formed the second part of a research project, which had begun the previous year when I conducted regular observation in the school. On both occasions, I discussed the research with the principal and with the teachers. It was agreed upon that I would undertake the research in the school.

I was aware that my personal identity was informed by the fact that I was a white, middle-class, middle-aged woman, with a husband and two grown-up children and that I had lived and worked in Jamaica for over twenty years. The teachers and many of the children and their families were aware of these facts; many of them knew my other family members. It was difficult to separate my role and identity at the Stan Amos Institute. My Jamaican identity had been formed through my work at the institute and my involvement in the lives of people from the inner-city. None of the management staff or teachers lived in the community. In this regard, we all start as outsiders in our relationship with the community, and the extent to which we become insiders is determined by our attitudes towards each other and mutual acceptance.

The Action Research Process

Having negotiated agreement to undertake the research, I met with the teachers to discuss the proposed project with them. We talked about the principles and process of action research and the way in which I hoped they would participate.

The Children's Experience of Community and Social Justice

The Grade 1 teacher chose to focus on community. She was using the Ministry of Education integrated curriculum for the first time and integrated her action research into this new curriculum. She used the action research cycle of planning, acting, observing and reflecting.

The curriculum theme for the first term was "myself." Initially the teacher developed a system for children to take homework to children who were absent from school. She also sent messages to these children, telling them what was happening in school, as a way of encouraging their speedy return and helping them to feel part of the classroom community during their absence.

In formulating a research question, the teacher said she was developing a community photo album and community corner in order "to build each child's confidence. To develop the ability to communicate. To enable children to find their place in the different communities to which they belong, starting with the community of the Grade 1 classroom" (Dodman, 2005: 134). She said that she wanted to find out "if and how children come to an understanding that they are real human beings with the ability to do things, not just for themselves, but which will benefit others" (p. 134).

She then formulated her research question; "To what extent can a focus on community in the classroom enable a sense of community to become a reality for the children within the different communities to which they belong?" (p. 134).

In her journal, she wrote that her aim was to develop a community corner in the classroom and a community relationship via the school. She wanted the research to impact positively on the children's parents and the wider community.

Over half the children brought photos of themselves for the "community photo album". The teacher placed the caption, "I am special" above the photo collage, which she mounted on a large sheet of paper on the wall facing the door, so that it was easily visible when people entered the classroom. She wanted her children to think of being "all of us together" (Dodman, 2005: 134). The teacher positioned each photo touching the one next to it, as this "depicts togetherness" (p. 135). She heard nothing but positive comments. The children kept going to the photos to look at them. They said that they and the other children "looked good" (p. 135).

Next, the teacher established a community corner where the children sat for story time. The teacher said that this was the place where children were encouraged to develop confidence—"the ability to talk out in the classroom" (Dodman, 2005: 135). She wanted them to find their place and communicate in both the school and the wider community.

At the start of each morning, as the children talked about the day of the week and the weather, the teacher also asked them how they were feeling. One day the children wrote "Today is Friday. We are at school. We are happy to be together again" (p. 135). This statement was seeking to encourage them to have positive feelings about the class as a community.

The curriculum theme for the second term was "the family" and as she began the second cycle of the research, the teacher moved beyond the community of the classroom and used the topic to encourage a sense of belonging to family and to the wider community.

She spent a lot of time talking with and listening to the children, as a class and as individuals. Sometimes she drew on her personal experiences, "when I was a little girl" to introduce a topic. Sometimes she used stories and information that the children shared with her, drawing on their personal experiences and knowledge learnt from their life in the community to work for change in their perceptions of family and community.

She had a discussion with the children about the other schools in the community. The children were negative about the government primary school near to the school. The children told the teacher that the children from this school were "rude . . . they like to fight . . . they fling stones" (Dodman, 2005: 136). When she asked the children how they saw the children from the other school, they said they saw them as boys and girls in their school uniforms. The teacher told them that they were boys and girls who attended another school. "They have feelings like you." The children responded, "But they are very rude," to which she responded, "So are some of you" (p. 136).

In a discussion about the neighboring community of Pitter Town, the children told her, "They are Labourites dem" (Dodman, 2005: 136). This statement refers to the fact that the particular community supported the Jamaica Labour Party (JLP). Residents of Beth Town were considered to be supporters of the People's National Party (PNP), the governing party at that time. It was evident that the children were already clearly polarized with regard to traditional political affiliations. These community alliances along partisan line have been known to have contributed to serious tensions and violence between communities.

The teacher explained that they were children like them. To illustrate this, she showed the children photos of some children from Pitter Town. These were children who were their classmates the previous year when they were in their final year of the Stan Amos Early Childhood programme. After prolonged violence in Beth City in the summer holidays, most of the children from Pitter Town moved to other schools as their parents were afraid for their safety. When the teacher talked with the children about the children from Pitter Town, they recalled them with positive memories and "spoke joyously, remembering the good times" (p. 136). Later, following a discussion with the children, the teacher added photos of some of these children to the photo collage. She told the children that they were still one big family even though they were no longer in school together.

In a class project on community helpers, the children imagined they were a community helper and said a sentence about what they did in the community. The children used titles such as electrician and carpenter. They were able to say that an electrician was someone who fixed lights. The children said positive things about the teacher, the nurse ("I take care of sick people"; and the fireman ("I put out fire"). They were more ambivalent about the policeman and the soldier. The teacher heard one boy, at his desk, say, "I am a policeman. I kill rapists." When it was his turn to come and talk to the class he said, "I am a policeman. I protect people." Another boy said, "I am a soldier. I walk around with a long gun" (Dodman, 2005: 137).

The teacher provided opportunities for the children to come to the front of the class and talk about themselves and give their address. She said that one day a boy came to the front and gave the name and number of his street, which was just over the border between Beth City and Pitter Town. The following week he would not give his address; he said that he lived down the road and across the street. On another occasion a girl made up a fictitious name for her community. The teacher thought that parents told their children not to tell people where they lived.

The teacher said that she used the words "community" and "family" almost interchangeably. She explained that the children were familiar with the word "family" and readily responded to it. They had three families—their home family, their community family and their school family. Sometimes people came and looked through the classroom window and when she spoke to them, they would reply that they were looking for their "cousin." The word "cousin" can be used to describe any distant relative. Part of the sense of community in a community like Beth City stemmed from the fact that many people were blood relatives. As the teacher said, "They were knitted together as families" (Dodman, 2005: 137).

At the beginning of the third term I asked the teacher if she could see any evidence of the sense of community becoming a reality in the classroom. She said that early in the school year the children had looked out for themselves. Now they were looking out for each other. She gave some examples:

- A child has no lunch. Another child will tell her that this boy/girl is not eating;
- Sometimes a child will take off his/her shoes and socks and put them in one of the boxes (used as both storage and seats) and forget where they have put them. Other children will search in all the boxes until the missing shoes and socks are found;
- Children will tell the teacher if a child is not working;
- If a child does not have a pencil the teacher will ask "Is there anyone with two pieces of pencil?" Children will offer, "Me, Miss"

(Dodman, 2005: 138).

The third cycle of the action research started at the beginning of the third term. The teacher's objective for this term was to "build up—what the children do as community, I want them to do it from the heart, to be genuine" (Dodman, 2005: 138). The curriculum theme was "living and non-living things." The teacher tried to relate it to community. The children told the teacher about a goat pen on one of the roads in the community and they also told her about the people in the community who kept goats and rabbits.

Toward the end of the research, the teacher gave definitions of community, which had emerged from the process. For the children, community was "finding a place where they belong . . . they are becoming part of the community" (Dodman, 2005: 138). A community is "the coming together of a group of people, living and sharing the facilities in a specific area—water, road, shop, supermarket, sharing company. The children want to know that they are not alone" (p. 138).

The teacher felt that the sharing of information by the children about what happened in the community had been particularly effective. However, there were some things which the children would not share publicly or only share partially with the rest of the class. They would whisper to the teacher or wait until the other children had left. When there had been soldiers in the community, a girl waited until the other children had left before telling the teacher in confidence that there had been a (dead) body in her yard. The teacher was aware of how the children were "patterning" what they saw happening in the community. For example, they used a handkerchief and made a triangular shape to imitate a gun. They walked and leant against the wall, imitating the way they saw the men in the community walk.

The teacher thought that the research had encouraged the children's interest in "academics." She talked about the ways in which the children had moved from focusing on their own work, to working in groups, as she had encouraged a sense of community in the classroom. She gave an example of six children who usually got the right answers, who had formed a group. The children were now more tolerant; they were not "talking out-right that they don't like someone" (Dodman, 2005: 139).

The teacher commented on the changes she had observed as a result of the research. "They [the children] were involved with each other. They were concerned about what each other was doing over the weekend and would report on Monday" (Dodman, 2005: 140). She thought that the children "start looking on each other as individuals who have feelings and not only when you hit the person that they can be hurt (as we also discussed that) and they were more willing to share" (p. 140).

As a result of the action research, the children changed their understanding of community. They experienced social justice as they learnt that they were special. This was particularly important given the negative attitude of many in the wider society towards people living in the inner-city. Through the class discussions and activities they came to appreciate the need for mutual dependency and care.

The Teacher's Experience of Community and Social Justice

Reflecting on what she had learnt from the research, the teacher said, "It has allowed me to think deeper; as you are imparting to the children, you think where you are and you are looking at the community" (Dodman, 2005: 139). She said she had not been a member of a community group in her home community, but she thought she should now join one. She told the story of a young man in her home community who had gone missing at sea. He was not someone to whom she normally spoke but she became very concerned for his well-being. When he returned home safely, she went to speak to him. She said that the teacher taught children, and now she was participating in what she was imparting to them.

She argued that it would make a difference if the wider society would focus more on community, on "everybody, not just family and friends" (Dodman, 2005: 139). It was important for children to understand the importance of each other's feelings so that they would learn to deal with different emotions and learn to respect differences. This would lessen incidents of violence in high schools.

At a meeting in the summer holiday, the teacher reiterated some of things that she had shared during the year. She wrote that the word "community" came alive "in practice when each one, including the teacher, shows an interest in each individual life as it relates to the school and where they live" (Dodman, 2005: 139). She felt that she was relating to her colleagues with more interest and each child had learnt to "look out for each other after school and during school hours" (p. 139).

In sharing her research with the school board, the teacher said she chose community because the Grade 1 children "wouldn't share with everybody at times, so I saw the need to pull everybody together as one" (Dodman, 2005: 139).

She reported that from a personal perspective the research had "allowed me to see my neighbor—not that I wasn't seeing before—but in a more closer way. I began to take part in my community, in that I became a member of my community club even though I am often not present, but I did find out now from the club members they were now free to come over and rap with me" (Dodman, 2005: 140).

The teacher used her effective listening and inter-personal skills to effect change through the research. She moved from a "banking" approach to a "problem posing" approach as she listened to the children's stories and encouraged them to think critically about their attitudes to and relationships with others in their community. She challenged them to change their taken for granted assumptions.

Through her own reflective practice, she realized that sometimes attitudes and events in the community hindered the children's ability to embrace fully what it meant to be part of a community. However, out of a concern for social justice, she attempted to challenge and change their perceptions and behavior and implemented classroom activities which created a climate for meaningful community. By presenting and encouraging positive feelings and attitudes to community, she was bridging the gap between social justice and exclusion and enabling the children to become agents of transformation in the school and the wider community.

A Personal Reflection

When I reflected on my identity as the research facilitator, I considered myself an insider. My long association with the institute, the school and the community located me in that position. However, when I interrogated my position further on the insider/outsider continuum, I recognized that there were two elements that moved me a little in the direction of the outsider; I was a senior manager and I no longer worked full time in Beth City. To be a full insider I would have needed to be a classroom teacher. I think that the research was more effective because the teacher was an insider, who knew the children and taught them every day. As she listened to and observed the children, she was able to identify issues that she could use in her research. The children knew and trusted her and were willing to share their stories with her. As the researcher facilitator, who was predominantly an insider,

I understood the context and was known by the teacher, who trusted me and participated willingly in the research project. Our different position-alities complemented each other and shaped the research intervention and the change process. I think that this collaboration provided a lesson for researching communities. Both the teacher who was a constant presence in the school and I, as the research facilitator, who was well known, yet did not have that permanent presence, made our own unique contribution to the research.

The indigenous knowledge that was produced by the research provided a counterbalance in a context where "many of the defining and classifying mechanisms used in [Caribbean] academic thought are remnants of a total-izing colonial discourse" (Dodman & Dodman, 2006: 94).

In terms of social justice, Griffiths (2003) argues that it "need to be understood in terms both of 'little stories' and the 'grand narratives'; that is both localized issues and large scale theorizing about them" (p. 55). Draw-ing on this terminology, it can be argued that the "grand narrative" of the legacy of colonialism provided the framework for working for social justice through the "little story" of the research in the school. In this way the action research became part of the process of decolonizing the context.

CONCLUSION

The action research effected change in a number of areas. In terms of her pedagogy, the teacher introduced new ways of talking with and listen-ing to the children; she changed from a predominantly teacher-centered approach to a more student-centered approach. The research supported the professional development of the teacher as it employed a problem-posing approach to learning and teaching. She became a self-reflective practitioner as she reflected on the impact the research was having on the children and herself. She helped the children to practice community in the classroom and to be more inclusive in their attitudes to people who were different. The teacher became more committed to social justice and to the practice of community in both the classroom and her local community.

It was more difficult to evaluate the change in the children. However, there was evidence that the children responded positively to changes in classroom practice. They learnt to appreciate themselves and were recep-tive to new ideas about people who lived in the community.

From my perspective as the research facilitator, I came to appreciate in a more focused way the teacher's commitment and dedication to teaching in this particular school and context. As my relationship with the teacher deepened, I came to appreciate her strengths and the way in which she con-tributed something unique to her own class and to the school community as a whole. She demonstrated the positive changes that can result from undertaking an action research project in the classroom.

REFERENCES

Austin-Broos, D. (2001). Race/Class: Jamaica's discourse of heritable identity. In C. Barrow and R. Reddock (Eds.) *Caribbean Sociology: Introductory Readings.* Kingston: Ian Randle, pp. 256–269.

Berge, B. and Ve, H. (2000). *Action Research for Gender Equity.* Buckingham: Open University.

Burns, D. (2007). *Systemic Action Research: A Strategy for Whole System Change.* Bristol: Policy.

Carr, W. and Kemmis, S. (1986). *Becoming Critical: Education, Knowledge and Action Research.* London: Falmer.

Chevannes, B. (2001). *Learning to be a Man: Culture, Socialization and Gender Identity in Five Caribbean Communities.* Kingston: University of the West Indies.

Dodman, J. (2005). A SLICE of life: Towards transformation in an inner-city preparatory school in Kingston, Jamaica. PhD thesis. University of Sheffield.

Dodman, D. and Dodman, J. (2006). "Nuff Respec"? Widening and deepening participation in academic and policy research in Jamaica. In J. Pugh and J. Momsen (Eds.) *Environmental Planning and the Caribbean.* Aldershot: Ashgate, pp. 93109.

Elliott, J. (1991). *Action Research for Educational Change.* Buckingham: Open University.

Evans, H. (2001). *Inside Jamaican Schools.* Kingston: University of the West Indies.

Evans, H. (2006). *Inside Hillview High School: An Ethnography of an Urban Jamaican High School.* Kingston: University of the West Indies.

Freire, P. (1996). *Pedagogy of the Oppressed.* Harmondsworth: Penguin.

Griffiths, M. (2003). *Action for Social Justice in Education: Fairly Different.* Maidenhead: Open University.

Griffiths, M. and Davies, C. (1993). Learning to learn: Action research from an equal opportunities perspective in a junior school. *British Educational Research Journal,* 19(1), 43–58.

Levy, H. (2001). *They Cry "Respect!" Urban Violence and Poverty in Jamaica .* Kingston: University of the West Indies, Centre for Population, Community and Social Change.

Nettleford, R. (1991). Education and Society in the Caribbean: Issues and problems. In E. Miller (Ed.) *Education and Society in the Commonwealth Caribbean.* Kingston: Institute of Social and Economic Research, pp. 15–25.

Nettleford, R. (2003). *Caribbean Cultural Identity: The Case of Jamaica.* Kingston: Ian Randle.

Reason, P. and Bradbury, H. (2001). Introduction: Inquiry and participation in search of a world worthy of human aspiration. In P. Reason and H. Bradbury (Eds.) *Handbook of Action Research: Participative Inquiry and Practice.* London: Sage, pp. 1–14.

Smith, L. (1999). *Decolonizing Methodologies: Research and Indigenous Peoples.* London: Zed.

United Nations Development Programme (UNDP). (2004). *Human Development Report.* New York.

Zeichner, K. (2001). Educational action research. In P. Reason and H. Bradbury (Eds.) *Handbook of Action Research: Participative Inquiry and Practice.* London: Sage, pp. 273–283.

7 Inclusion, Narrative and Voices of Disabled Children in Trinidad and St. Lucia

Michele Moore

INTRODUCTION

This chapter aims to examine opportunities and possibilities for advancing inclusion of disabled children in schools in Trinidad and St Lucia. Organization of Eastern Caribbean States (OECS) Reform Strategy has identified "inclusive" special educational practice as central to raising standards for *all* children in the region (OECS, 2000). The chapter is concerned with the interface between understandings of disability and attempts to set up decolonizing community based work to create inclusion in schools in Trinidad and St Lucia. It begins to explore the actuality of disabled children's experience of schools and communities in these locations, recognizing these deeply reflect the legacy of colonialism in the sense that disabled children are members of communities from which they are excluded by dominant voices and practices. Yet, in settings in which disabled children do not have access to the same education as their non-disabled contemporaries, many of their teachers and other allies seek to intervene and to create ways of advancing an agenda for inclusive education which emphasize the importance of self-expression and self determination through raising children's own voices (Julien, 2008). The commitment of teachers, to raising the seldom heard voices of the disabled children they work with, launched me on a journey of school visits intended to inform my understanding of the circumstances in which disabled children learn in Trinidad and St Lucia. In this chapter I try to illustrate how this journey produced stories which enabled a "constructive process . . . inspired by partial happenings, fragmented memories, echoes of conversations" (Sparkes, 2007: 521) through which an agenda for collective action research was forged offering new possibilities for decolonizing work involving disabled children, schools and communities.

I acknowledge, as do other writers (Armstrong & Barton, 1999; Kaomea, 2004), that this discussion is limited by its personal and specific nature. Hopefully however, it might contribute in a small way to the transformation of disabled children's struggles in a range of community contexts.

INSIDER / OUTSIDER PERSPECTIVES

My starting point for becoming involved with disabled children and their allies in Trinidad and St Lucia was through delivery of a University of Sheffield Masters programme for teachers interested in special and inclusive education. I was apprehensive about this, knowing from previous experience that my own perspectives on disability, social justice and education are full of tensions and contradictions and that these have been particularly perplexing in new cross-cultural contexts (Moore & Dunn, 1999). I needed to engage with the actuality of what would be involved in Trinidad and St Lucia for those seeking to apply the theories and practices of inclusive education which I espoused, though brought with me no previous experience of working in postcolonial settings. Predictably, the teachers had one question in mind; how to bridge the gap between the theory of inclusive education with which I sought to engage them, and the actuality of disabled children's opportunities for learning and schooling in their contexts. The chapter is based on visits subsequently made at the request of the teachers, to six schools in both Trinidad and St Lucia.

The teacher's invitation to make the visits both inspired and filled me with dread. Being urged to visit schools and *then* work with local practitioners to articulate strategies for transforming a culture of segregation experienced by disabled children and young people in Trinidad and St Lucia acutely exposed the limitations of my outsider gaze. In this chapter I try to explore the multiple complexities which faced me as a non-disabled, white academic from Britain seeking to advance an agenda for disabled children's inclusion in a shared project of development with indigenous teachers who are "insiders" in this project—whereas I am forever and unmistakably an "outsider."

Smith (2005) makes plain the importance of being *reflective* in our engagements with communities. The need to continually think critically about processes, relationships in the field and the way in which these determine what we see and claim cannot be overemphasized. She argues there are different considerations for "insider" indigenous community researchers who have to live with the consequences of their engagements, as do their families and communities. "Outsiders," it is argued, are differently accountable to the communities with whom they are working by virtue of the possibility of separation—or even severance from the community—the consequences of their activities the distance of their position allows. The notion of "lines of relating" is used by Smith (2005) to offer a way of articulating the relative nature of insider—outsider distance. While I am not an insider in terms of indigenous membership of the communities in which the teachers are working, I do claim some meaningful "lines of relating." Through my status as the mother of children with impairments, for example, the consequences of my engagements in schools impact on my own children's destinies. During the visits I could not always claim the detachment of an outsider's gaze because my own children *do* live with the consequences of barriers which impede a global vision of inclusion. An element of muddle has to be recognized as embodied in the multiple—and confused—dimensions of insider / outsider status. On most critical lines of relating I was an outsider; a visitor, not an indigenous member of the community; an academic not a practitioner. Yet in other ways I shared experiences and held commitments which perhaps lessened the remoteness of my encounters with children and adults in the schools.

UNEQUIVOCAL COMMITMENTS

I have long been conscious that placing an unequivocal "headline" focus on "inclusion"—as I was doing with the teachers in Trinidad and St Lucia—can seem to complicate the task teachers face in attempting to make children's experiences of education satisfactory, particularly when children are placed in segregated settings. It is well known that "inclusive thinking and practice are hard work" (Barton, 2004: ix), fraught with complexity and often contradictory tensions. In addition, postcolonial identity politics have served to create and sustain segregation of disabled people throughout the Caribbean. Yet, what I have come to realize through my work with teachers in many countries is that deeply felt views—and oftentimes reservations—about the varied challenges a requirement for inclusion engenders—can open up routes to inclusion. I approached the school visits in Trinidad and St Lucia with this potential solace in mind. I was troubled though, because my own interpretation of disabled children's experiences would continue to function as a dominant representation at least as far as the original group of teachers involved were concerned. And further, the location of these interpretations and representations within the academic discourses of this book recycles the voice of a white British academic so that possibilities for contesting Western theories of disability through the visits are necessarily inadequate.

Nevertheless, two general principles frame my thinking about disability and inclusion which shaped my approach to the visits. First, I am unequivocally committed to a social model of disability (Oliver, 1996) and to the development of schools and communities in accordance with this model. Second, all of my work promotes an agenda for inclusion. Yet I constantly wonder whether the encroachment of my own theoretical (and activist) principles should be resisted if community based work is to claim any decolonizing dimension. Am I, as a white British academic, seeking to reaffirm "the colonizer's behaviors and tastes, including language" (Freire and Macedo, 1998: 184) or, since the principles I promote are articulated by disabled people who have experienced centuries of oppression themselves, is there some legitimacy in seeking to bring their voice and experience to the project of reducing segregation in disabled children's education in Trinidad and St Lucia? There is confusion here but, as with the issue of lines of relating, the predicament reveals another way in which decolonizing community-based work around disability and exclusion is bound up with real difficulties in real lives which cannot be subordinated to a clear line of postcolonial or disability studies analysis.

The social model of disability (Oliver, 1996) provides a way of understanding and responding to the task of teaching disabled children. It emerged in the 1970s as disabled people struggled to understand their own situations, to define their own problems and to develop their own aspirations for change. It is based on the idea that:

> Disability is something imposed on top of our impairments by the way we are unnecessarily isolated and excluded from full participation in society.
>
> (Union of the Physically Impaired Against Segregation, 1976)

The social model contrasts with the traditional "medical" model of disability which tends to see children with impairments as "having something wrong with them." Most policy relating to disabled and vulnerable children and young people, including education policy, has been based on a medical-model approach. Consequently, education services have historically focused on children and young people as "having problems" and this has blocked a creative approach to tackling the barriers that permit segregation and exclusion and create disablement. I have found that the social model of disability helps practitioners and disabled children's allies to think beyond the apparent functional limitations of an individual child or young person that relate to the specifics of impairment and to look more creatively instead at ways of circumventing problems caused by disabling environments, attitudes and cultures (Dunn & Moore, 2005). I want to persuade teachers of the efficacy and applicability of this model for their contexts.

Disabled people, including children and young people, taught me the power of the social model of disability:

> It is not impairments—which are what we have—that make us disabled children. For me, my impairment will always be with me and is a part of me and I can live with that. It is society which makes me disabled by not letting me join in.
>
> Claire, aged 14 years (Office of the Deputy Prime Minister, 2003)

Thus I plainly did have commitments of my own, which I argue are informed by the voices of disabled people who continue to feel and articulate that they matter less than their contemporaries. Whether or not as a non-disabled person (and irrespective of being white and British) I am qualified to advocate on behalf of those disabled people who are the principle architects of a social-model agenda for inclusive education is another moot point. But here I call upon particular determinants of identity and biography to assert my "right" to engage in social model transformations of exclusions in disabled children lives. Parenting children with impairments, and relationships with disabled people have taught me to view medical understandings of disability, and the segregation which a medical approach cultivates, with contempt. Thus when teachers say:

> "But Miss, these autistic children are the ones that no one wants to work with"
>
> or
>
> "we cannot help *those* children in my school, we have no resources." Their mothers cry and beg us but we say "go to the special school they may be able to help you but here we have nothing. . . ." . . . so they have to go to the special school and beg corporate Trinidad.
>
> Teachers in Trinidad and St Lucia

I feel ashamed of the discriminatory structures, oppressive attitudes and isolating practices which stem from the "colonizer's behaviors and tastes" and which are still evident in the British context today (Armstrong, 2007: 552). I therefore felt emboldened to put the abovementioned social model principles for inclusive practice to the test of relevance to the lives of disabled children and young people in Trinidad and St Lucia because these are born out of the priorities of disabled people who have resisted exclusion through segregated education elsewhere in the world and somewhere along the "lines of relating" (Smith, 2005) I *claim* an insider perspective when it comes to threatened exclusions of disabled children.

Through the visits I wanted to become able to identify and describe what I saw as the *problem* of segregation experienced by disabled children in Trinidad and St Lucia. I was interested in perceptions about entitlements for disabled children in comparison with entitlements afforded to their non-disabled contemporaries. I wanted to explore ideas on how disabled children's learning and lives are constructed through examining presence or absence of particular children in particular settings and reflecting on ideas about difference. I was conscious of needing to understand what the implications of the legacy of colonialism are for disabled children in the cultural locations in which I was working. There seemed to be useful possibilities associated with these questions; gaining insight for example, into education policy and practice that might add to understanding of inclusions and exclusions of disabled children. And, where following on from colonial models disability is configured in ways which promote segregation and oppression within schools and communities, or is perpetually connected to narratives of charity and benevolence as teachers were describing, what ways of thinking might assist the process of transforming such dominant modes of disabling thinking?

Teaching and talking from the relatively safe landscape of a British university encouraged me to agree with Smith (2005) that reflectivity and reflexivity help manage the tensions embedded in the insider / outsider dichotomy. But the narratives of reflection and representation constructed through my visits do unmistakably reproduce Western perspectives. Thus I am bound to make a host of problematic conjectures in the remainder of this chapter. These conjectures have, however, functioned as "frictional platforms for resistance" (Burman et al., 1996: 200); by putting representations of the visits into a shared space of teaching and learning new possibilities for teachers seeking to transform the education of disabled children in Trinidad and St Lucia have been opened up.

Everything I thought I "knew" about the question of inclusive education for disabled children mutated in front of my eyes as a result of these visits into—for me—unknown worlds of special and inclusive education. The visits became part of an unsettling personal journey. There have been moments of acute political shame, such as when buses pulled up outside a playground full of local boys to drop tourists off from the cruise ships that dock in the harbor for the day. I often feel my research accounts and encounters exit in shifting landscapes of thinking around inclusion. Just as I think I understand the barriers that impede a global vision of inclusion I find myself encountering a different gaze; "there is no room for complacency" (Barton, 1998: 36).

Extracts of narratives I wrote during the visits raise questions about opportunities and possibilities for the project of inclusion in Trinidad and St Lucia and about the importance of raising voices of disabled people and their allies in decolonizing community work. Few answers, or even good practice pointers can be provided but through sharing the stories, action research for inclusive education has evolved which will set about "changing places, changing practices, changing minds" (Armstrong & Moore, 2004: 15).

I deliberately open the next part of this discussion with a controversial problem-oriented extract from the first visit I made. I shuddered to share this story with the teachers who sent me to collect it because it so easily betrayed my inability to separate the fundamental emotionality I attach to children's lives from clear thinking about either decolonizing practice or disability issues. Further, it uncovered my deficit view of segregated education contexts in which some of the teachers were working and undoubtedly reaffirms the legacy of colonialism in disabled children's lives. Helpfully, Walker (2007) argues "stories help us to think well and more wisely about ourselves and our practice." The discussion now builds on ideas presented previously about the power of story telling for promoting change (Clough, 2002; Goodley et al., 2004), extending these to a new cultural situation.

THE *PROBLEM* OF SEGREGATION
EXPERIENCED BY DISABLED CHILDREN

> Inclusion is impossible. I am the Dean of Correction so I'm the only one allowed to hit pupils in school. That boy George, he's like a regular child and him and his friends beat up on each other. He said "you can't hit me" to the teachers. But I said "I *can* hit you because I am the Dean of Correction." But I thought "hitting this child won't make a difference." He said "you can take things from me, and stop my privileges . . ." but I thought "that won't hurt you." So I noticed his weak hands and how he can't hardly stand if he don't lean on his hands and I said "pick up them telephone directories and hold them up over your head and keep doing." And I said "that's your punishment. And also you have to sit with me for the whole afternoon." And when the afternoon finished I said to the House Mother "please don't include him in anything until tomorrow morning."
>
> (From notes on a visit to a segregated school for disabled children)

I have no sense of the "validity" of the above account. I tried to write down just what I saw and heard and claim not to have altered or embellished events. I was disturbed to realize the huge negative implications embedded in portraying *this* image from my first visit to a segregated school in the Caribbean. I asked myself and my students "what tensions and contradictions does the narrative betray? Does this story help to shift some of those boundaries that shore up exclusion of disabled children and young people in Trinidad and St Lucia? And, if so, how?"

When the teachers reflected on this story the power of narrative practices as a vehicle for transformation of exclusion came immediately to the fore. They found an authenticity in the story and the "frictional platform" that it provided enabled troubling implications to be first realized and then resisted.

Teachers who read the story articulated feelings of guilt and blame in relation to elements of the extract they said they recognized or practices with which they felt they colluded. These reflections increased motivation and hope for change, so that stories of the visits, complete with all the problematics of one person's inadequate personal rendition, opened up a dialogic space in which teachers could think about practices in segregated settings to generate views more in accordance with how they would wish to experience inclusion themselves.

Thus, stories allowed impressions of the actuality of disabled children's experience of segregated education to be shared; meaning could be negotiated and applied to understanding individual and social worlds of experience (Goodley et al., 2004). The narratives disturbed and compromised my own theory making as well as the contexts in which the teachers operated, thus opening up a much more equal platform for discussion within which, my affinity with the academy no longer provided a guarantee of safe passage.

Part of the process of sharing the stories involved accepting that any commentator will bring their own meanings to the story; we might reject a story or look at it differently, but through discussion new possibilities for developing inclusive practice could be opened up. Working with "the story" reminded us that all stories are socially constructed and must be interleaved with other stories (Goodley et al., 2004). The focal extract, for example, is part of a principal's longer story reflecting on culturally dominant accounts of what a good principal should do, referencing locally held beliefs such as "adult authority must not be contested." Behind the extract lie other stories, for instance that an individual principal is responsible for setting the standards of behavior in a school, and failure to do this will be criticized. Other narrative extracts from the same visit were labeled "loving and caring practice"—the Dean was, after all, explaining they are not reduced to beating a disabled child. The stories help create understanding but are both partial and partisan. It would be impossible to convey the actuality of the Dean of Corrections conduct, but by making explicit our *own particular witnessing* of what occurs we may be able to open up routes which will allow for possible applications of inclusive thinking.

What the teachers felt most strongly, was that sharing these observations of practice affirmed the critical importance of (i) opening up segregated spaces to the gaze of outsiders and (ii) raising disabled children's own voices. They reflected upon their own shared history of oppression and being silenced to realize the imperative for transforming the experience of disabled children.

So, despite our frustrations about the difficulty of reconciling a theory and practice of inclusive education with the actuality of teachers and disabled children's lives in Trinidad and St Lucia, through identifying and analyzing our concerns, the road to inclusion was being opened up. "That boy George" said one of the mainstream teachers "he's like a regular child in my school."

In notes from a mainstream infant school's "Special Needs Assessment Unit," I had written:

> I can't pick out anyone who would really be a candidate for segregated schooling as I know it. The deciding factors seem to be "he's a bit slow" or "he doesn't remember very well." Apparently all parents want their children to stay at this school but the principal says "they are in denial. They say their child must stay here but they stay and they don't learn anything."

One of the teachers immediately dissected "the problem" in the above extract saying "then our teaching problems are the root of children's exclusion" at which point the potential of social model thinking for inclusive practice seemed plain—and appropriate.

INCLUSION OF DISABLED CHILDREN
IN TRINIDAD AND ST LUCIA

"There are many challenges here," says the principal, "We are the only school that will take many of these pupils. We can't leave them on the corridors of a school that doesn't want them."

The school runs a feeding programme. Some families can't pay but the school divides food paid for amongst all who need it. This displeases some parents who work hard to send their dollar for their own child to have a dollar's worth of food but the principal says "if we see there's a child with their head on the table we try to feed them." In every class there are children with their heads on the table. The principal says it is difficult to pull the parents in to a close relationship with the school, though most of them attended the school themselves.

The principal, the deputy and a passing PE teacher all agree the school tries to welcome any and every child. They talk about a boy in standard three with a cleft palate and the deputy says "we try to teach them [the children] to love him." They talk about an ex-pupil named Jewel whom they are very proud to have included right through her primary years. Jewel, they say, is autistic and has severe learning difficulties. By the time she was in standard three "she was a big, big girl and if she raged the teacher would have to sit on her to keep her down." "But we worked with her" said the PE teacher, "and her mother came in with her every day and we got used to her and she got used to us." Currently, there is great disappointment because Jewel has not gone on to secondary school. Only one segregated school has offered her a place but her father insists she must go to a mainstream school. Because no school will accept her she now stays home and has done so for nearly two years. The principal says this is wrong because there is meant to be universal secondary education but nobody takes any notice of the absence of Jewel.

When the topic of children with special needs comes up most people interpret this in terms of literacy or behavior problems. In Mr David's class I see a boy who cannot stand unaided who is being helped by his classmates: "Oh that boy is Kevin" says Mr David, "He has arthritis and he cannot walk." And then he remembers there's also Felix who mostly uses echolalic speech, twin girls who won't speak and of course all the hungry children who can barely lift up their heads to learn. A group is changing for PE but one boy lies across the table with his head down. The PE teacher has her arm round him and is trying to get him to nibble some cereal "come on, if you have a little munchy you might be able to do it" she urges.

And then, from the upstairs veranda there is great excitement because Jewel and her mother are coming across the yard. The principal, the deputy and the PE teacher hurry down to bring Jewel over to meet me. She shuffles over but looks to the ground. They insist she greets me and tells me her name. Without looking up she says in a straight American TV style "Good morning, I am a thirteen-year-old girl." Her mother urges her to "say good morning properly." She repeats her greeting, twiddling her dress and looking at the ground: "Good morning, I am a thirteen-year-old girl. Good morning, I am a thirteen-year-old girl." The staff are very proud Jewel is here so that I can see for myself the complexity of impairment they are willing to accommodate.

Jewel's mother cannot praise the school highly enough. She says Jewel begs her to bring her back to the school. She feels desperately disappointed that Jewel is missing so much school as she now spends her time staying home watching TV. Her father is adamant she cannot go to a segregated school but nothing else is on offer. Jewel's mother says people in the community came to know Jewel when she was at the primary school and she had friends who would help her if they saw her in the street. But now all her friends have gone onto secondary school and she doesn't know them anymore.

We walk across to the Special Education Unit as Jewel makes known she wants to see the teacher there. Jewel clutches and strokes the teacher's arm but does not look at her. She's still saying "Good morning, I am a thirteen-year-old girl."

(Extract from mainstream Junior School)

Again, the teachers said "that's authentic—you can see what we're up against now Miss." The stories from the visits were beginning to attach credibility to my own outsider theory making and to function as a site of transformative thinking; the rhetoric of inclusion could be applied to local practice in tangible ways.

Following on from the first story, this one generated further discussion about the invidious purposes of segregated schooling. We learn from this brief glimpse of a mainstream primary school that there are daily impressive things to see concerning the inclusion of disabled and vulnerable children in Trinidad and St Lucia. Teachers have quietly and diligently rolled out inclusion initiatives over the years often at their own expense and at the cost of their own career progression since academic attainment is the dominant focus of education in the region. The teachers agreed there are "a large number of children with special educational needs already included into the public education systems in almost every country in the Caribbean" (Armstrong et al., 2005). They could see the origins and significance of an action research project in which they could themselves be the pioneers of a movement to challenge socially constructed barriers which create exclusions. They felt medical constructions of disability, such as relegate Jewel to segregated provision, reflect colonial ways of organizing teaching and learning and that education systems which shore up these constructions have no place in contemporary aspirations for children in the East Caribbean countries (OECS, 2000).

The teachers noticed my failure to adequately engage with the voices of disabled children and young people. I had noticed from the mapping of my visits around schools that disabled children's voices were not privileged by staff. Teachers said they feel themselves to be working in a context where children's views are seldom sought. The question of *how* to enable children's own voices to determine the most appropriate and adequate support in their own terms is not easy to address. The teachers felt there to be a strong imperative for accessing Jewel's own perspectives even though communication with her was clearly neither an easy or comfortable process. It was noted Jewel's preferred mode of communication may be tactile as she stroked the sleeve of the teacher she liked and questions were raised about the nature of "voice" and the necessity of making children's communication difficulties our own communication responsibilities. The importance of accessing the perspectives of parents who are reluctant to be in a close relationship with schools was brought into the debate. It seemed through shared reflections on what we had agreed to term "images of actuality" the teachers had entered into a "culturally curious questioning" of their own which they very quickly saw as enriching possibilities for advancing the project of inclusion.

The "exceptional" cases of Jewel, Felix, the twins and their peers were taken by the teachers as points of entry into possibilities for inclusion of other children and thus, the platform for resistance of exclusions, whilst threatened initially by frictions arising from the distance between our insider / outsider perspectives, began to coalesce. My anxieties concerning the limitations of my exposure to the settings in which the children and teachers were situated had been profoundly unhelpful; a much more productive dialogue had ensued from acknowledging the fragility of my own perceptions and assumptions. And likewise, the teachers gained confidence through knowing I had to some small extent now entered into their circumstances, including seeing first hand the sparse material base and resource constraints in which most of them do their jobs. As they recognized the applicability and relevance of principles pertaining to a social model of disability, and the opportunities it affords in the project of inclusion, they in turn enabled me to gain confidence in the relevance of the claims.

The extracts in the following section provide a context through which the teachers located connections between inclusive education and social justice.

FORGING THE AGENDAS OF SOCIAL JUSTICE AND INCLUSION

The principal says there is uncertainty about the age of some pupils because they were abandoned as babies with no record of date of birth. Some of the children attend from a psychiatric hospital where they live. Three pupils live in a "geriatric home." "But then," says the principal, nodding towards the window, "all of our children should be out there. They should all be out there." It can work, but with support. Our community isn't ready for our children yet. Then she told the story of the boy taken on an outing to the Savannah. "Another boy in the park was eating a hot-dog—our boy went over and took the hot-dog and you should have seen the way they jumped on him. But we love them and learn. You learn more about yourself. As a teacher here you learn more than anything else I think."

(Extract from visit to a segregated school)

The teachers reflecting on this story fell into a shared realization that excluded children are excluded adults:

[W]hat will happen to him when he graduates from school and is also asked to leave the orphanage where he lives? His heart and his head are in a different place. We can't reach him though we can try to show him that we love him . . .

(Segregated school teacher)

While the stories were found to be interesting because they record real accounts of experience within the context of special and inclusive education it was clear that they were also generating new ideas about how teachers can forge the agendas of social justice and exclusions:

"Some are older than seventeen" says the principal, by which she refers to something said in other segregated schools; as these children have nowhere to go once they reach school leaving age they continue coming to school although there is no funding to support this: "[R]ather than leave them in an institution we have them back here. Some come back to see us on their birthdays, one brought his new baby in and one came back recently to tell us about his job as a coastguard."

(Extract from a segregated school)

When the pupils reach school leaving age we try to let them stay on anyway if they have nowhere else to spend their time. Some, like the receptionist, the cake baker, one of the teaching assistants and several of the gardeners became permanent fixtures and work here. We are really proud of our teaching assistant—she is an ex-pupil with Downs Syndrome. She doesn't speak but has a great rapport with a couple of the boys with Autism.

(Extract from a segregated school)

The narratives encouraged the teachers to reflect on particular ramifications of disabled children's experiences. The "problem" of inclusion continued to be highly motivating including for those who had originally felt uncertain about their commitment to reducing exclusion. The teachers began to "re-write" the stories to raise possibilities for inclusion and to tell stories of their own.

CONCLUSION

In my mind it is still clear that:

> the only people who can successfully engage fully with local people, and get them to reveal their true thoughts and feelings, are people who are truly from and still part of the community.
>
> (Braithwaite et al., 2007: 73)

Yet in the work which has been the focus of this chapter, the sharing of narratives told and aired through very different eyes has given a special way of sharing multi-layered reflections on possibilities for practice. This in turn generated specific ideas for projects involving the teachers in insider action research. When lack of research funding obstructed plans, the teachers undertook to construct all of their remaining assignments for their Masters programme as action research endeavors to raise seldom heard perspectives on inclusion in the schools and communities in which they work. This collective project will generate a huge amount of new knowledge from the insider perspectives of some of the most excluded children and marginalized teachers in Trinidad and St Lucia; through five assignments each, twenty teachers will engage in one hundred efforts to raise insider perspectives on special and inclusive education in the region within two years. Bland and Atweh (2007) acknowledge the power of teacher's working "collaboratively towards positive outcomes for the participants and their schools" through such action research initiatives. Many of the teachers will work with disabled people and their representative agencies to extend and highlight understanding of the wider politics of participation. Some of the teachers, of course, *are* disabled people or parents of disabled children.

There is much that has been left out about the journey teachers have taken me on as part of the process of consolidating our commitments to inclusion. We found the challenge of story making and sharing opened up a rich seam of possibilities for widening inclusion. Together, we found the stories help to make visible sources of exclusion so that it then becomes possible to set about dismantling these.

Through recognizing and building on the distance between our respective perspectives we have been able to acknowledge discomfort but still to find routes towards inclusion. There are many unresolved questions including what do we mean in theoretical and practical terms by the "voices" of disabled children? (Moore, 2000). And what are the implications for practice offered by the raising of voices of disabled children that we will need constantly to interrogate?

Two images from the school visits prove poignant as I reflect back on the central discoveries of the school visits discussed in this chapter. First a memorable classroom poster provides testimony to the power of narrative:

> *A story is a wonderful thing*
> *The ones that I have read . . .*
> *They do not stay inside the book*
> *They stay inside my head*

(Classroom poster)

But as I turned to go, with a head full of questions about disabled children's entitlements, another poster, unforgettable for different reasons:

> *You are the U in ToUrism!*
> *Be a good host.*
> *YoU will benefit.*
> *Tourists fund our schools.*

(Classroom poster)

Clearly there is no room for complacency in the project of decolonizing children's lives.

REFERENCES

Armstrong, A., Armstrong D., Carlyle Lynch B. and Severin, S. (2005). Special and inclusive education in the Eastern Caribbean: Policy practice and provision. *International Journal of Inclusive Education*, 9(1): 71–87.

Armstrong, F. (2007) Disability, education and social change in England since 1960. *History of Education*, 36(4): pp. 551–568.

Armstrong, F. and Barton, L. (Eds.) (1999). *Disability, Human Rights and Education: Cross Cultural Perspectives*. Buckingham: Open University Press.

Armstrong, F. and Moore, M. (2004). *Action Research for Inclusive Education: Changing Places, Changing Practices, Changing Minds*. London: Routledge-Falmer.

Barton, L. (1998). *Developing an emancipatory research agenda: possibilities and Dilemmas*, in P. Clough and L. Barton (Eds.) *Articulating with Difficulty: Research Voices in Inclusive Education*. London: Sage.

Bland, D. and Atweh, B. (2007). Students as researchers: engaging students' voices in PAR. *Educational Action Research*, 15(3): 337–349.

Braithwaite, R., Cockwill, S., O'Neill, M., and Rebane, D. (2007). Action researchers: The experiences of community members as they become community-based: Insider participatory action research in disadvantaged post-industrial areas. *Action Research*, 5: 61–74.

Burman, E., Aitken, G., Alldred, P., Allwood, R., Billington, T., Goldberg, B., Gordo Lopez, A.J., Heenan, C., Marks, D., and Warner, S. (1996). *Psychology, Discourse Practice: From Regulation to Resistance*. London: Taylor & Francis.

Clough, P. (2002). *Narratives and Fictions in Educational Research.* Buckingham: Open University Press.

Dunn, K. and Moore, M. (2005). Developing accessible playspace in the UK: What they want and what works. *Children, Youth and Environments,* 15(1): 331–353.

Freire, A.M.A. and Macedo, D. (Eds.) (1998) *The Paulo Freire Reader.* London: Continuum.

Goodley, D., Lawthom, R., Clough, P. and Moore, M. (2004). *Researching Life Stories: Method, Theory and Analyses in a Biographical Age.* London: Routledge Falmer.

Julien, G. (2008). Street children in Trinidad and Tobago: Understanding Their Lives and Experiences. *Community, Work and Family,* 11(4): 475–488.

Kaomea, J. (2004). Dilemmas of an indigenous academic: A native Hawaiian story, in K. Mutua and B. Blue Swadner (Eds.) *Decolonizing Research in Cross-Cultural Contexts: Critical Personal Narratives.* Albany: State University of New York Press.

Moore, M. (Ed.) (2000). *Insider Perspectives on Inclusion: Raising Voices, Raising Issues.* Sheffield: Philip Armstrong.

Moore, M. and Dunn, K. (1999). Disability, human rights and education in Romania, in F. Armstrong and L. Barton (Eds.) *Disability, Human Rights and Education: Cross-cultural Perspectives.* Buckingham: Open University Press.

Office of the Deputy Prime Minister (2003). *Developing Accessible Play Space: A Good Practice Guide.* Twoten Publishers.

Organization of Eastern Caribbean States (OECS) OECS Education Reform Unit. (2000). *Pillars forPartnership and Progress.* St Lucia, OECS Secretariat.

Oliver, M. (1996). *Understanding Disability: From Theory to Practice.* London: Macmillan Publishers.

Smith, L. (2005). *Decolonizing Methodologies. Research and Indigenous Peoples.* London: Zed Books Ltd. Union of the Physically Impaired Against Segregation (UPIAS) (1976). *Fundamental Principles of Disability.* London: Union of the Physically Impaired Against Segregation.

Sparkes, A. (2007). Embodiment, academics, and the audit culture: A story seeking Consideration. *Qualitative Research,* 7: 521.

Walker, M. (2007). Action research and narratives: Finely aware and richly responsible. *Educational Action Research,* 15(2): 295–303.

8 Inclusion of Disabled Students in Higher Education in Zimbabwe

Tsitsi Chataika

INTRODUCTION

Zimbabwe, whose estimated population is 12, 236, 800, is a non-coastal Southern African country located north of the Tropic of Capricorn between Zambezi and Limpopo Rivers (World Fact Book, 2006). It is bordered by Zambia to the north, South Africa to the south, Mozambique to the east, and Botswana to the west. Zimbabwe is part of a great plateau, which constitutes the major feature of the geography of Southern Africa. Zimbabwe is a nation being overwhelmed by a plethora of challenges where its citizens are increasingly disenfranchised, profoundly frustrated and feeling a sense of hopelessness. The level of political instability, economic disintegration and poverty, which characterize everyday life in Zimbabwe, virtually relegate issues pertaining to the rights and needs of people with impairments to the lowest "rung" of the national priority ladder.

The economy has shrunk by over 40% in the last ten years, as the unemployment stands at 80%. Official statistics reported in October 2008 put Zimbabwe's annual inflation in July 2008 at 231,000,000 % (Central Statistical Office, 2008), although independent economists estimate a much higher inflation rate. Undoubtedly, such hyperinflation has caused widespread cash shortages. Zimbabwe is being ravaged by HIV and AIDS with over 3,000 people dying every week from AIDS-related diseases (Munro, 2005). The once cherished family and community ties are fast diminishing because of socio- economic hardships and "forced" migration in search for greener pastures (Munro, 2005). The one time "breadbasket of Africa" is faced with severe shortages of all staple items, and the once admired African health system has almost collapsed (Lang & Charowa, 2007). The usual closely-knit family institution has been substantially weakened by this lingering humanitarian crisis (Mpofu, 2001). This is like a country under siege and where a time bomb awaits to explode and wipe away the entire nation. Given the above situation, the challenge is on how disability issues are ever going to be prioritized within the context of other development priorities.

Inclusion of disabled students in higher in Zimbabwe is situated in the midst of intolerable social ills, poverty, political instability and community disintegration. The chapter brings to light the personal experiences of disabled students in higher education in Zimbabwe based on findings from my qualitative doctoral research project (Chataika, 2007). The study focused on personal experiences of disabled students' from the University of Zimbabwe. As the aim of this book is to reposition the idea of community and consider implications of change for a wide audience of those committed to pioneering an agenda for social justice within educational organizations and their wider communities; it is essential to understand this chapter in the context where Zimbabwe is experiencing political instability and economic melt-down and the challenges presented by such circumstances. Disabled students' experiences presented in this chapter highlight issues they grapple with in their day-to-day living. Theoretical perspectives, innovative practice and policy are interrogated, and some ideas to enhance inclusive practices are provided.

PROVISION FOR DISABLED STUDENTS IN HIGHER EDUCATION IN ZIMBABWE

Higher education is usually considered an imperative opportunity to a better future. It has been well documented that employment opportunities are most likely to double or treble judging against those without higher education qualifications (Magnus, 2006). In addition, the Department for Education and Skill [DfES] (2002) found those who have degree qualifications earn on average, 50% more than employees without degrees, and have better chances of having job promotions compared to non-graduates.

Unlike the long-standing debate over mainstreaming within the school system, higher education has hardly committed itself to the education of disabled people (Borland & James, 1999). Since 1995, there has been a rapid expansion of a higher education system in Zimbabwe in response to a huge demand that has increased since independence (Kariwo, 2007). Currently, there are nine state universities, four private universities and one specializing in distance learning; bringing the total to thirteen. It is however estimated that every year, Zimbabwe has an excess of 8, 000 students who meet the criteria but fail to secure a university place (Kariwo, 2007). In addition, there are eleven state and three private teachers' colleges; 279 private and ten state polytechnics and industrial training centers across the country (Chataika, 2003).

Despite efforts to deliberately widen access in tertiary and higher education, disabled students are still under-represented. Zimbabwe is one of the few countries in sub-Saharan Africa with legislation on disability. The Disabled Persons Act was passed in 1992 and amended in 1996, to make provision for the welfare and rehabilitation of disabled persons. The Act was enacted with the disabled war veterans in mind, and as a result, has no mention of the education of disabled people (Mpofu, 2000). Consequently, any social group denied access to further and higher education is likely to be excluded from the social and economic development of society (Borland & James, 1999). This seems to be the case with disabled people in Zimbabwe. In 2003, the student population in universities, technical and teachers' colleges was 78,481; unfortunately, disabled students constituted less than 1% of this figure (Zimbabwe National Report of Education, 2004). At present, there are only two universities with Disability Resource Centers: University of Zimbabwe and Midlands State University, the former having a longstanding establishment. However, comparing to the student population, the number of students who declared a disability in the 2004–2005 academic year at the University of Zimbabwe is insignificant (sixty students) in comparison to the entire student population of about 12,000 (Kariwo, 2007).

THE UNIVERSITY OF ZIMBABWE
DISABILITY RESOURCE CENTRE

In 1978, a few disabled students with physical impairments regarded not to require special academic and physical accommodations were admitted at the University of Zimbabwe. Despite the absence of a disability policy, in 1982, the first students with visual impairment were enrolled, which was a challenge as these students required specialist services such as Braille material, assistive technology and other forms of relevant support services (Disability Resource Centre, 2006). In 1987, the Disability Resource Centre was officially set up and a Disability Coordinator's position was established (Disability Resource Centre, 2006). In 2004, Midlands State University started admitting disabled students, enabling disabled scholars to at least have some form of choice between the two universities. However, my study focused on the former as it was operational before the latter.

In 2005, the University of Zimbabwe Disability Resource Centre presented a draft policy to the Senate. The policy document was endorsed in the same year, and this was a major breakthrough in the education of disabled students, and a milestone towards inclusion of disabled students in Zimbabwe (Disability Policy, 2005). However, with the current situation in Zimbabwe highlighted earlier on, the implementation of the policy at the moment is highly unlikely as the university is grappling with the economic woes facing the country. Worse still, the absence of a mandatory policy such as the British Special Education and Disability Act 2001 (SENDA, 2001), Americans With Disabilities Act [ADA] 1990, and Australian Disability Discrimination Act [DDA] 1992 derails the inclusion process. Without such policy, it could be concluded that it is not mandatory for higher education institutions in Zimbabwe to admit disabled applicants. Unfortunately, lack of legislation that promotes the inclusion of disabled students in higher education militates against inclusionary practices (Chataika, 2007).

METHODOLOGICAL RESOURCES

What has been of concern throughout the study is the lack of empirical research evidence on lived experiences of disabled students in higher education in Zimbabwe. It was therefore imperative to engage with methodological resources that enabled disabled students to share their personal experiences—hence the use of narrative and ethnography. Narrative inquiry allowed me to consider informants' educational experiences leading up to, during and in some come cases, beyond university. In the study, narrative research and ethnography allowed me to:

(i) Collect stories and reflect on the expertise and experiences of disabled students in higher education.
(ii) Explore life stories of disabled students in a family, educational context, and the society at large.
(iii) Gather invaluable insights into the inclusion of disabled students or lack of it, and attempt to influence change through recommendations;
(iv) Evaluate the impact of policy and practice on educational experiences;
(v) Produce data that enabled me to develop and explore the social ecosystem framework.

Fifteen students initially registered interest in sharing their life experiences. Since the in-depth study only required five key informants, variables such as type of impairment, age, year of study and faculty were considered in order to have some variation of issues. The key informants were Edmore, Fortune, Peter, Rudo and Mufaro. The remaining ten students agreed to share their experiences in focus groups. Data reported in this chapter is that of the five main key informants.

Interviews were held to collect participants' experiences. There was no interview schedule, but informants talked through their life experiences, and the researcher probed for further information and clarifications. Interviews varied in length, depending on the amount of information an interviewee was prepared to share. Interviews were audio taped and transcribed, and later turned into narrative stories. Written stories were then emailed to students for verification, which they approved, some with minor alterations. Eventually, all the five informants agreed finished versions of the stories conveyed their reflections.

Analysis of the stories was based on Kidder and Fine's (1997) argument that analysis strengthens stories and meaning. Data were analyzed using the narrative analysis (Bell, 1999), which was "theory-driven" through the use of the social ecosystem framework guided by theoretical resources of disability studies, inclusive education, and postcolonial literatures (Chataika, 2007). Thus, narrative analysis allows the researcher to be explicit about the political and cultural location of both the narratives of participants and the researcher. The methodology utilized is similar to, and expands on the analysis strategies of grounded theory (Strauss & Corbin, 1990; Glaser, 1978), and thematic analysis (Bell, 1999). Narrative analysis shifts the focus of the research from what participants and the researcher say to how they tell their stories (Bell, 1999; Chataika, 2005).

LIVED EXPERIENCES OF DISABLED STUDENTS

Barriers to accessing higher education throughout the world are in most cases, due to inequalities inherent in the educational systems (Leicester & Lovell, 1994; Borland & James, 1999). Therefore, obstacles arise from the ways in which higher education institutions are structured and function and from the dominant attitudes that inform and shape the practices of institutions. Institutional barriers identified in this study, which have also been identified in other studies include lack of access (Riddell, Tinklin & Alistair, 2005), lack of disability awareness (Wolfendale, 1996; Borland & James, 1999), undermining the potential of disabled students (Riddell et al., 2005), and failure of an institution to publicize services and facilities available for disabled students (Borland & James, 1999; Wray, 2003). In addition, students lack support and guidance when applying to higher education institutions. Above all, problems experienced by disabled students are often attributed to inadequate support services and resources in the form of assistive devices or technical equipment. It is important to bear in mind that although students are now accessing higher education in Zimbabwe, there are some for whom higher education is still inaccessible (Chataika, 2007). For those fortunate to proceed to higher education, it became clear from what the interviewees said that access issues affect them at every stage of their university life:

> When I wanted to go to university, I applied to the university of my choice, however, the Registrar there referred me here [University of Zimbabwe].
>
> (Rudo)

Other students did not address the issue as Rudo did, probably because the University of Zimbabwe was their first choice, or maybe they knew it was the only university with facilities for disabled students at the time of applying. If the latter is true, disabled students have therefore to assess very carefully the built-in environment and the availability of support such as assistive provision prior to making applications (Riddell, et al., 2005; Howell, 2006). Two participants were unaware of the existence of disability services at the University of Zimbabwe. A lack of knowledge regarding provisions universities have for disabled students, or lack of provisions altogether can adversely impact on progression into higher education. This raises serious concerns about the provision of equal opportunities, and the extent to which inclusion is embraced within the higher education sector in Zimbabwe.

The stories I collected revealed disputes between students and academic staff about the student's choice of courses:

> The main problem that I had was that of being accepted into the Law faculty. They tried to brush me off until I was helped by one lecturer, who is also a practicing lawyer, who had to appeal to the Admissions Office.
>
> (Peter)

Challenges related to admission are familiar to me since I have worked as a Disability Coordinator at the University of Zimbabwe before. I remember writing numerous memos and making emotionally laden telephone calls to various academic departments, and at times having to approach the heads of departments face-to-face so that disabled students could be admitted. This process was tiresome and in most cases, due to continuous persistence, disabled students were eventually accepted. The main hindrance, from my understanding, was lack of a disability policy to guide admission of disabled students. There was a culture of "supposed ineligibility" which can be directly linked to the dominant discourse of disability and special needs, which provides the basis for a segregated and inadequate schooling system (Howell, 2006). While higher education institutions have not been separated into "special" and "ordinary" institutions, the overriding medical discourse around disability (Oliver, 1996) has placed the emphasis on the nature of the learner's impairment and the extent to which this impairment is perceived to limit particular capabilities, including academic pursuits (Howell, 2006). In line with Howell's analysis, Fortune had this to say:

> The people at the University of Zimbabwe had a tendency of looking down upon us such that even if you were studying for the same degree as theirs, they would assume and conclude that you reached that level of education through charity marks or favors.
>
> (Fortune)

Three participants felt that the registration process was cumbersome and time consuming. Rudo commented:

> The Disability Resource Centre staff took me to countless offices to register and the registration offices were scattered and the process was very tiring. A lot of time is wasted by moving from one office to the other.
>
> (Rudo)

Registration barriers are usually exacerbated by higher education registration arrangements that are very inaccessible to many disabled students (Howell, 2006). These arrangements leave disabled students physically and emotionally drained by the time they complete the registration process.

Depending on their particular impairment, students experienced barriers because of inaccessible physical environment or teaching and learning methods (or both) at some point during their studies. Once they "got in" to university, participants wanted to "get on" and pursue their studies, but access and mobility difficulties presented obstacles to overcome in pursuit of ordinary involvement in university life. For Mufaro, access to physical space and events was fraught with limitations and became an obstacle to her full participation in both social and academic activities:

> This university is not very accessible, even places that they classify as accessible. If you were to be in our shoes one day, you will see that it's not all that accessible.
>
> (Mufaro)

Physical access was a huge concern to Mufaro since she is a wheelchair user, and therefore, spent enormous amounts of time and energy negotiating many seemingly accessible buildings. This illustrates how students with mobility difficulties face substantial challenges, and in some cases, have to make long journeys to try to get one accessible entrance into a building (Riddell et al., 2005; Howell & Lazarus, 2003). The University's Disability Resource Centre, in most cases, liaises with various departments to make sure that a lecture is located in a more accessible venue. However, Mufaro described limited responses:

> There are extreme cases where venues for lectures are upstairs and then if you bring that up with the Disability Resource Centre, alterations are sometimes made. But if not, you may just leave it as it is and devise a way of getting there.
>
> (Mufaro)

Apart from lecture theatres, most faculty offices are inaccessible and therefore it becomes difficult for students to access them if need arises:

> They [university] could look at putting at least office receptions on the ground floor and then maybe the other offices can be upstairs, avoiding inconveniences.
>
> (Mufaro)

Access goes beyond physical access to support services, resources, teaching and learning methods (Borland & James, 1999). Once physical access was addressed, students could still have difficulties in their experience of learning because of inaccessible teaching and learning methods (Hall & Tinklin, 2002; Howell, 2006). Unquestionably, lack of, and/or inadequate equipment and resources disadvantage disabled students. Students, particularly with visual impairment appreciated the provisions from the Disability Resource Centre. Peter indicated a decrease in the challenges with the help of assistive devices:

Since I started university education, when writing my assignments and examinations, I have been using a Braille output gadget called a Eureka A4, which is then connected onto an ordinary printer and this has made my life very easy.

(Peter)

This confirms the facilitative role of assistive devices which can have a positive impact on an individual's functioning (Schneider, 2006). Appropriate technology makes studying a lot easier. I noticed, as the former Disability Coordinator, that disabled students regularly struggle with inadequate equipment. I observed disabled students having to share tape recorders, Perkins Braillers, and typewriters for example, which made it difficult for them to study at their own convenience. The arrangement at the University of Zimbabwe is that the Disability Resource Centre should, in principle, supply appropriate equipment and resources to disabled students. However, in practice, budgetary constraints do not allow this to happen so that lack of equipment creates a barrier that adversely affects students' academic performance. Appropriate and adequate provision should not be additional extra, but a core element of the overall service that an institution should make available to disabled people (Wray, 2003). Considering the small budget allocation for the Disability Resource Centre however, it is very difficult to secure adequate equipment, especially bearing in mind that most of this equipment is not locally available. The situation becomes more complicated with Zimbabwe's current economic downturn (Lang & Charowa, 2007) and it is difficult to allocate foreign currency to the Disability Resource Centre. Unless political leaders put their political agendas aside and concentrate on improving the current Zimbabwe's humanitarian crisis, disabled students may only dream of making it to higher education. For those disabled students already in the system, they may continue to study under exigent circumstances.

Problems experienced by disabled students in the classroom are often purely attributed to lack of necessary assistive devices to meet the potential demand, and those that are available are far too expensive for the large majority of Zimbabweans to afford (Chataika, 2007). While such facilities may form an important part of the enabling conditions necessary to support students in their studies, limited attention is paid to the actual teaching and learning process, and the extent to which it may marginalize or exclude some learners (Howell, 2006). As a result, pedagogical issues become apparent. Pedagogy encompasses all instructional ideas, the range of approaches, strategies, competencies, skills, tactics or organizing ideas that a teacher can do to improve student outcomes (Corbett, 2001). Research has shown that the effect of the teacher is the largest single factor affecting students' achievement and that some inclusive pedagogical practices are more powerful or effective than exclusive ones since one size hardly fits all learners

(Moore, 2000). From what disabled students have told me, much of the variability in their academic experiences was determined by the pedagogies used by individual lecturers. According to the students some lecturers were positive and understanding and others much less so:

> Of all my first year lecturers, Mr Makanaka was the only one who knew and understood about my hearing problems; he was very good and supportive.
>
> (Edmore)

Peter was very enthusiastic about the support he got from his academic department:

> Most of them understand us, researching is a little bit difficult and different in that we depend on others to read for us and record the material and at times, braille it. Therefore, they give me more time before I submit my assignments.
>
> (Peter)

However, where lecturers lacked awareness or specific knowledge of disability and appropriate support, students reported adverse experiences. A typical example is where a visually impaired learner is part of a class where the lecturer makes use of overhead projector slides without reading out or describing what is contained in the slides, on the assumption that all the students have access to the visual material. For students with visual impairment and those with hearing impairment, reflecting on access to their learning experiences is important (Fuller, Bradley & Healey, 2004). Students with visual and hearing impairments identified a number of common issues in relation to teaching and assessment where lecturers were not engaging in inclusive pedagogies. Students with hearing impairment pointed out the absence of sign language interpreters at the university for example. Rudo and Edmore explain how some lecturers did not consider their hearing impairment during the teaching and learning:

> Bearing in mind that I do not hear it is bad sometimes when attending lectures. I don't hear what they say. During lectures, I rely on my friends from whom I copy lecture notes. I suppose I would prefer to have an interpreter during lessons.
>
> (Rudo)

> The most difficult part of my university studies was third year because most of the lecturers did not give notes but there would only be discussions in class, and therefore I did not benefit.
>
> (Edmore)

A lack of public and professional awareness of disability formed the generative core of participants' difficulties in accessing knowledge and information:

> The learning process is a painful one; a lecturer writes notes on the board and you will have to ask someone to read for you.
>
> (Fortune)

Such treatment demonstrates a lack of awareness and understanding as Edmore, who has hearing impairment, described in an ordeal during an examination:

> I was robbed of a distinction because the paper had gross errors, they [invigilators] instructed us to leave some of the questions while corrections were being made, then we could continue later. I did not hear it when it was announced over the PA system. When corrected questions were then brought in, it was too late. It affected my approach to all the remaining papers.
>
> (Edmore)

Edmore was disadvantaged during his examination because the university did not have the services of sign language interpretation to assist deaf students. As a result, Rudo and Edmore had to put up with communication barriers in lectures, seminars, group work, oral presentations and examinations. Edmore identified large classes and tutorials based on discussions or dictation as inaccessible. Dictation is unquestionably, geared towards hearing students. Through lack of attention to inclusive pedagogy, opportunities for disabled students to contribute to sessions are severely restricted (Fuller et al., 2004).

The above analysis implies that lecturers should be aware that inappropriate teaching methods are bound to erect unnecessary learning barriers that grossly interfere with one's intellectual capabilities (Hall & Tinklin, 2002). Thus, an understanding of the power of questioning one's practices is central to teachers' practices. Increasing instructional repertoires contributes to inclusive practice that takes into account the abilities and learning styles of all learners (Bennett & Rolheiser, 2001).

In terms of accessible reading materials, Fortune remembers how his journey to success became "thorny and hilly" at the University of Zimbabwe:

> The university had no reading materials for the blind [*sic*] and I had to depend on my friend who would read for me.
>
> (Fortune)

The students incurred extra financial costs as a direct result of disabling educational environments (Riddell et al., 2005). It was essential for them to be able to meet these costs in order to access their course(s). Although the students were getting some government grants and loans for their day-to-day upkeep, this was often not adequate and they had to find additional funding from other sources and forego other things:

> Whereas the other students would use their grants to buy jeans, I would buy study material because I knew I had to depend on myself for studying.
>
> (Edmore)

The Higher Education Funding Council for England (HEFCE) introduced Disabled Students Allowances in 2000–2001 based on the argument that disabled students are most likely to incur disability-related costs that warrant spending more than non-disabled students (DfES, 2002). These may include extra travel costs, a need for specialist equipment such as voice recognition software, or personal assistance such as a note-taker or interpreter (DfES, 2002; Skill, 2003). The rationale behind these allowances is that if impairment related needs are met, disabled students can operate from the same baseline as other students.

Government involvement in supporting disabled students in higher education in Zimbabwe is minimal, living them to struggle with disability related expenses. Despite the endorsement of the Disability Policy at the University of Zimbabwe, the inexistence of a public policy that promotes the education of disabled people in Zimbabwe makes it almost impossible for the needs of disabled students to be genuinely addressed (Howell, 2006).

While some disabled students will always require additional, and often more cost-intensive support to access the curriculum, such support has to be seen as part of academic development services and integrated into the general academic planning process (Riddell et al., 2005; Howell, 2006). It is known that disabled students incur substantially greater costs when participating in higher education (Howell, 2006). The Disabled Students Allowances (DfES, 2002; Skill, 2003) allocated to British Higher Education students reflects this. Resource mobilization and allocation in most cases is made possible through mandatory legislation like the SENDA (2001), the ADA (1990) and the Australian DDA (2005). Lack of such obligatory pieces of legislation means governments are not obliged to fund the higher education of disabled students. I have argued elsewhere (Chataika, 2007) that it is appropriate legislation, political will, appropriate resources, information and technology which promote inclusive practices.

Nonexistence of an obligatory legislation protecting the educational rights of disabled students means responsibility will lie on individual students to fit into the university system with little reciprocal adjustments (Riddell et al., 2005). This is deeply problematic because barriers that disabled students experience in higher education institutions can then contribute directly to negative attitudes among staff and students towards their participation in the institution. Lack of participation by disabled students in decision-making processes and structures within university settings effectively removes these issues from debate and discussion in institutional planning and resource allocation (Howell & Lazarus, 2003).

Lack of disability awareness and negative attitudes undoubtedly compound most of the barriers identified above. The attitudes of significant others can act as a barrier to inclusive practices and some of the students reported experiencing prejudice, and hostility. Fortune experienced patronizing, stereotyping, negligence, and stigmatizing encounters:

> It was ironical [sic] at this institution of higher education that the ugly head of segregation began to pop up, leaving me feeling totally out of place. Life was different. Students had an indifferent attitude that amounted to "your existence does not bother me."
>
> (Fortune)

IMPLICATIONS AND CONCLUSION

Although the University of Zimbabwe is seemingly inclusive as it accepts disabled students on some of its programs, those same students experience marginalization and disempowerment (Oliver, 2004). In Fortune's case, the struggles and challenges he encountered reflect a deficit or medical model approach to disability. The disabled students' experiences presented in this chapter reveal the need for appropriate legislation, resources, information and technology, and above all, a political will to make inclusive education a reality. Without a change of attitudes, disabled students in Zimbabwe are justified in saying:

> To really talk of inclusion in Zimbabwe might be an overstatement and too strong for the Zimbabwean higher education system.
>
> (Peter)

The challenge for disabled students and their allies in Zimbabwe is to break down barriers within the higher education system. Through individual determination, some of them have made it into higher education despite operating under challenging circumstances, and despite having to continually overcome social injustices they face. This type of determination has seen disabled students managing to go through systems that are not inclusive as Edmore realizes:

> I don't apologize for being deaf, and I have no excuses. I have done a lot that some of the hearing people have not achieved . . . excelling in a system geared towards the hearing.
>
> (Edmore)

The situation Edmore describes evidences attitudes that require disabled students to work much harder than their non-disabled peers in order to prove their capability; attitudes which are characteristic of an individual deficit model of disability (Barnes, 1993). Fortune also reflected on this:

> I shined and glittered like a diamond, powered on my journey of hunting for wisdom through book reading . . . but it sent the right message to the populace in general by dispelling the misconception of looking down upon the blind and disabled people.
>
> (Fortune)

To promote inclusive practices in higher education, Zimbabwe needs to enact mandatory policies. A code of practice needs to be developed that details a range of issues, including funding processes for disabled students entering higher education, as legislation without financial backing will not promote change. Until such a vigorous policy commitment is in place, Higher Education in Zimbabwe will unfortunately continue to be accessible to only a few disabled people (Engelbrecht, 1999). Zimbabwe's disabled people's organizations have to be proactive and put pressure on government for a national policy formulation that compliments efforts of higher education initiatives.

It is clear is that disabled people who have managed to proceed into higher education in Zimbabwe feel that the energy, emotional resources and levels of stress involved in dealing with the overwhelming range of barriers that confront them are extremely undermining. Unfortunately, these barriers force them to perform at a level not expected from other students. If they perform below par, the prevailing attitudes and prejudices towards their abilities are regrettably reinforced (Howell, 2006).

What is clear from the voices of disabled students presented in this chapter is that disabled people encounter multiple attitudinal, environmental and institutional barriers that militate against their effective inclusion within the Zimbabwean society. What can be achieved, in short to medium-term, with the regard to the development of disability policy and practice is the challenge, based on the current situation where communities are struggling to put food on their tables and accessing basic health facilities. Until there is political commitment to the current socio-economic and political crisis in Zimbabwe, disability issues look likely to remain at the bottom of the priority list. Zimbabwe cannot, however, afford to keep disabled people on the periphery because of the prevailing social and economic woes. As Edmund Burke's famous quote rightly puts it: "Nobody makes a greater mistake than he [she] who does nothing because he [she] could only do a little."

Mainstreaming disability issues into local and national activities is not an optional strategy for the empowerment of disabled people, but rather a requirement (Oliver, 2004). In Zimbabwe, action is required to ensure that disabled people are able to participate fully in community activities and claim their rights as full and equal members of society (Butler & McEwan, 2007). In this process, there is need to conceptualise a new society that is inclusive and planned for all the people; and, central to this process should be the principles of "universal design" (Butler & McEwan, 2007). Such arrangements are indeed likely to benefit all people of all ages, abilities or circumstances in Zimbabwe.

REFERENCES

Americans with Disabilities Act. (1990). *Pub. L. No. 101–336.* (ERIC Document Service Reproduction No. ED 323 679). Available at the ERIC Document Service Web site: ttp://www.eeoc.gov/policy/ada.html.

Barnes, C. (1993). How the media presents "Disabled Images." *British Polio Fellowship Bulletin*, 31(9): 30.

Bell, J. (1999). *Doing your Research Project: A Guide for First-time Researchers in Education and Social Science.* Buckingham: Open University Press.

Bennett, B. and Rolheiser, C. (2001). *Beyond Monet.* Toronto: Bookation Inc.

Borland, J. I. and James, S. K. (1999). The learning experience of students with disabilities in higher education: A case study of a UK university. *Disability & Society.* 14(1): 85–101.

Butler, R. and McEwan, C. (2007). Disability and development: Different models, different places. *Geography Compass*, 1(3): 448–466.

Central Statistical Office. (2008). Income, *Consumption, and Expenditure Survey,* (ICES) Report. Harare: CSO.

Chataika, T. (2003). Policy and provision for disabled students in higher educational institutions in Zimbabwe. Unpublished Masters Dissertation, University of Leeds.

Chataika, T. (2005). Narrative research: What's in a story? Paper Presented at the Nordic Network Disability Research Conference, April 14–16, Oslo: Norway.

Chataika, T. (2007). Inclusion of disabled students in higher education in Zimbabwe: From idealism to reality—A social ecosystem perspective. Unpublished PhD thesis, University of Sheffield.

Corbett, J. (2001). *Supporting Inclusive Education: A Connective Pedagogy.* London: Routledge Falmer.

Disability Discrimination Act [Australia]. (1992). *Disability Discrimination Act Section 22*, Division 2. Cauberro: Australian Federal Government.

Disability Discrimination Act. (2005). *Disability Discrimination Act Section 22*, Division 2. Available at the Australian Federal Government Website: http://www.austlii.edu.au/legis/cth/consol_act/ddaa992264/S6.html.

Disability Policy. (2005). Available at The University of Zimbabwe Disability Resource Centre site: http://www.uz.ac/institutions/drc/disabilitypolicy/2005.

Disability Resource Centre. (2006). *Disability Resource Centre History.* Available at: http://www.uz.ac/institutions/drc.

Department for Education and Skills. (2002). *Bridging the Gap: A Guide to the Disabled Students in Higher Education in 2002/2003* London: DfES.

Engelbrecht, P. (1999). A theoretical framework for inclusive education, in P. Engelbrecht, L. Green, S. Naicker, and L. Engelbrecht (Eds.) *Inclusive Education in Action in South Africa*. Pretoria: J. L. van Schaik Publishers, pp. 3–11.

Fuller, M., Bradley, A. and Healey M. (2004). Incorporating disabled students within an inclusive higher education environment. *Disability & Society*, 19: 5–9.

Glaser, B. G. (1978). *Theoretical Sensitivity. Advances in the Methodology of Grounded Theory*. Sociology Press: Mill Valley, CA.

Hall J. and Tinklin T. (2002). *Disabled Students in Higher Education Scottish Council for Research in Education*, Edinburg: SHEFC.

Howell, C. and Lazarus, S. (2003). Access and participation for students with disabilities in South African higher education: Challenging accepted truths and recognizing new possibilities. *Perspectives on Education* 2(3): 59–74.

Kariwo, M. T. (2007). Widening access in higher education in Zimbabwe. *Higher Education Policy*, 20: 45–59.

Kidder, L. and Fine M. (1997). Qualitative methods on psychology: A radical tradition, in D.R. Foxand I. Prilletensky (Eds.) *Handbook of Critical Psychology*. Thousand Oaks, CA: Sage.

Lang, R. and Charowa, G. (2007). *DFID Scoping Study: Disability Issues in Zimbabwe Final Report*. DFID.

Leicester, M. and Lovell, T. (1994). Disability voice: Educational experience and disability. *Disability & Society* 12(1): 111–118.

Magnus, E. (2006). Disability and higher education—What are the barriers to participation? Paper presented at the Disability Studies Conference, September 18–20, Lancester, UK.

Moore, M. (Ed.) (2000). *Insider Perspectives on Inclusion: Raising Voices, Raising Issues*. Sheffield: Philip Armstrong.

Mpofu, E. (2000). Rehabilitation in international perspective: A Zimbabwean experience. *Disability and Rehabilitation* 23, 481—489.

Munro, L. T. (2005). A social safety net for the chronically poor? Zimbabwe's pubic assistance programme in the 1990s. *The European Journal of Development Research*, 17(1): 111–131.

Oliver, M. (1996). *Understanding Disability from Theory to Practice*. London: McMillan.

Oliver, M. (2004). If I had a Hammer: The social model in action, in C. Barnes and G. Mercer (Eds.) *Implementing the Social Model of Disability: Theory and Research*. Leeds: The Disability Press, pp. 18–31.

Riddell, S., Tinklin, T. and Alistair, W. (2005). *Disabled Students in Higher Education: Perspectives on Widening Access and Changing Policy*. New York: Routledge.

Schneider, M. (2006). Disability and the environment, in B. Watermeyer, L. L. T. Swartz, M. Schneider, and M. Priestley (Eds.) *Disability and Social Change: A South African Agenda*. Cape Town: Humanities Sciences Research Council Press, pp. 8–18.

Skill. (2003). *Auditing Change: National Bureau for Students with Disabilities*. London: Skill.

Special Education Needs and Disability Act (SENDA). (2001). London: HMSO.

Strauss, A. and Corbin J. (1990). *Basics of Qualitative Research: Grounded Theory Procedures and Techniques*. Newbury Park, CA: Sage.

Wolfendale, S. (1996). Learning support in higher education: Principles, values, and continuities. In S. Wolfendale & J. Corbett (Eds.) *Opening Doors—Learning Support in Higher Education*. London: Cassell.

World Fact Book (2006). *Zimbabwe*. Available at: http://www.cia.gov/cia/publications/factbook/geos/zi.html.

Wray, M. (2003). *SENDA Module*. Available at: http://jarmin.com/demos/index.html. http://www.cia.gov/cia/publications/factbook/geos/zi.html.

Zimbabwe National Report of Education (2004). The National Report of Education: Ministries of Education, Sport and Culture and Higher Education and Tertiary Education: *Zimbabwe Presentation at the 47th Session of the International Conference of Education* 8–11 September, 2004 Geneva: UNESCO.

9 Diversity, Democracy and Change in the Inner City

Understanding Schools as Belonging to Communities

Evelyn Abram, Felicity Armstrong, Len Barton and Lynne Ley

INTRODUCTION

In this chapter we consider the changing nature of populations in inner-cities, and the implications, in particular, for the building of school communities based on democratic and participatory principles. The relationships forged through the many outcomes of colonialism, globalization and migration are continuously present and changing and connect to contemporary questions of inclusion and exclusion in education. How, for example, does the curriculum in schools relate to their diverse communities? What are the implications for the way "history" is conceptualized and how it is taught, and for the recognition of different forms of knowledge and cultural and linguistic heritage? What are the essential features of the culture and ethos of school life? What challenges does "diversity" present for the values, practices and pedagogies which underpin the daily lives of schools, and to what extent can schools respond to these in positive ways?

In writing this chapter together we recognize the importance of acknowledging, and giving space to, the different perspectives of each one of us as contributors. At the heart of our chapter is a case study of a primary school in Sheffield, Sharrow School, where two of the contributors to this chapter, Felicity Armstrong and Len Barton carried out some "field work,", as part of a wider project on inclusive schools, last year. The idea that two people from a university department should spend a few days in a school and then go away and write about it became increasingly incongruous as the relationship between the "researchers" and those working in the school developed. When Lynne Ley and Evelyn Abram, headteacher and deputy headteacher at Sharrow School, came to talk to students on the MA in Inclusive Education in that department, it was evident that *they* should write about their own school, and that this chapter urgently needed their participation. This raises important issues about the relationship between researchers and "researched"—those who share their knowledge, ideas and experiences—in whatever form these take. This "sharing" is not generally reciprocated and it is usual practice for researchers working in academic institutions to "go in" to the research field, carry out interviews, observations and perhaps distribute questionnaires, and then return to their desks to write about "their" research for publication in scholarly books and journals. (It is worth noting in passing that in this sense, qualitative research is potentially far more invasive than quantitative research in terms of dealing with the personal and professional lives of individuals and groups.)

Questions of whose voices count in the research process, and who controls the way the research is conceptualized and carried out, how accounts of particular research settings and processes are drawn up, in whose interests and with what purpose, and the very nature of research itself, have become the subject of critical enquiry within the wider research community in recent years (Bines, Swain & Kaye , 1998: Armstrong, Dolinski & Wrapson, 1999: Moore, 2000; Youdell, 2006; Allan, 2008). We cannot claim that the conceptualization and *design* of the fieldwork involved both "researchers" coming in from the "outside," and "practitioners" on the "inside." However, the writing of our chapter has been done collaboratively. While it is true that there has been some division of responsibilities in terms of the different sections of this piece of writing, (Felicity Armstrong and Len Barton have written the first and final sections, Evelyn Abram and Lynne Ley have written the case study of their school), we believe that the conversations and reflections we have shared during the research process, and through the teaching session at the Institute and the writing process, have probably had some influence in the way we have conceptualized the chapter and questions relating to community and diversity as individuals and collectively.

EDUCATION AND CULTURAL DIVERSITY: GOVERNMENT POLICY

England—like many parts of the world—has always been the "recipient" of newcomers who have arrived in many different ways and circumstances—as invaders, slaves, as "displaced persons" following war and turmoil, or migrants in search of security and work or other opportunities. Historically, cities such as London, Liverpool, Sheffield, Bristol and Manchester have been subject to continuous transformation in terms of their character, populations and activities. There have always been "refugees" and itinerant peoples, or those who came to cities in England against their will—peasants who were unable to make a living from the land, people escaping wars and possible extermination, others arriving from the British colonies to seek work and what they hoped would be a better life in "the motherland." Thus, while it may be true that since the mid-twentieth century the populations of towns and cities in England have become increasingly culturally and ethnically diverse, England has always been a country made up of many different cultures and histories. The effects of the arrival of the

Goths, the Roman Occupation, Britain's colonial past and intimate connection to slavery, and the arrival of migrants and refugees over thousands of years mean that England is not ethnically or culturally homogeneous. This rich historical landscape is frequently overlooked in debates about what it means to be "English." However, whereas in the past English communities were segmented primarily along divisions of class—and England is still very much a class-based society—urban communities, in particular, are now more than ever before characterized by ethnic and cultural differences as well as those of class. Global events and developments have an important impact on identities and relationships within and between groups in English society—so civil wars, economic instability, occupations and wars such as those in Iraq and Afghanistan, acts of terrorism and representations in the media of "other" places, events and people—all leave their imprint on a rapidly changing society.

There have been periodic outbreaks of debate in the media about the status of incoming groups—described as "immigrants," "asylum seekers," "refugees"—and questions raised about their rights and potential to contribute to, or undermine, the economy and the (mythical) "traditional British way of life." Significantly, a report commissioned by the British government in the spring 2008 suggested that schoolchildren should take part in citizenship ceremonies and a new public holiday should be introduced to celebrate "Britishness" as part of wide-ranging proposals to strengthen British citizenship and identity, although these ideas appear to have been shelved for the time being. Living in a culturally diverse society brings enormous richness to that society in multiple ways. However, the changing character of England and recent global events have, according to some sections of the media, brought a sense of alienation to certain groups in the population, and possibly more general feelings of instability, fear and anxiety within the wider population. From a very different perspective, Derrida (1994: 207, quoted in Catterall, 2007) sees immigrant peoples as belonging to " . . . a time of disjunction, to that 'time out of joint' in which is inaugurated, laboriously, painfully, tragically, a new thinking of borders, a new experience of the house, the home, and the economy." It is helpful to hold onto these very different perspectives and ways of reading the world when we think about communities and questions of inclusion and exclusion.

The government has gradually recognized the relationship between globalization, increased migration and greater social and cultural diversity and education. In the past, responses to cultural and linguistic diversity have been limited to providing support for learning the English language and assimilationist assumptions—but just recently there has been a new emphasis on responding to broader and deeper issues relating to ethnicity and culture and educational outcomes. The government has focused on what appears to be a revised approach designed to foster greater understanding of diversity and promote greater social cohesion.

This has been prompted by a number of factors:

- Concerns about the low levels of performance of some ethnic groups in England and their over-representation in statistics for "special educational needs" (First Release, 2007).
- The apparent disaffection and lack of motivation ascribed to many young people belonging to different cultural groups.
- Fears of social disorder, linked to a range of factors including—religious, political, social and economic.
- Heightened levels of racial tension and racist attacks in some areas.
- A desire to build a cohesive society in which everyone feels they have a place.

The government promotes a vision of a society in which all members understand common values and beliefs, and are able to share a "British" perspective on global developments. The Education and Inspections Act 2006 introduced a duty on all maintained schools in England to promote community cohesion. It states:

> Education that develops cultural understanding and recognises diversity is crucial for the future wellbeing of our society. Schools have a duty—not least for community cohesion—to ensure learners in every school gain a broad understanding of the country they are growing up in, how it has evolved to be as it is and how they are able to contribute to its future development. Ultimately they should be able to comprehend the values of the United Kingdom in a global context and understand UK society from a variety of viewpoints.
>
> (www.teachernet.gov.uk/wholeschool/Communitycohesion)

While this approach is fundamentally concerned with peaceful assimilation, it has conspicuously avoided framing minority ethnic groups as "the problem" and attempted to place "cultural diversity" as concerning all members of the community. Take for example, its guidance on the curriculum in schools.

Developing a Curriculum that Supports Identity and Cultural Diversity

In order to develop learners' understanding and appreciation of identity and cultural diversity, they should have opportunities across the curriculum to:

- Discuss the origins of diversity in the UK and how different cultures and groups have shaped the UK.
- Explore different racial, ethnic, cultural, religious and non-religious groups in the UK and the wider world, and the similarities and differences within and between those groups . . .
- Develop an understanding of how diverse people, places, economies and environments in the global community are interconnected.

- Develop an understanding about the consequences of racial and religious intolerance and discrimination, and how to challenge discrimination, including racism.
- Develop a critical capacity to reflect on multiple identities, their own cultural traditions, and those of others.
- Investigate how ideas, including those that are mathematical and scientific, reflect diverse cultures and traditions.
- Explore and appreciate the art, artifacts, literature and music of different cultures.
- Explore how technology has transformed ways of working together to create knowledge and the sharing of ideas and information.

The document adds:

> Teaching about identities and cultural diversity may provoke extremely strong sentiments in some learners. There are a number of specific ways in which teachers can encourage learners to value diversity and challenge racism.
>
> (www.teachernet.gov.uk/wholeschool/Communitycohesion/)

This policy is more radical than anything which has gone before in that it appears to recognize that *all* members of the community are implicated in the development of a harmonious, culturally diverse society. In this respect it is to be welcomed. However, there are some serious problems. The first is the possibility that the government will take a "low key" approach in disseminating such guidance because it is unlikely to be popular with all sections of British society and may lose electoral support. Secondly—and crucially—the present English National Curriculum and system of national testing and the obsession with meeting "attainment targets" do not harmonize at all with this new guidance. Because of the large amount of material to be covered and targets to be met, teachers find it very difficult indeed to widen and differentiate the curriculum. Indeed, there is little time for discussion about the kinds of topics relating to culture and diversity. A third issue is that there appears to be no suggestion at this stage that the proposed changes will be made compulsory or enforceable.

Cultural Diversity and the Inclusive School

The starting point for developing culturally inclusive schools is an understanding of the dynamic relationship between schools, communities and the broader social context. Tony Booth describes participation in the inclusive classroom in the following terms:

> It (. . .) implies learning alongside others and collaborating with them in shared lessons. It involves active engagement with what is learnt and

taught and having a say in how education is experienced. But participation also means being recognized for oneself and being accepted for
oneself: I participate with you when you recognize me as a person like
yourself and accept me for who I am.

(Booth, 2003: 2)

Sharrow School, the focus of our chapter, exemplifies this statement by
its ongoing commitment to celebrating cultural diversity, and this includes
seeking to prevent, and address, all kinds of discrimination which might
arise in the teaching and learning process, the daily life of the school, and
in the local community.

The social demographic and economic life of cities and rural areas in
England has changed and continues to change as new communities arrive,
often along circuitous routes, in response for example, to war, persecution, poverty, changing boundary structures and regulations. Phillmore
and Goodson (2008) have explored the background to policy-making and
the impacts that recent policies have had with regard to the situation in the
UK based on an investigation of the lives and experiences of new migrants.
They maintain:

New communities are forming in urban and rural areas where there
was, and still is, little infrastructure to support their development and
little experience of integrating newcomers, certainly on the scale now
being seen in the regions. Questions need to be asked about the kinds
of support these newcomers are receiving, their aspirations for the future, the types of provision they are seeking and the extent to which it
is being provided? How are newcomers to the region fairing? Are they
able to access education, training and employment? What mechanisms
have been put in place to help them to integrate via these means?

(p. 2)

This study recognizes the complexity of the factors that have contributed
to what became known as the "refugee crisis.". These included, extensive
increases in poverty and political instability worldwide; the demise of com-
munism in the Soviet Union and the inter-ethnic violence in Eastern Europe.
They contend that, the ever widening demographic and development gap
between the North and the South has encouraged increasing numbers of
migrants to flee to the rich North in search of improving their current life-
chances and future prospects. These developments involve new challenges
with regard to social conditions, relations and experiences including the
changing nature of inequality, discrimination and exclusion.

An issue which has received scant attention from policy makers and in
debates on immigration and asylum, is the experience of asylum seeker and
migrant children. Yet, in their study Sporton, Valentine and Bang Niel-
son (2006) report "in 2002 the UK received over 100,000 applications for

asylum and over one-fifth of these were made by those aged 20 years or under, and of these 6,200 were unaccompanied children (Asylum Statistics, 2002). Indeed since 2000 an estimated 15,000 unaccompanied children have entered the UK without identification, documentation or guardians" (p. 203). Sporton et al. observe that the experience of asylum seeker children are little understood and there is a general ignorance about how such children come to be in an English classrooms and the journey they have made to get there, or what their needs might be. Nearly all of asylum seeker children will have lived in camps for displaced people, experienced extremes of hardship and fear, lived among strangers, and been separated from familiar surroundings, family, culture and language.

EXCLUSION AND INCLUSION

One of the crucial challenges which this new context raises is the pervasive fact of inequality. We live in unequal societies, which are part of an unequal world. These inequalities cover, for example, health, welfare, education, income, respect, safety and care. These are reflected in class, ethnicity, gender, sexuality, disability and age differences and experiences. Inequality needs to be understood as complex, deeply rooted and stubborn. In their report *Education and Poverty: A Critical Review of Theory, Policy and Practice*, Raffo et al. (2007) concluded that only by understanding, and challenging, the structural and systemic features and power relations which underpin the link between education and poverty can meaningful change come about. Different aspects of discrimination and exclusion interact and compound the complexity of the issues involved, resulting in what has become known as simultaneous oppression. In the struggle for inclusion, inequalities in their varied forms are not to be viewed as natural, inevitable or unchangeable facts of life. They are social creations and thus amenable to change, no matter how difficult this may seem at times. Finally, no single factor can effectively remove these inequalities, discriminations and exclusions. Writing on the question of equality, Baker et al. (2004) have developed a series of questions which they contend, need to be seriously examined. They include:

What are the central, significant, dominant patterns of inequality in our society?

What are the best ways of explaining these inequalities, using which overall frameworks?

What are the best institutional frameworks for advancing equality in different spheres and contexts?

What policies would best promote equality?

What are the best political strategies for promoting equality?

(pp. 14–17)

The necessity of understanding the dynamic relationship between exclusion and inclusion is reinforced through the assumptions informing these significant questions. Also, the question of the position and function of education in contributing to challenging barriers to inclusion, as well as developing more inclusive ways of thinking and behaving needs to be understood as a fundamental task in the pursuit of transformative change. These factors have a number of implications. For example: for governments in terms of their decision-making over policy developments, priorities and the allocations of scarce resources, as well as for schools and teachers in terms of their purposes, cultures and expectations, involving external relations with the local community and the wider society. This entails more than issues of access or placement and is centrally concerned with questions of community, diversity, citizenship and the establishment and maintenance of inclusive cultures and relations.

Writing on the question of inclusion in education, Booth (2005) contends, that values underpin all policies, actions and practices within education. Furthermore, he emphasizes the need to understand inclusion in terms of:

> . . . particular values in action including equity, participation, community, compassion, respect for diversity, honesty, rights, joy and sustainability.
>
> (p. 153)

The pursuit of inclusion, he contends, is to be viewed as critically challenging all forms of conditions, relations, experiences that are discriminatory and exclusionary. This approach necessitates such advocates making public their values and learning how to clearly and effectively relate their practices to inclusive values.

It is crucial therefore that education is viewed as a human rights issue, an entitlement, not a privilege for a select few, nor a matter of charity. No child is viewed as uneducable. All children are entitled to quality education. Thus, a human rights approach to education entails issues of access to education, fair treatment with regard to learning, and fair access to the outcomes of education including the world of work (Unterhalter, 2006). The question of rights is derived from the qualification of being human. However, recognizing the formal equality of citizenship rights, does not necessarily lead to equality of respect, opportunities and resources. Too often there is a gulf between rhetoric and practice.

Focusing on the global dimensions of these issues in a very important report of a study entitled "Education's Missing Millions" (World Vision UK, 2007), the question of inclusion and its implementation is viewed as crucial in relation to achieving the Millennium Development Goal of universal primary education by 2015. While some progress has been achieved, the report highlights the alarming figures, that an estimated 77 million children remain out of school worldwide. The study seeks to critically identify attitudinal, environmental, legal, institutional and resource barriers to inclusion in education. In the report, inclusion is identified as involving:

- A recognition of the right to education and its provision in non-discriminatory ways.
- A common vision which covers all children of the appropriate age range.
- A conviction that schools have a responsibility to educate all children.
- A process of addressing and responding to the diversity of needs of all learners, recognizing that all children can learn.

(p. 8)

What this report vividly reminds us, is on the one hand, the seriousness of the issues involved in the pursuit of inclusion in education, and on the other, the unacceptable gulf that often exists between laudable statements, claims and policy directives and the actual practices and degrees of their implementation. This in itself is sufficient to reinforce a recognition of the urgency, complexity and contentiousness of these issues.

While transformative change is central to an inclusive approach, it must not be understood as a smooth linier process. Rather it is characterized by developments, contradictions, setbacks and uncertainties. It inevitably involves identifying, understanding and challenging all forms of barriers to inclusion, in all spheres of society, including education. It is about maximizing the participation of all people in more empowering and liberating ways of living and behaving. Thus exclusion and inclusion must be understood in terms of a complex dynamic relationship to one another.

So, education has a part to play in the struggle for change, but it cannot do it alone. Education must not be conceived in a social vacuum, but rather, intrinsically related to the historical, social, economic and political relations of a given society. In the remainder of this chapter, drawing on a research project in a primary school in a northern city in England, we will seek to explore some aspects of the process and experiences of the participants in their struggles to be more inclusive in their everyday practices and relations.

SHARROW SCHOOL—A CASE STUDY

Sharrow School lies in the south west of Sheffield, approximately half a mile from the city centre. Sharrow is a vibrant, multi-ethnic community or collection of communities. The school is in the heart of the area, surrounded by rows of red brick terraced housing, council owned tower blocks, low rise flats, a vast array of small shops, fast food outlets, restaurants and a small park—one of the few green spaces in the area. Much of the catchment lies within an area of deprivation with higher than average levels of unemployment, over crowded households and high rates of mental ill health amongst adults and children.

Two schools, Sharrow Nursery Infant and Sharrow Junior, were amalgamated in May 2005 and opened as a new Local Authority primary school in September 2007. The new school now provides extended services for children aged three months to eleven years and is open daily from 8 a.m. to 6 p.m. The school includes the Performing Arts Space which is also used by the community.

The design of the new school reflects the ethos and vision of its occupants. Light, open and welcoming with a range of sustainable features incorporated. Its facilities invite families and visitors to celebrate the diversity of the community within it.

In the early 1980s the old nursery infant school had a very child centered approach to educating young children. It had a clear vision and from its early days could have been described as inclusive. Children with special educational needs were welcomed, 50% of the pupil population was made up of Pakistani children. There were also small numbers of children of Bengali, African Caribbean, Chinese families and isolated learners of English. There were several black staff already employed and positive discrimination was used when employing new support staff particularly. An atmosphere of respect for all children and their families was evident throughout the school.

There was generally good community cohesion, with the white population accepting of the new Pakistani community. The Pakistani families had opened one or two corner shops and several were still working in the steel industry. Although many of the Pakistani families were living in poverty in terms of economic income, there was a richness in relation to strong family relationships and aspirations for their children. The Pakistani families at that time were not seen as a threat to the white British community, the latter enjoying the differences the Pakistani community brought, in their restaurants, for example.

The following twenty years have brought about significant developments. Policies and initiatives were rolled out at regular intervals by the new Labour government from 1998 onwards. The Government were determined to raise attainment in maths and literacy, at the same time attempting to remove the barriers that were contributing to the widening attainment gap across class, gender and ethnicity.

Local demographic changes also required the school to consider the needs of a more diverse community and a wider inclusion agenda. Sheffield's Labour council introduced a policy of re-housing families from the high-rise and maisonette accommodation in the area to houses in other parts of the city. This resulted in white working-class families particularly, leaving and falling rolls in school. At the same time a housing modernization scheme was introduced to improve the rows of terraced houses around the school. Many houses were emptied; families offered alternative accommodation in the city's housing stock with a promise of a return to the area on completion of the work. However, many of the families chose not to return and the houses were bought by private landlords at a time when the city's two universities were expanding their student population. Subsequently, many houses were let to students, asylum seekers, families on low income as well as foreign students and their families coming to the city to complete further degrees for short periods of time.

Other communities also began to move into the local area. Somali families living in other parts of Sheffield had now moved into the catchment area of the school. Many of these families had arrived as asylum seekers and refugees via Scandinavia. More recently families from different parts of the Arabic-speaking world have come to live in Sharrow as asylum seekers, refugees and families of students.

The pupil population was changing and "white flight" set in. White British families were choosing to send their children to non catchment schools where the numbers of black and ethnic minority children were far fewer than at Sharrow school.

By 1998, 80% of the children had English as an additional language (EAL), with more than twenty different languages being spoken. In addition, there were an increasing number of children with special educational needs attending the school, several with very complex needs. Although the school had a stable core pupil population, pupil mobility was relatively high.

The school had to rethink its way of working and become more effective in meeting the new challenges. Staff were finding it increasingly difficult to engage parents and carers in the life of the school in a meaningful way.

A number of strategies were developed to overcome the communities' perceptions of the school and for the staff at the school to develop a better understanding of the more diverse families it now served. The introduction of these strategies coincided with government funding via Education Action Zones (EAZ) and later the Excellence in Cities (EiC) projects, which the school actively took part in.

Staff developed a series of activities to encourage parents and carers into school. A number of courses were developed, initially focussing on family literacy and later, film making. These were usually a series of up to ten workshops and were targeted at particular groups within the community. For example, sessions were run for Pakistani, Bengali and Somali families separately. Interpreters were available, often school staff but sometimes parents took on this role. In addition to these more formal courses, a number of activities were developed which were more open, less threatening, sessions. These included a homework club, Friday morning reading sessions, arts weeks and design weeks. Families could opt in and out of these ongoing sessions as they chose. Initially, only one or two parents might turn up, but as word got round, these courses and activities became increasingly popular. The key feature of all these activities was that they were run by teachers and teaching assistants working in the school. Funding from the EAZ and EiC was used to provide resources and supply cover, enabling the school staff to plan and run the courses and events.

Alongside these activities, the school began to develop some extended care facilities for families. This began in a small way with a lunch club for nursery children which extended the children's two-and-a-half hour session by one hour, to include lunch. This initiative met the needs of parents, usually women, who were beginning to take training courses.

It was through such activities that school staff began to develop a better understanding of the differing communities it was serving. The activities provided opportunities for dialogue, in an informal way, between parents/carers and staff. Directing the activities at particular groups ensured that no one group became dominant and enabled staff to have a conversation with each group separately, all voices being heard. Some groups were easier to engage than others. This was due to a number of different reasons. Within the Somali group, one parent became an advocate for the school. She had an outgoing personality and was able to approach Somali families whom she did not know directly. She would talk to the parents about the benefits of becoming involved in the family activities on offer in school. She was very inclusive in her approach. As this parent also spoke Arabic, she encouraged many Arabic speaking women to join in too. It was important to recognise key members of the community who understood the need for and could support the change.

School staff became more aware that one size did not fit all. It became clear that different ethnic groups, including the white British group of families, had very different starting points. Some had no understanding of the British education system—but had been educated in their own country. Some were illiterate in their first and second language and had no concept of how important their role was in supporting their children's learning. Some had been through the British education system but had not really engaged with it. Others had experienced very interrupted education as well as great trauma. The factor that they all had in common was their enthusiasm to enhance their children's and their own learning. The school had to become more flexible in its approach towards families and its policies had to be more adaptable.This work led to a better understanding by staff of the needs of the families and a number of further developments.

The impact was noticeable as new staff who shared families' first languages were employed. Hence, when a Somali support worker first was employed, communications and confidence between the Somali community and the school increased immediately. Chinese, Bengali, Arabic and more recently Polish speaking support workers were employed by the school. The families appeared to relax as they were able to communicate with staff in their first language. It also gave families a sense that their community was respected and valued by the school which went beyond the opportunity to have someone translate for them.

As part of its drive to increase standards, the government began to insist on a more detailed analysis of data of children's achievement, attainment and attendance by ethnicity. Initially the school's senior management team was daunted by the increased workload. However, as they engaged with the process, patterns began to emerge which needed further exploration and understanding. The significance of the children's individual circumstances began to stand out. Boys with older female siblings who had been through the English education system, boys whose fathers were actively engaging in their children's education and children whose mothers had experienced the English education system tended to perform better at school. Other questions that this process raised were why were children from the more recently arrived Somali families more likely to succeed than children from Pakistani families, who had been established in the community for some time? Why was school attendance valued more by some families than others? The impact of family involvement in children's learning was crucial for significant improvement in children's attainment, achievement and attendance. A real partnership had to be developed and support for families needed to be clearly targeted.

The amalgamation of the two schools was a key factor in moving the schools forward. Staff from the former nursery infant school began to see much more clearly the impact on children at the Junior school [Key Stage 2] who had not attained age expected levels at the end of their time in the infant school [Key Stage 1]. The former Junior school staff were developing a better understanding of children's early learning. They were better placed to identify gaps in learning and could seek specific support from colleagues to fill these gaps. Staff became more aware of the need to accelerate learning for all children. Parents of children in Key Stage 2 began to re-engage with the school. All staff had the opportunity to understand the communities from a different perspective. Nursery and Key Stage 1 staff had learnt about the communities from the parents and carers, whilst the Key Stage 2 staff had learnt from the children themselves. By amalgamating, staff could now put these two perspectives together and they gained a more complete picture. All this led to better more effective targeting of support, a higher priority now given to attendance and more targeted and focused family work, with a degree of insistence on participation. This had not been there previously.

Local Sure Start Programmes were rolled out by the government to encourage more effective partnership working between agencies to better meet the needs of families with children under 5 years. Although Sure Start had been set up in early 2000 with links to the school, it was only in more recent years that a working relationship was established. Sure Start had identified speaking and listening as one of its priorities and employed a bilingual communication therapist to work with the families. It quickly became clear that many children in the community had poor and delayed communication skills not necessarily always linked to having English as an additional language. They would struggle to access the nursery and school curriculum. The Sure Start team and the nursery staff, with the support of the communication therapist, began to develop a clear language programme to accelerate children's communication skills. This intervention programme is now being extended throughout school.

The process of understanding the needs of the local communities and how to be an effective, inclusive school is not complete. The influences of government initiatives, such as the Every Child Matters agenda, Local Council policies including housing, and demographic changes continue to impact on the school and its inclusive ethos.

CHALLENGES AND PRACTICES

This brief overview of a number of aspects of life at Sharrow School provides a rich source of insights and examples of challenges and practices. For example:

- Teaching staff and support staff represent a wide range of cultures and backgrounds and many people working in the school live in their local community. This immediately creates informal "lines of communication" between the school and the different cultural groups who make up its pupil population.
- A very important aspect of the development of more inclusive thinking, relations and practices within the school has been the contribution made by key members of the community. Through their enthusiasm, knowledge, linguistic and interpersonal skills they have been able to foster and maintain, more informed, interested and respectful relations between parents pupils and the school. They have been a vital element in the struggles for change.
- Teaching is based on the wider principles of social inclusion and respect for diversity which underpin the ethos and practices of the school. It is planned on the principle that learning takes place in different ways. There are many opportunities for *collaboration* and attention is given to grouping children according to perceptions about which groups, or pairs, of children would work best together. Sometimes children are grouped according to ability for some activities. For other activities groupings may take into account factors such as personality or language. Thus, in one class we observed, a group of four boys were working at a table on a collaborative activity and they were speaking Arabic. They explained that one member of the group had "just arrived" from Libya and spoke little English. By working together in Arabic, their new friend was able to participate in learning.
- One important aspect in developing inclusive practices in education is a willingness on the part of teachers to respond positively to differences in knowledge and experience and—in particular—differences in learning styles between children. Rather than trying to force

children into a particular learning mould which the teacher would, perhaps, expect to adopt as "good practice" in another context, at Sharrow School a serious attempt is made to adopt approaches which children find meaningful and motivating. As one teacher explained, there are particular challenges presented by the very diverse nature of the groups of children who make up the classes in the school, such as their very varied backgrounds and experiences and approaches to learning which children have encountered in their different cultures and communities and in their day-to-day family life.

Recognizing the differences in learning styles among a diverse group of children sometimes involves reassessing professional knowledge and pedagogical practices. Similarly, recognizing the ethno-centric nature of the English school curriculum, and that there are other forms of valued knowledge and culture which children and their communities possess, must lead to a reappraisal of what is taught, and who can teach it, on the part of teachers and planners. These issues raise fundamental questions about curriculum and pedagogy which need to be addressed at every level of the education system, starting with a critical re-evaluation on the part of teachers themselves of their own beliefs and practices.

At Sharrow School children communicate with each other in different languages spontaneously—often switching between English and Arabic, or Somali or Urdu—drawing on their own knowledge in the process of explaining, interrogating and negotiating. There appears to be a balanced mix of approaches to teaching and learning, which take into account pupil diversity. There is an emphasis on "visual" input, used to back up language-based material, which is particularly appropriate in such a diverse classroom in which some children struggle with language comprehension.

Children take national tests at the age of eleven—the Standard Assessment Tests (SATS)—and much of the work done in class is compiled with consideration to the requirements of the tests. These tests do not take into account factors such as a child's first language or level of literacy. They reflect the monocultural nature of the National Curriculum which fails to recognize the "rich repertoire" of forms of communication (Lambirth, 2006) and kinds of knowledge and experience that children belonging to a diverse range of cultures and traditions bring to the learning process. At Sharrow the diversity of the school population and its neighborhood communities are regarded as important resources which are central to its ethos and character.

CONCLUSION

Inclusivity is a demanding and disturbing process of change. The participants in this school testify to the extent and degree of hard work involved in the struggle for change. It is a perennial process of active engagement in the endeavor to establish and maintain alternative ways of thinking and being educationally and socially both within the school and the community. The impacts are very real in terms of the extent of the intellectual, emotional, physical and time demands involved. Great effort is focused on providing and encouraging a sensitive and supportive culture, without which effective change could not be realized and sustained.

Disappointments, setbacks, unanticipated issues of both an internal and external nature continue to remind the participants and observers that there are still important tasks to be undertaken and barriers to be removed. Nevertheless, Sharrow School can be characterized as an exciting, vibrant, creative and innovative setting. There is a serious concern with the well-being of all learners and their entitlements, which provide the motivation for developing flexible and innovating forms of teaching and learning. There is a sense of belonging and of learning to live with one another in more inclusive ways within the school and in its relationship with the community.

England is facing an interesting and challenging future in terms of the kinds of fundamental transformations in policy, law, culture and practices which will have to be envisaged if the country is to develop harmoniously with full recognition of the rights and aspirations of all groups in society—some of which may, initially, be in conflict with each other. Education and schools clearly have a unique role to play in developing cultures, curricula and pedagogies which recognize and celebrate diversity in all its forms. Such a task will inevitably mean reconceptualizing the nature and purposes of education, and must involve all groups in the community in the critical discussion that this will open up. This study provides an example of a school and its participants seeking to begin this journey and dialogue and thereby experiencing both the exciting developments and demanding work of confronting and removing the varied and damaging nature of discriminations and of building an inclusive and democratic community.

Finally, it is important to remind the reader that this is the first time that the four of us have worked together on the task of identifying, discussing issues, practices and questions over the struggle for inclusive conditions and relations in this particular school and community context. Endeavoring to understand for example, the nature of inequality, discrimination, exclusion and inclusion in their varied forms and expressions is an immensely difficult undertaking. Thus, the degree and quality of the time we have spent discussing our ideas and writings, is far from sufficient. This is a project in the early stages of development, and the degree to which our relationship is an example of inclusive practice, is open to question. What we are convinced about, is that the work we have been able to do, including this form of outcome, provides us with a real incentive for continuing this very challenging, exciting learning process of engagement.

REFERENCES

Allan, J. (2008). *Rethinking Inclusive Education: The Philosophers of Difference in Practice*, Dordrecht. Springer.

Armstrong, D., Dolinski, R. and Wrapson, C. (1999). What about Chantal? From inside out: An insider's experience of exclusion. *International Journal of Inclusive Education*, 3z(1): 27–36.

Baker, J., Lynch, K., Contillon, S. and Walsh, J. (2004). *Equality from Theory to Action*. Basingstoke. Polgrave Macmillan.

Bines, H., Swain, J. and Kaye, J. (1998). Once upon a time: Teamwork or complementary perspectives and critique in research on special educational needs, in Clough, P. and Barton, L. (Eds.) *Articulating with Difficulty: Research Voices in Inclusive Education*. London. Paul Chapman.

Booth, T. (2005). Keeping the future alive: Putting inclusive values into action. *Forum*, 47(2&3): 151–158.

Booth, T. (2003). Inclusion and exclusion in the city: Concepts and contexts, in P. Potts (Ed.) *Inclusion in the City: Selection, Schooling and Community*. London: RoutledgeFalmer.

Catterall, B. (2007). Is it all coming together? Thoughts on urban studies and the present crisis: From Neoliberalism towards a paradigm for a New International. *City*, 11(2): 245–272.

Derrida, J. (1994). *Species of Man: The State of the Debt, the Work of Mourning, & the New International*, translated by Peggy Kamuf. New York. Routledge.

First Release (2007). *Special Educational Needs in England*, January 2007. 26 June 2007. SFR 20/2007. London: Department for Education and Skills.

Lambirth, A. (2006). Challenging the laws of talk: Ground rules, social reproduction and the curriculum. *The Curriculum Journal*, 17(1): 59.

Moore, M. (Ed.) (2000). *Insider Perspectives on Inclusion: Raising Voices, Raising Issues*. Sheffield: Philip Armstrong Publications.

Phillimore, J. and Goodson, L. (2008). *New Migrants in the UK: Education, Training and Employment*. Stoke-on-Trent: Trentham Books.

Raffo, C., Dyson, A., Gunter, H., Hall, D., Jones, L. and Kalambouka, ? (2007). Education and Poverty: A Critical Review of Theory, Policy and Practice. York: Joseph Rowntree Foundation. Available at: www.jrf.org.ukSporton, D., Valentine, G. and Bang Nielsen, K. (2006). "Post conflict identities: Affiliations and Practices of Somali asylum seeker children. *Children's Geographies*, 4(2): 203–217.

Unterhalter, E. (2006). *Gender, Schooling and Global Social Justice*. London: Routledge.

World Vision UK. (2007). *Education's Missing Millions*. Milton Keynes: World Vision UK. Available at: www.teachernet.gov.uk/wholeschool/Communitycohesion/.

Youdell, D. (2006). *Impossible Bodies, Impossible Selves: Exclusions and Student Subjectivities*. Dordrecht. Springer.

10 Decolonizing the Contexts of the Subaltern Academic Teacher Communities through the Genealogical Method

Sechaba Mahlomaholo

INTRODUCTION

Colonization, in its worst version called apartheid, suffused the lives of all South Africans especially black/African people. Blacks were denied optimal access and participation in formal education (Potgieter, 2002; Saul, 2007) and they have remained a perpetual underclass, swelling the subaltern grouping that would forever remain dependent and serving as a source of cheap menial manual labor. This to date has resulted in their under-representation in all employment positions requiring high and intensive skills training such as academic teaching roles in South African universities. Recent statistics still show this anomalous situation where the whole academic community does not reflect the demographics of the country (Potgieter, 2002; Saul, 2007). The situation gets even worse when one looks at the extremely skewed under-representation of black people in senior academic positions.

Through the National Plan on Higher Education, the South African government reduced the number of universities from thirty-six to twenty-three by closing down some predominantly black universities which were underfunded due to apartheid history and had hoped that mainly black academic teachers from these closed universities would be merged with and into predominantly white universities. To some extent this "integration" seems to have happened (if one chooses to be optimistic), but the fact of the matter is that the majority of academics in senior academic teaching positions are still not black and therefore the subject content enshrined in what is taught at South African universities is still removed from the experiences of the black communities (Potgieter, 2002; Bereng, 2007; Hongwane, 2007; Liphapang, 2007; Matobako, 2007; Saul, 2007) in spite of the calls for transformation, Africanization and inclusion of indigenous knowledges. Curriculum is thus still colonized as the black academic teachers are still marginalized.

It is therefore my view that by introducing black and African discourses, their experiences, fears and aspirations into the curriculum of the South

African higher education, as a starting point, it may be possible to consolidate the successes of the democratic agenda and thereby assist in advancing a decolonization project. Otherwise the euphoria of the so-called South African miracle or rainbow nation (Potgieter, 2002; Bereng, 2007; Hongwane, 2007; Liphapang, 2007; Matobako, 2007; Saul, 2007) will remain but a mirage.

CONCEPTUALIZING THE COMMUNITY OF SUBALTERN TEACHERS

The focus of this chapter is to use Michel Foucault's genealogical method to explore discourses of the community of the subaltern (black/African) academic teachers at two universities in the Free State province of South Africa. I do so by using the genealogical method as both the organizing principle for a discussion of, and as an instrument for, decolonizing the contexts of the community of the subaltern academic teachers.

By way of introducing my argument it is important to explain that I use the concept "community of the subaltern academic teachers" in this chapter to refer firstly to the community of practice of the subaltern academic teachers who are black/African academics. Secondly, I refer to their black community that gave birth to them and to which they are eternally located in terms of experiences, fears and aspirations. I use the phrase "academic teachers" advisedly to emphasize the point that these academics share common roles and responsibilities with teachers at other levels of education, although in their situation their practice includes research and community work at an advanced level.

On the other hand the concept "decolonization" for me refers to a desire and wish that the South African nation will be less euro-centric in all its discursive and non-discursive practices; that especially in its higher education sector, it will show a preponderance of blacks (Africans) and thereby reflect the demographics of the country in terms of staffing, curriculum, outlook and knowledge content; that there will be full participation of black academics as well in decision making processes; that there will be greater awareness and acknowledgement of blacks, more respect for them and their history; and that there will be greater care for their plight.

In this chapter therefore I argue that the Foucauldian "genealogical method" (Aronowitz, 1979; Donelly, 1979; Foucault, 1980; Dreyfus & Rabinow, 1989) seems to be one of the most potent research approaches for analysing, hence decolonizing the contexts of the subaltern academic teachers' communities by creating "critical spaces in which struggles for indigenous knowledge within a community context are articulated, valued, heard and responded to" (Lavia and Moore, "Preface," this volume). Although the analysis in this chapter is carried out on the South African (SA) higher education experiences, it is possible that the same findings and outcomes may be achieved in other similar contexts around the world where overt and/or subtle forms of colonization are still rampant.

This argument is supported by the view that typically human issues, that include attempts to decolonize the contexts of subaltern academic teachers' communities in SA higher education, require typically human methodologies. These help to analyse and understand the human being's subject-ness as well as his/her multiple and fluid identities. At the same time I want to hasten to add that research that foregrounds typically human methodologies also seems to be geared towards the decolonization and empowerment of the subaltern groupings, by advancing an agenda for social justice and creating spaces for the voices of the marginalized while being methodologically consistent.

In order to systematically pursue the argument of this chapter, I specifically focus on the discourses around learner guides. The learner guides in SA higher education in particular are used by the academic teachers as the primary mode of disseminating, sharing and facilitating learning of their students. It is on learner guides that there are competing discourses between the communities of the subaltern academic teachers on the one hand and the forces of domination on the other (Bereng, 2007; Hongwane, 2007; Liphapang, 2007; Matobako, 2007). Thus if research wants to facilitate the decolonization of the community of the subaltern academic teachers, it is important for it to analyse, thereby amplify the voices of this subaltern group, perhaps as a starting point. In this way research will contribute towards making these voices heard regarding higher education (HE) discourses on learner guides.

Furthermore, research that focuses on the transformation of learner guides in this manner will also go a long way towards effecting the much needed positive educational and political changes. As argued elsewhere in this chapter, the learner guides are important pedagogical media in HE. Analysing the competing discourses surrounding them also provide opportunities for analysing similar contestational discourses in the larger South African community. In fact, the learner guides tend to mirror in the same way the experiences, fears and aspirations competing politically and educationally in the larger SA nation.

This could be achieved if these learner guides could include and valorize the views of the community of the subaltern academic teachers, which encompass their concerns, fears and aspirations (thus constituting their indigenous knowledge). These discourses are important because the academic teachers are at the operational level of teaching and learning where these learner guides have to be used for the enhanced, effective and efficient learning of their students. Teaching and learning are thus primarily made up of the dissemination, sharing and facilitation of the South African culture and national identity, as the starting point.

CHANGES REGARDING LEARNER GUIDES
IN FREE STATE HIGHER EDUCATION

Research on the discourses around the learner guides from the perspective of the communities of the subaltern academic teachers in South Africa, is currently still thin (Bereng, 2007; Hongwane, 2007; Liphapang, 2007). What are in abundance are research findings and reports, policy documents and workshop materials on learner guides from the dominant discourses.

For example since 1994 higher education in South Africa has been undergoing significant changes. Many directives from the government through the Department of Education (DoE) in particular have been forth-coming and they constitute part of the dominant voices. These dominant voices are re-enforced (to varying degrees) by the Council for Higher Education (CHE) through the Higher Education Quality Committee (HEQC), the South African Qualifications Authority (SAQA), and higher education management structures within the academy. Change in higher education and reforms resulting from such change have been directed to compliance regimes within the academy that is mandated by a policy regime. The pleth-ora of policies can be seen by the publication of the White Paper 3: A Pro-gramme for the Transformation of Higher Education (DoE, 1997a), Higher Education Act in 1997 (DoE, 1997b), National Plan on Higher Education (DoE, 2001), the New Academic Policy for Programmes And Qualifications in Higher Education (DoE, 2002), An Interdependent National Qualifica-tions Framework (DoE & Department of Labour, 2003) and the Higher Education Qualification Framework (HEQF) (DoE, 2007).

The tenets of these changes in Free State caused to be initiated: (i) reduc-tion in the number of higher education institutions in the province from seven to approximately three (if one counts in the University of South Africa's Distance Education), (ii) merging of some institutions with others and incorporating others into some, (iii) changing the names of such newly constituted ones and (iv) directly micro-managing curricula, their design, constitution as well as their offerings.

In as far as curricula changes are concerned notice is taken of concerted efforts towards heightened levels of steering (a euphemism for government interference) in education in general but especially in higher education as well as the heightened levels of centralization by the National Department of Education (DoE).

Higher education institutions, for instance, are allocated fixed and specified programs and qualification mixes (PQM) (DoE, 1996). Adding any qualifi-cation and/or programme to the PQM has to be approved firstly at the level of Senate of the institution wishing to effect such a change. The application then has to serve again (at the second level) at the Senate(s) of other universi-ties in the vicinity or region of the applying institution. These have to satisfy themselves that there is no other similar programme or qualification in their respective PQMs already. If approved then the application has to be sent to the following national bodies for the final level of approval; (i) the National Department of Education—to satisfy itself that the proposed programme is worth funding and investing in, financially, (ii) the South African Qualification Authority (SAQA)—for cross-checking for possible duplication as they include the proposed programme or qualification into the national register and (iii) the Higher Education Quality Council—for ascertaining compliance with all the requisite standards, hence quality of the proposed programme (Hay, Mahlomaholo, Van der Merwe, Brussouw, Lampbrecht & Badenhorst, 2004).

Special forms have to be completed in the case of any curricula changes. An example of one such form is the so-called HEQC-online (Council for Higher Education, 2004) which is an electronic document asking questions which are designed to help the mentioned structures to decide whether or not to fund a newly designed programme or qualification as well as to decide whether or not to register and/or accredit it.

What is of interest to me in this chapter though is the place of the learner guides. Many names are and have been used to refer to these documents, for example; the learning manual, the student manual, the course manual, the teacher's guide, the year guide, the module guide and so on (Hay et al., 2004). The learner guides are of interest because they constitute a significant part of the evidence to show that the HEQC has considerable powers to accredit or de-accredit a programme, qualification or module (Council for Higher Education, 2004). These learner guides also serve as evidence to central quality assurance concerns within the academy that teaching and learning do take place along prescribed lines in specific modules constituting certain qualification(s) and/or programme(s). The new policy configuration has had the effect of portraying the Department of Education as micro-managing what happens in universities.

These learner guides also detail the outcomes of "learning" at the various National Qualification Framework (NQF) levels. They outcomes are fashion by dominant discourses about: (i) the whole process of education from the cradle to the grave through the Critical Cross-Field Outcomes (CCFO) prescribing the development of desired characteristics for citizenship by the dominant discourses; (ii) institution specific graduate qualities; (iii) the conceptual sophistication of the learning content as well as the cognitive demands on the learner as ranked and prescribed on the National Qualification Framework (NQF); and (iv) the module specific learning outcomes (Hay et al., 2004; Mahlomaholo and Matobako, 2006).

Apart from the nested outcomes derived from the mentioned and prescribed NQF level descriptors explained above, the learner guides also describe and prescribe in detail how an academic teacher/lecturer should organize learning opportunities through activities and resources towards the attainment of each module specific outcome. This is called facilitation (Hay et al., 2004). Finally how assessment is done is also described and prescribed in detail for the information of both the supervisors (who will from time to time review the facilitation within the modules, hence the qualification, to ensure that they meet and comply with the prescribed requirements) and the learners who will be subjected to it. These detailed facilitation procedures linked to assessment procedures and outcomes, account for the prescribed number of hours for learning per module, per day, per week and per teaching and learning year respectively in a cumulative manner. These are called credits which indicate the amount of time each topic, each page, each book and so on is supposed to be learnt/studied on the average by an average learner (Hay et al., 2004).

Given the previous scenario it seems that learner guides have more than before become the most significant instrument/mechanism for "change" in the Free State and South African higher education. The guides are discussed by many affected and involved individuals and groups of people having a stake therein.

In this chapter I argue that Foucault's genealogical method can be instrumental in developing an approach to exploring the varied and alternative understandings that communities of subaltern academic teachers in merged and incorporated Free State higher education settings.

COMMUNITIES OF THE SUBALTERN ACADEMIC TEACHERS GENERATING THE DISCOURSES

Hongwane (2007) conducted a study detailing the identities and experiences of academic teachers all of whom work closely from two of the three remaining universities in the Free State. Hongwane provides a rich and detailed description of the identities of these respondents which I totally agree with but will not repeat here. One thing I'd likek to point out is the fact that the whole group can easily be split into two main categories, primarily in terms of their meaning-making strategies around the learner guides. The two categories into which the discourses of all the aforementioned academic teachers could be classified, according to Hongwane are; (i) the one espousing and promoting the dominant view of the learner guides and (ii) the "other" amplifying and supporting the alternative and subaltern position around the learner guides.

The dominant category seems to be generating discourses agreeing more with the canonized information or knowledge (Aronowitz, 1979; Foucault, 1980; Donelly, 1979; Dreyfus & Rabinow, 1989; van Dijk, 2004, 2006; Hongwane, 2007) that learner guides are justifiably dictated to by the instruments of steering and centralising tendencies in higher education.

On the other hand the dominated category of these academic teachers, seemed to be firmly located within the subaltern community which was without power (as defined in Aronowitz, 1979; Foucault, 1980; Donelly, 1979; Dreyfus & Rabinow, 1989; van Dijk, 2004, 2006; Hongwane, 2007) and was generating problematized understandings of the learner guides. They were questioning the genesis as well as the dissemination of the learner guides' information and/or knowledge. This community seemed to be asking difficult questions such as; whose knowledge was contained in the learner guides, whose cultural experiences, aspirations and fears (indigenous knowledge) were accommodated in the learner guides and whose were excluded. These questions seemed to be posed with the declared and stated aim of underlining the incongruence of the learner guides to the processes of Africanization of the curriculum.

In my reading, the latter questions seemed to be more rhetorical as the status of the subaltern community of academic teachers was clear that in spite of the lip service paid by the powers that be, the declared curriculum changes in post apartheid SA higher education sector were more cosmetic than real, at best. In reality they seemed to be pointing out to the fact that the instituted changes in higher education curriculum since 1994 which are enshrined in learner guides are neo-liberal in nature and void of the counter-hegemonic, poor, working class, women and African people's imaginings and theorization. This community seemed to be concluding that this state of affairs is due to the fact that the process of compiling learner guides in the merged higher education institutions in the Free State province of SA, have not transcended the dominant presence and representations that are still white and euro-centric male seniors (Hongwane, 2007). The demographic figures of the proportion and number of black academics as reflected in the most recent international higher education publication, (MacGregor, 2008) confirm this claim.

In my view, the loaded counter-hegemonic interpretation and reading that Hongwane (2007) makes of the discourses of the community of the subaltern academic teachers, which concurs with their personal profiling, *vis-à-vis* the dominant category, attest to the point that; through making the past as unfamiliar as advocated for by the genealogical method (Aronowitz, 1979; Foucault, 1980; Donelly, 1979; Dreyfus & Rabinow, 1989; Hongwane, 2007), processes of decolonization are initiated. Decolonization begins when the community of the subaltern academic teachers starts to ask difficult questions, through the application of the genealogical method, about the reasons for the exclusion of their history, culture, knowledge, views, experiences, fears and aspirations from the design and use of the learner guides.

This reading also enhances quality in practice as seen from Meulenberg-Buskens'(1997) definition of quality as it seems to be geared towards the decolonization and empowerment of the subaltern groupings, advancing the agenda for social justice and creating spaces for the voices of the marginalized while being methodologically consistent.

THE GENEALOGICAL METHOD ON DISCOURSES

Several writers concur (Dreyfus & Rabinow, 1996: Donelly, 1979; Aronowitz, 1979) that deconstruction of structures of power. Hongwane (2007: 86), in his explanation of the genealogy method writes:

This is a model that is used to critique the certainty of absolutes. It is a method that seeks to record the singularity of events outside of any universality. According to this method there are no fixed essences, no underlying laws, and no metaphysical realities. The method seeks discontinuities where other traditional historical methods found continuous development. It is also meant to find recurrences where other methods found progress and seriousness. It avoids the search for depth; instead it seeks the surface of small events, small details, minor shifts and subtle contours. It aims at tracing the constitution of categories, with their shifts and turns over time. This method shuns the profundity of great thinkers the tradition has produced and revered. This method seeks to account for events and objects on the basis of circumstances under which they were produced or emerged.

What stands out very clear in this definition is that the genealogical method is couched in a critical emancipatory theory (Satterwaite, Watts & Piper, 2008) which thematizes power (Ivey, 1986; Wuthnow, Hunt, Bergensen & Kurzweil, 1985; Held, 1993; Mahlomaholo & Nkoane, 2002; Fairclough, 2004). Its theoretical origins and method are about interrogating power and advancing the transformation agenda towards decolonization and empowerment of the subaltern communities which in this case is made up of the academic teachers from "previously disadvantaged communities" (black/African and female). The voices of these individuals are not represented in the learner guides in Free State higher education mainly because of their demographic under-representation especially in senior academic positions where decisions, about what constitutes knowledge to be included in learner guides, are made (Bereng & Mahlomaholo, 2006; Bereng, 2007; Hongwane, 2007). If these individuals teach, they are merely foot soldiers implementing the canon as designed invariably by the white senior academics, vicariously by their proxies or being back-stage directed by them in these merged or incorporated higher education institutions.

What the genealogical method does is therefore to deconstruct the absolutes of the so-called true knowledge as prescribed by the dominant discourses in the mentioned government documents that prescribe as to what has to be taught and how it has to be taught, and thus included in the learner guides. By adopting a disposition of excavation and unearthing, academic teachers have the right to question the canon and re-interpret policy agendas. In this way, by their practice they express a sense of academic freedom which is impossible if permanent surveillance situations where every crevice of teaching and learning is micro-managed are not interrupted. The conditions of subalternity make this task difficult since there is the constant watch and gaze on what all the academic teachers do to check to see whether what the teachers do through the learner guides is compliant with the canonized view as prescribed by the HEQC, SAQA and the DoE.

In doing all these, the genealogical method thus manages to demonstrate that there is nothing essentialist, sacrosanct and with intrinsic fixed existence about learner guides or "true knowledge" for that matter. This method convincingly shows that, even the learner guides are constructed in the relations of power that have "veiled" the agenda of continuing the marginalization and exclusion of the discourses of the subaltern communities, even in the context of the so-called democracy and Uhuru in SA.

THE GENEALOGY METHOD ON POWER RELATIONS

Looking at discourses in Free State higher education (Hongwane, 2007) one notices that the dominant voices echo and are compliant with prescriptions of the the the DoE and its Parliamentary Acts, the HEQC and SAQA. One such policy relates to official theory of learning as articulated by the DoE. This policy adopts a philosophy of social constructivism, which provides a seamless framework for learning that informs all educational policy, procedure and practice from the cradle to the grave. In this light, learner guides are to be represented on the basis of principles of social constructivism (DoE, HEQC & SAQA websites focusing on the CCFO in particular; Hay et al., 2004).

Perhaps this decision was informed by the preponderance of the globalization debates and its effects on local constructions of policy. The debate is not with any robust objection to social constructivism. Indeed, social constructivism may seem to resemble some of the home grown theories for learning like people's education and may leave room for exploration of curriculum that may be indigenous based. What is at stake here is policy process, its origins; and the absence of the voice and imagination of the academic teacher in setting the curriculum agenda. In a sense it is designed and nurtured in foreign countries of Europe and elsewhere (Hay et al, 2004). In my view the question of origin is important in designing anything especially a theory of learning because the product will always mirror this origin.

The power play between Europe and Africa, or South Africa in particular, has never ended. The disrespect in which the still imperialist Europe has always looked down upon anything and everything African has been documented sufficiently (Mahlomaholo, 1998). Besides, most of the products designed in Europe seem to also always need extensive adaptation to the "colonized" African needs and requirements. Furthermore the same imperialist or more clearly the neo-imperialist agenda is still much alive. For example the discussions around poverty and marginalization that went on in the G8 meeting in Doha (Sampson, 2008) demonstrate this point. The story is infinite, it would seem. Europe (sometimes called the West) as "the center" whose interests and agendas supersede everybody else's, continues to prescribe to all, to expect conformity to its own "regime of truth" to the exclusion of and/or distortion of the views of the "other."

There should be no wonder that research, education, and curriculum guides seem to be suffused by the imperialist or neo-liberal discourse which Smith in talking about indigenous communities says " . . . postulates that indigenous beliefs were considered shocking, abhorrent and barbaric by western epistemologies" (Smith, 1999: 7).

The genealogical method proves its worth and value by pointing out to the voices of the subaltern academic teachers who are without power but who clearly see and articulate how powerless and excluded they seem to be from influencing knowledge and its production at their place of work. The learner guides are thus looked at as foreign because they are designed using foreign (Eurocentric) theories of learning as templates to the total exclusion of what is African (Hongwane, 2007).

Knowledge, hence learner guides are thus not a-political as construed, but through the lens of the genealogical method they seem to be infested and invested with power that marginalizes and antagonizes the subaltern discourses. Therefore the learner guides become a mirror of, and a site for, these contestational and competing discourses through the exclusion of the subaltern while valorizing, validating and affirming the dominant discourses. The interesting point is that this "veil" is removed from covering the mentioned discourses in the context of democracy and Uhuru which seems to be using "Orwellian newspeak" (Orwell, 1949) to advance the steering and centralising tendencies by a government which is supposed to be more democratic and representative.

DECONSTRUCTION OF CONVENTIONAL HISTORY AND MAKING THE PAST UNFAMILIAR

The genealogical method's strong point as formulated by Foucault (1980; see also Dreyfus & Rabinow, 1989; Donelly, 1979; Aronowitz, 1979) and previously discussed, lies in the linking of its pronouncements on power relations to its deconstruction of history by also making it (history) unfamiliar.

In this way the previous subheading has assisted me in getting closer to being able to show that the narrative I made at the beginning of this chapter regarding changes in higher education generally in South Africa (but with a specific focus on the Free State) and their implications/effects on learner guides was at best merely telling half of the story. This half of the story is the dominant half which supposes history is linear, that is, the changes as conceptualized and implemented represent advancement in human history and the story of the practice of (higher) education in South Africa. This half of the story creates the illusion that apartheid in South Africa was bad but that the new dispensation ushered in with the elections of April 27, 1994 is an improvement thereof and that somehow as a country and perhaps the Free State higher education in particular, is moving towards an utopia of some kind with regard to education. That part of the story was unproblematized. It was neat and sanitized of any impurities of doubt and contestation.

The other part of the story is not neat, is unfamiliar, is surprising, is thought provoking, is unusual, is non-conventional and is incoherent. The mentioned method interrupts the smooth conceptualization and theorization which is unproblematized as readers become aware that what seems so obvious about learner guides may actually have some unclear motives with regard to the subaltern categories. The interruption makes the reader(s) aware of a hidden agenda which seems to be driven at the expense of the subaltern academic teachers at least, with which they are expected to comply through the application of disciplinary and normalization influences/forces of the dominant discourses.

The subaltern academic teachers seem not to be allowed to, or are unable at first to question and to interrogate their own exclusion from designing the learner guides. Their discourses are also not reflected in the content of the learner guides which are designed with/without them (Bereng & Mahlomaholo, 2006; Bereng, 2007) but are said to be designed so that they meet with international academic standards (social constructivism and curriculum alignment as operational international learner guides design concepts, see Hay, et al., 2004). This is what the genealogical method demonstrates as the taken for granted "truth" which is now being exposed for what it is not (see Hongwane, 2007).

The "international academic standards" referred to as the norm, fail to point out to the fact that they exclude the local African voices. Seemingly, for the voices of the subaltern academic teachers to be heard as well as represented in the learner guides, they need the canonized and approved megaphones/amplifiers of the colonial dominant discourses which ultimately render them (the voices) undecipherable as they are inauthentic, unoriginal and irrelevant to their own selves and own communities. The discourses of the community of the subaltern academic teachers as Spivak (Montag, 1997) contends can thus not be heard, maybe because they cannot speak or because they are muffled and diluted with/by the medium through which they are made to speak. The colonial language, both literally and figuratively speaks through them. "Their" ideas, experiences, fears and aspirations which they articulate, are borrowed and couched in foreign epistemologies. The genealogical method assists us to come to this uncomfortable realization, a catch twenty-two situation of some kind, (for this chapter as well). The process of decolonization seems to demand the re-appropriation of the original "own" voice and discourses, by the communities of the subaltern academic teachers. This however does not seem to be very easy to accomplish, but it has to happen through the interruption of the current dominant discourses, so as to create spaces for the alternative subaltern in the interest of decolonization.

THE PROBLEMATIC ISSUES, THE PRINCIPLES OF
REVERSAL, DISCONTINUITY AND SPECIFICITY

The other pillar of the genealogical method is its advocacy for not taking anything at face value. What this implies is that in applying the genealogical method one needs to look at all sides of the story especially the problematic and uncomfortable side. Hongwane's study (2007) demonstrates how the communities of the subaltern academic teachers look at the learner guides as instruments of oppression and exclusion. Their discourses clearly question the exclusion of the African experiences which they could have readily supplied were they allowed to participate in the design of this guides. The smooth progression from design to implementation of the learner guide is questioned in these discourses which tend to reverse the process to show how by omission, oppression, hence colonization and apartheid are perpetuated. It is by exclusion of the experiences, fears and aspirations (culture) of the majority that the learner guides continues to negate the democracy obtained in 1994.

The traditional and conventional wisdom espoused by the dominant discourse is that learner guides are objective, that they are custodians of pure and untarnished knowledge for all learners, but the subaltern discourses (according to Hongwane) come to the fore to show the opposite of that which is conventional as discovered by the subaltern communities of teachers. In the words of MacLean (1970: 6–9):

> The principle of reversal where we recognize the source of discourse, the principles behind its flourishing and continuity, we traditionally think of the positive role of author, disciplines, and will to truth; instead, we must recognize the negative activity of cutting-out and of rarefaction of discourse.

From the above reflection it becomes apparent that the communities of the subaltern academic teachers tend to base their argument on the fact that current learner guides need to be opened up for processes of Africanization, wherein the new South African nation may be reflected, recognized and valued. The value of indigenous knowledge is once again reiterated from this perspective as an important part of decolonization. Africanization in this sense seems to be referring to African academic teachers participating in decision-making processes regarding learner guides as an example.

These academic teachers are at the same time challenged to create knowledge that will mirror their communities and worthy of being included in the learner guides. Indigenous knowledge thus included in the learner guides seems also to be seen as a vehicle for creating among all, including the subaltern communities; self-reliance, self-awareness, consciousness raising, self-lessness, commitment, respect, resourcefulness, integrity and care for the plight of others less fortunate (Bereng, 2007; Hongwane, 2007; Liphapang, 2007; Matobako, 2007).

Linked to the above is the principle of specificity which argues that "a particular discourse cannot be resolved by a prior system of significations; discourse does not work hand in glove with what we already know. We must conceive of discourse as violence that we do to things, or, at all events, as a practice we impose upon them" (MacLean, 1970: 6). From the discussion of the discourses of the community of the subaltern academic teachers made in Hongwane (2007), it becomes clear that the understandings that these teachers bring with are relatively "new" and that they represent a disruption of conventional "knowledge" about learner guides as innocent and pure instruments. This "new understanding" argues that the exclusion of the African voices indirectly, by excluding African teachers themselves, may seem logical due to the low status, the relative poor academic qualifications and powerlessness of the community of these subaltern teachers. However this new understanding continues and it interrupts this logical flow by showing that the same limitations for which the subaltern teachers are accused of, are due to the creation of the same logic that now seems to exclude them. For example that the mentioned teachers are in inferior positions is a historical outcome of the distorted apartheid/colonialism already alluded to earlier. The cycle is now complete and it tends to repeat and re-enforce itself and that is why the genealogical method is useful in terms of breaking it and attempting to set all free in terms of thinking and re-theorization of their roles.

The analysis shows the importance of reflecting on specific and particular situation(s) and instance(s) of the academic teachers involved. Their discourses, though indirectly referring to the bigger picture of colonization versus decolonization, directly talk to the specificity of their situation in terms of participation and informing their process of teaching.

CONCLUSION: THE NORMALIZATION TECHNOLOGIES AND THE "REGIMES OF TRUTH"

The previous discussion has indicated how learner guides could be embedded with processes operating at the macro level, like colonization. The hold of colonization through its harshest version, apartheid, has been almost complete in the South African setting. This hold has even permeated the everyday practice of teaching and learning. What is sad though is that as a nation we have not been able to lift ourselves out of its hold in spite of the efforts that culminated in the 1994 democratization of the country. Today talk is rife about how the new South African state has "slipped", (Kraak, 2001) on the initial objectives of the liberation struggle in education. The neo-colonial-apartheid residues referred to above are still operational in the design and use of learner guides. In this light, subaltern academic teachers experiences, fears and aspirations of their communities are still excluded, showing how deeply colonization is entrenched.

It would seem that another, more focused struggle for decolonization of educational practice that ensures inclusion of the discourses of the subaltern has begun. There seems to be need to extricate the practices of learning from the subtle forms of colonization that have created the new "regime of truth" wherein what counts as valid knowledge worthy. Inclusion into learner guides in this light means inclusion of the experiences of socially lowly stationed subaltern communities. What the information in this chapter tends to point out is the need and the possibility of using the genealogical method to unearth the alternative discourses that could be included in understanding the processes of developing learner guides so that they become representative of the majority and their culture(s) into the mainstream of teaching and learning.

It seems full democracy will only be possible once learners take pride in what they learn. Through the participation of the communities of the subaltern academic teachers in the design of learner guides, all learners, including those from the poor, marginalized, black communities could see themselves and their history validated, valorized and reflected in what is termed mainstream "knowledge." The possibilities are infinite if this could be achieved since learners will be more propelled to do even better in their own learning as role modelled by their black academic teachers. Such a new regime of truth is necessary towards Africanization of the curriculum which will facilitate and entrench democracy and decolonization. At present, the ghosts of apartheid colonialism still hold us captive, but the discourses of the communities of the subaltern academic teachers laid bare through the genealogical method, hold a promise and hope for a better future.

REFERENCES

Aronowitz, S. (1979). History of disruption on Benjamin and Foucault. *Humanities in society*, 2: 125–147. Bereng, T. (2007). Interrogating the absence of African-authored research-based textbooks and journal articles in South Africa's education system. Unpublished PhD thesis, Central University of Technology. Bloemfontein.

Bereng T. and Mahlomaholo, S. (2005). Interrogating the absences of African-authored research-based educational texts in South Africa. Paper presented to the South African Association for Research Development in Education (SAARDHE), Pretoria, June 26–29.

Council for Higher Education. (2004). *Framework for Programme Accreditation.* Available at: http:/ http://www.che.ac.za

Council for Higher Education. (2008). *Higher Education Qualification Framework. (2007).* Available at: http:/ http://www.che.ac.za

Department of Education. (1997a). *White Paper 3: A Programme for the Transformation of higher Education.* Available at: http://che.ac.za/documents/d000148.

Department of Education. (1997b). *Higher Education Act 101.* Available at: http:// che.ac.za/ documents/ d000148.

Department of Education. (1997c). *Higher Education Quality Committee.* Available at: http://che.ac.za/ documents/ d000148.

Department of Education. (2001). *National Plan on Higher Education.* Available at: http://che.ac.za/ documents/d000148.

Department of Education. (2002). *New Academic Policy.* Available at: http://che. ac.za/documents/d000148.

Department of Education and Department of Labour. (2001). *South African Qualification Authority.* Available at: http://saqa.com.

Department of Education. Higher Education Quality Council. (2004). *Criteria for Programme Design and Evaluation.* Available at: http://che.ac.za/documents/ d000148.

Donelly, M. (1979). Foucault's genealogy of the human sciences. Economy and society, II, in B. Smart (Ed.) *Michael Foucault (I): Critical Assessment. Vol. II.* London: Routledge, pp. 363–380.

Dreyfus, H. and Rabinow, P. (1989). *Michael Foucault: Beyond Structuralism and Hermeneutics.* Sussex: The Harvester Press.

Fairclough, N. (2004). Critical discourse analysis. Aalborg University PhD Workshop. Available at: http://diskurs.hum.aau.dk/English/seminar/FaighloughPoster.

Foucault, M. (1980). *Power and Knowledge.* Toronto: The Harvester Press.

Hay, H., Mahlomaholo, M., Van der Merwe, B., Brussouw, S., Lampbrecht, G. and Badenhorst, J. (2004). *Manual for Learning and Teaching.* Bloemfontein: Unit for Academic Development.

Held, D. 1983. *Introduction to Critical Theory: Hockheimer to Habermas.* London: Hutchinson and Company Ltd.

Hongwane, V. (2007). Free state higher education discourses: Analyzing the positioning of learning guides. Unpublished PhD thesis, Central University of Technology. Bloemfontein.

Ivey, G. (1986). Elements of critical psychology. *Psychology in Society,* 5: 63—81.

Kraak, A. (2001). *Policy Ambiguity and Slippage: Higher Education under the New State, 1994—2001.* Pretoria: Human Sciences Research Council.

Liphapang, M. (2007). Inclusive education in the South African context: Analyzing how cultural diversity is accommodated in five former Model C schools in Bloemfontein. Unpublished PhD thesis, Central University of Technology. Bloemfontein.

MacGregor, K. (2008). Challenges of equity, ageing, expansion. *University World News. The Global Window on Higher Education.* Available at: http://www. universityworldnews.com/topic.php?topic=SpecialReports&page=6.

Mahlomaholo, S. (1998). Signification of African cultural and individual African identity and performance in mathematics among some Standard Nine African pupils in Mangaung High Schools. Unpublished DEd thesis submitted to the University of the Western Cape. Bellville: Cape Town.

Mahlomaholo, S. and Nkoane, M. (2002). Traditional approaches to learning and instruction, in J. Elen (Ed.) *Learning History: Language, Instructional and Assessment Issues.* Leuven: University of Leuven, pp. 7–13.

Mahlomaholo, S. Matobako, S. 2006. Service learning in South Africa held terminally captive by legacies of the past. *Alternation,* 13(1): 203–217.

Matobako, S. (2007). The positionality of the euphemism of Service Learning at selected Higher Education Institutions in South Africa. Unpublished PhD thesis, Central University of Technology. Bloemfontein.

McLean, B H . (1970). *Discourse on Language.* Paris: Gallimard. Available at: http://individual.utoronto.ca/bmclean/hermeneutics.foucault_suppl/DOL_outline.pdf.

Meulenberg-Buskens, I. (1997). Turtles all the way down? On a quest for quality in qualitative research. *South African Journal of Psychology*, 27(2): 111–116.

Montag, W. (1997). Can the subaltern speak and other transcendental questions. *Cultural Logic*, 1(2): Available at: http://dogic.eserver.org/1–2/montag.html.

Orwell, G. (1949). *Nineteen Eighty-Four*. London: Seeker and Warberg.

Potgieter, C. (2002). *Black Academics on the Move. How Black South African Academics Account for Moving between Institutions or Leaving the Academic Profession.* Pretoria: Center for Higher Education Transformation (CHET).

Satterwaite, J., Watts, M., and Piper, H. (2008). *Talking Truth to Power.* Stoke on Trent. Trentham Books

Saul, J. (2007). The strange death of liberated southern Africa. *Transformation: Critical Perspectives on Southern Africa*, 64: pp. 1–26.

Sampson, G. (2008). G8 Summit, Doha Agenda and the Future of the WTO. Special supplement to the *Japan Times*. Yokohama. Available at: http://search.japantimes.co.jp/cg:-bin/eo20080528a1html.

Tuhaiwi Smith, L. (1999). *Decolonizing Methodologies: Research and Indigenous Peoples*. London: Zed Books.

Van Dijk, T. (2004). *From Text Grammar to Critical Discourse Analysis.* Barcelona: Universitat Pompeu Fabra.

Van Dijk, T. (2006). *Discourse and Manipulation.* Barcelona: Universitat Pompeu Fabra.

Wuthnow, R., Hunter, J., Bergensen, A., and Kurzweil, E. (1985). *Cultural Analysis: The Work of Peter L. Berger, Mary Douglas, Michael Foucault and Jurgen Habermas.* London: Routledge-Kegan Paul.

11 Adult Education and the Project of Widening Participation

Anita Franklin

INTRODUCTION

In this chapter I will describe and analyze the University of Sheffield's Working With Communities Programme and particularly its Foundation Degree. I will describe the Foundation Degree and its place within the university's commitment to widening participation, and within the context of the changing role of adult education in the UK. As a programme director on a part time university tutor contract I am well placed to look at the ways in which the programme is caught in a web of dilemmas and contradictions which challenge taken-for-granted ideas about the accessibility of education and its relationship to social mobility and social justice. This discussion draws on the work of a range of writers who have asked searching questions about the changing role of higher education and the role of adult education in the process of widening participation.

The narrative has three sections; first, an autobiography that identifies some of the factors that have shaped my perspective during the twenty-five years that I have taught in higher education institutions in the UK. Second, a section that looks at the origins of the programme and its function within the university. Finally, in the third section I ask questions about the significance of the programme and allow students' voices to join in the discussion. I conclude that Foundation Degrees are a site of struggle within higher education, especially within elite institutions.

AUTOBIOGRAPHY

When I was a Politics postgraduate at the University of Leeds in the mid-1980s a lecturer told me and others from my cohort a story. Such was the power of this story that it has remained with me for years. In the story, a professor from an elite university, someone quite dear to us for her rigorous attacks on imperialism, was asked by colleagues for her views on positive action in education to bring forth more black and Asian students into courses and in time, more such scholars into the academy. Her response was "it's dangerous to take people out of their natural class position." Her theory of the world assigned me (a black American novice academic) and people like me as "un-natural in the class struggle. Her orthodox Marxist view would have us "struggle without concessions." Those of us privy to this story were made to understand that from her point of view and presumably from others in the academy we, as anomalies were dangerous—not so much to higher education institutions but to the class struggle itself.

This story has remained with me through the years as a reminder of so many things—the arrogance of the well-respected professor who would crush the aspirations of others because of ideas that allowed her to decide who mattered and who did not in the world's future. It reminded me of the way in which what is supposedly natural is more often than not socially constructed. But perhaps most importantly the story has always kept me alert to questions about my (ambiguous) place in the academy, what I teach and how I teach it. To what extent am I participating in oppressive practices, to what extent is education a practice of freedom (Freire, 1970) for myself, my colleagues and my students?

As an educator in higher education, over the years I have been engaged in teaching and research in development studies (especially, but not exclusively in relation to Southern Africa), identity politics, women's studies and now community development. The underlying theme connecting what may look to some as a patch-worked intellectual career is an ever-evolving concern with social movements. And my longstanding concern with social movements reflects my personal background as an African American who was born into and shaped by two key social movements, the civil rights movement and the women's liberation movement. As a teenager it seemed to me and my peers inevitable that I would be involved in anti-apartheid protests, in anti-U.S. foreign policy demonstrations of various kinds and indeed in community development (Franklin, 1999).

Given my personal and professional autobiography perhaps it is not surprising that I am in the academy. However in the UK, black women working in the academy are still rare and our experiences have not always been very pleasant (THES, 2000; THES, 2004).

Still, I have been much more comfortable with my role as a teacher than as a researcher. As a black woman growing up in New York City neighborhoods that were field work for the nation's budding urban sociologists I have been of the view that much that has passed for research is often oppressive to the researched. So I have been careful in my own work to try and cause the least damage possible and indeed to try to use the intervention to do some good. But teaching too can be harmful—every course, every lesson, every letter home to a student is an intervention (Franklin and Channer, 1995). The following authors have been important in shaping my pedagogy: Edward Said, bell hooks, Frantz Fanon, Aime Cesaire, Paulo Freire, Manning Marable, Walter Rodney, Steve Biko, Patricia Hill-Collins and most recently Linda Tuhiwai Smith. All have all encouraged me to think long and hard about the purpose of education and its relationship to marginalized groups.

The next section of this chapter describes the history and development of the Working With Communities course which started in 2006. My purpose is to demonstrate how the creation and directorship of the course reflects not only the university's ambivalence about Foundation Degrees but also reflects my own ambivalent and marginalized position within the academy.

THE FIRST FOUNDATION DEGREE AT SHEFFIELD UNIVERSITY

The Foundation Degree in Working With Communities has the distinction of being Sheffield University's first Foundation Degree course. The Foundation Degree qualification, especially within the context of the Russell Group, is a relatively new qualification. Although Foundation Degrees have been a part of the curriculum of many colleges and newer universities since their launch in 2001, it is only recently that older universities like the University of Sheffield have begun their validation. The combination of vocational and academic skills and knowledge promised by Foundation degrees is a combination advocated by the New Labour government DfES (2004). The financial support given to institutions with Foundation Degrees has become increasingly important to Higher Education Institutions (HEI), even traditionally rich ones like The University of Sheffield, where the volume of money coming in from research contracts is among the highest in the world. The government has pledged to support 100,000 Foundation Degree places by 2010 (DFES, 2004)). The creation of Foundation Degrees could mark a radical new departure for many of the older universities. But to embark on Foundation Degrees calls for serious reflection on its distinguishing features.

First, and most obviously the addition of a strong vocational element within an undergraduate context challenges the skills and knowledges traditionally held within the academy. This includes its administrative culture and its priorities which are dominated by the needs of young undergraduates and the research funding agendas of academics.

Secondly, the subject areas covered by Foundation Degrees are often shaped by pressures on the local economy and demography surrounding the university. Ours is a quickly shifting demography which has seen the settlement of various "new" immigrant groups into the city and region. Yorkshire is under pressure to increase the HE participation rates of its populace (Learning and Skills Council, 2008). While having some accountability to local needs is historically a feature of many of the newer universities which in the past were funded through local authorities, such accountability has not really been deeply embedded in the contemporary work of most traditional universities.

Finally, and most profoundly, Foundation Degrees have at their center the purpose of widening participation among those communities that are traditionally under-represented in universities (HEFCE, 2000; DFES, 2003; Gorard, 2008). This too challenges the university's traditional elite culture, this time its dominant upper-middle-class biases about what the purpose of higher education is and who can benefit from it. But on a deeper level, widening participation may not simply be about allowing in groups previously kept out. It also challenges the academy to dare itself to a makeover. Much has been said about what society expects in the qualities of graduates. Indeed a renewed focus suggests that we need to begin conversations about the qualities we expect from academics and administrators as well if widening participation is truly to be a radical new departure in spear heading mass higher education in the UK. The work of Trow (2000) has been crucial on the necessity of higher education to give up its elitist culture if it is to provide mass higher education. Some institutions have been quicker than others to imbibe the lessons in Trow's work.

Of course we need to remind ourselves that universities are not monoliths and from time to time there are departments and courses that work to reverse the general trend. For example at The University of Sheffield, The Institute for Lifelong Learning has worked for years with local communities, providing flexible, accessible, often work-related courses for adults in the region. And this has been true of many Adult Education departments, at least those that managed to survive the various economic restructurings which have taken place in universities over the last twenty years (Martin, 2003).

The Institute for Lifelong Learning (TILL) is the part of Sheffield University that provides part time undergraduate courses. Therefore our students are mostly adult (age twenty-five and up), local to the region, employed and/or with adult responsibilities. We have been engaged in widening participation activities before WP was mandatory. We provide a range of named awards: natural and human environment, social and political studies, modern languages, literature and creative media, to list a few of the more prominent areas. In the past we ran both undergraduate and postgraduate courses in Community Development. TILL is clearly an obvious home for the first Foundation Degree. Nevertheless TILL's core courses and funding has up until now come from the middle classes. Recent policies on Equivalent Level Qualifications have begun to price this traditional adult education cohort out of the market (House of Commons Innovation, 2008). So whereas in the past we widened participation *alongside* catering for the middle classes we are now forced to re-structure our provision to increase participation among those who do not possess previous experience of HE.

I became deeply involved in co-designing the Foundation Degree Working With Communities in 2005. My part-time work on the Women's Studies BA in TILL was coming to an end as that area had failed to recruit students after thirteen years. I was partnered with another colleague. Several years ago as most adult education departments were closed TILL lost its autonomy and as a consequence TILL was joined together with the Department of Education to create The School of Education. This was a formulation that had been used in a few other universities, that did not dismantle adult education altogether. While some of our values overlap, it is to be expected that the different cultures and priorities of the two departments would make integration difficult, though not insurmountable. Therefore, in addition to the Foundation Degree being the first Foundation Degree at the university, it is also the first major (and visible) initiative involving both departments of the school.

My background included work with a range of black and Asian groups in the city, women's groups, and involvement with community development workers' education that went back twenty years. My colleague was involved in work with families and also with groups active around disability issues. Even with such rich backgrounds in the field, in the run-up to validation it was important for both my colleague and I to undertake outreach activities in the region. We needed to get a sense of what was already in place for students of community development. We needed to obtain information about what prospective students on a community development programme wanted. We also needed to obtain information about what current and prospective employers wanted. What we found out inspired the design of the course.

One of the most important ideas that came to us from prospective students was the need for an MA qualification in addition to an undergraduate qualification. We also learned that there were lots of courses around but that most did not lead to a recognized qualification. This led us to thinking about how to help progress students from some of those courses on to the Foundation Degree. We also had to think about how some prospective students who may not be ready for the Foundation Degree could be steered to other courses at lower levels. Finally, we created an MA award for the Working With Communities Programme in addition to the Foundation Degree.

We learned how important it was for this course to be family-friendly. This meant that classes needed to be held during hours that take child-care issues into account. It was also the case that prospective students did not want classes during the evening—which immediately challenged the adult education norm of providing classes in the evenings. Prospective students told us they liked the idea of "tasters" (orientation workshops) that would give them a chance to sample the teaching and learning experience without commitment. They also wanted re-assurance that Foundation Degrees were seen as serious qualifications, with the academic prestige and freedom awarded to other students on conventional BAs. They did not want their course work to be seen by or controlled by employers and they wanted to be able to do assignments that were connected to other aspects of their community profile, not just that associated with their paid work.

From employers we learned that changes in funding streams were imminent. With the end of New Deal Programmes and Objective 1 initiatives, the voluntary sector which is where most community development workers are based will be facing new financial challenges. Those workers without qualifications will not be able to position themselves positively for the restructuring ahead. The Skills Council informs many aspects of the curriculum, in terms of its content and delivery through our involvement with the Federation for Community Development Learning. We have involved some employers as guest speakers, as advisors to the course, etc., but in general ours is not a typical Foundation Degree. For instance most of our students are not funded by their employers. Employers are not involved in the design of the assessment nor are they involved in the moderation of students' work.

The course's bottom-up design is unusual. Our tendency to privilege the needs of marginalized groups over those of employers is again counter to the direction policy would have us take. The academic input to the course is interdisciplinary with research-led teaching from colleagues whose specialisms include postcoloniality, disability, health, children and families, identity politics, development studies, new literacies, arts and communities. In other words much of our academic input is intended to be multi-and inter-disciplinary and heavily informed by critical traditions within the social sciences. The field of community development is particularly interesting in relation to the issue of widening participation. The opportunities and constraints around community development as a vehicle for democratic social change are key parts of the course and the topics we teach.

Together the academic and vocational work form the intellectual basis for the MA and the Foundation Degree in Working With Communities. In addition all Foundation Degrees must offer a top-up year which leads to a BA. The top-up year is an additional programme of 120 credits which convert a Foundation Degree to a Bachelor's Degree.Unlike Foundation Degrees in most other HEIs we are creating a BA year that is customized for our Foundation Degree students and hopefully (pending a massive change in regulations) welcoming to other students from Foundation Degrees in this field. In this way we seek to avoid the pitfalls of most other Foundation Degrees whereby students finish the award and then transfer onto the third year of another course only to find themselves ill-supported to cope with the demands of final year study (Dodgson and Whitham, 2005; Gorard et al., 2006.)

DILEMMAS

As I write we have begun our third year of the programme. We have exceeded our targets for both the Foundation Degree and the MA named awards. We are seen in some quarters as a success because of our steady recruitment of students who bring in HEFCE money. Still there are problems that we have had to overcome.

First, other local universities have begun offering similar Foundation Degrees. Newer universities with more nimble bureaucracies and a longer history of teaching during a third semester have come out with Foundation

Degrees that take less and less time. Shorter courses are likely to be more attractive to students. We have responded to this by offering an accelerated route—the first course in the university to do so.

Secondly, students with vocational qualifications often come onto university courses expecting more help with assignments than those with an "A" level background or indeed only a General Certificate of Secondary Education (GCSE) background. This may be due to the way students are taught on vocational courses in colleges, where tutors comment on many drafts of an assignment until the student is awarded a satisfactory grade. Also many students will have done National Vocational Qualifications (NVQ) at their workplace and the method of commenting on draft after draft is a part of that pedagogy as well. This is in marked contrast to undergraduate practice where the emphasis is very much on producing one's own work.

Thirdly and perhaps most urgently, Foundation Degree students on Working With Communities come from parts of the city and region beleaguered by all the problems that belie marginalized communities. As a result our course and our students are sometimes hyper-visible and at other times totally invisible. Their working-class accents and multi-cultural looks and languages and vast age and (dis)ability range has sometimes sat uneasily with some staff who are used to a different ethnic and socialclass norm. Their very presence is a reminder of all the groups who are not usually included in higher education in more traditional universities.

Fourth, for all of TILL's work in widening participation, because we are a part of a very old and traditional university, our department is not often locally recognized for what we do well. Many colleges in the city still steer their students in an almost knee-jerk fashion to newer universities. There is also an assumption that class- and race-based bigotries are still largely uncontested in older HEIs. Having worked on both sides of what used to be called the binary divide, I can say that in my experience such assumptions are terribly misleading. Both new and old HEIs are having tremendous difficulties in widening participation. The fact remains that academic culture in the UK at least, has yet to fully embrace diversity within its staff and student body.

Fifth, elite university culture has prioritized research. However, widening participation is an end in itself and requires more attention than preserving the status quo. If the Foundation Degree is to flourish, it may at least in early stages need to be protected from being subsumed to the needs of research.

Perhaps these difficulties are not surprising. Mass higher education is a relatively new concept in the UK and no sooner are we trying to get to grips with 'massification,' than the impetus to universalization comes along. Moreover increasing and widening participation is a policy that has come about politically to help the country in the wake of increased international competition (Scott, 1995; Trow, 2000). It has become clear that there is no other way to attain the goal of one-third of the population having higher education without encouraging participation from non-traditional groups.

But in terms of a slow moving conservative, traditional, academic bureau-cracies, plus a demography that is shifting more towards an aging popula-tion, the non-traditional cohorts are students of the last resort.

Additionally, the consequences of "opening doors" to groups histori-cally not welcomed have not been followed through sufficiently in higher education. As long as the fortunes and reputations of elite universities are tied to indicators around research and not to other kinds of work then wid-ening participation will be done as efficiently (read cheaply) as possible—so as not to detract from core business. In this context many institutional obstacles can arise which makes widening participation an uphill task.

When I think back to the outreach work we did prior to validating the Foundation Degree and I look at the literature on Foundation Degrees—both groups, that is to say potential students and academics shared similar skepticism about the new qualification. Potential students asked a series of high-caliber questions about the Foundation qualification. "Who is it for? Why not a BA? What is it (the Foundation Degree) good for? What does it lead to? Why can't a BA do all of that? Why does the government want to sponsor what employers want when there is no guarantee that employers will want to sponsor their workers?"

Academics also asked important questions about the relationship between employers and the new qualification, and queried the way the government's emphasis on "employability" was being set up almost in opposition to uni-versities' emphasis on academic skills and knowledge. Researchers of Foun-dation Degrees have found over the years that employers have not always sponsored their workers and that many Foundation Degrees are sitting on college and university shelves, figuratively speaking. Students from many Foundation Degrees have failed to progress onto their final BA top-up year and as a consequence do not enjoy the full advantages of higher educa-tion and are therefore chronically underpaid (Dodgson & Whitham, 2005; Doyle, 2003; Foskett, 2005).

Most worryingly, some of the literature suggests that Foundation Degree students benefiting the least materially from the university system tend to be working class, mature, female and members of ethnic minority groups, and often are raising children on their own. (Webb et al., 2006).

I am therefore left with a number of questions. What is the significance of adult education for my students on the Working With Communities Pro-gramme, the majority of whom are women of color? What is the significance of me, a black female foreigner on a part-time, teaching-only contract, as co-designer and director of the programme? How am I meant to manage such an onerous assignment from my deeply marginalized position? And if I am as I have been told the best person for the job what does that mean for my future progression? How might I build a critical mass within the institution and beyond that could ensure the programme's survival and further development?

I have responded to these questions by working to protect the pro-gramme in a variety of ways. My experience and these reflections tell me that the university as a whole was not interested in the Foundation Degree qualification but that the institution was also keen to be seen to use the Foundation Degree to widen participation. As universities continue to be asked questions about their role in communities, being seen to be widening participation—especially through community development fulfils that brief. On the other hand, widening participation is not a core policy and it is not a policy that is intended as yet to shape any other department but that of TILL. In a sense TILL was the most reasonable place to house the new award(s) although there has been critical resistance to this- as represented in the literature. But in creating Foundation Degrees we may run the risk of increased marginalization from the university's central work—teaching young, academically gifted, middle-class individuals from the UK and from all over the world, and chasing funding to do world-class research.

In protecting the programme from failure I have welcomed (a) critiques of the Foundation Degree award which have alerted us to the sometimes cynical use of the award in luring in students into HE simply because of the funding they represent with scant attention to the quality of the course and the teaching and learning experience of the students; (b) the course's interdepartmental nature and the way that has allowed us to expand the programme by linking it to other courses, and to community development initiatives outside of the UK; and (c) I have also sought to protect it by using TEL to enhance the learning experience of students and by encouraging other more senior academics to contribute to the course (even if their presence is only the MA part of the course). In other words I have sought to integrate what is otherwise an isolated Foundation Degree award into the mainstream academic community. I'm looking to connect the programme internationally with a community development course in the U.S., the Caribbean, and in continental Europe.

STUDENTS' VOICES

As the first group of Foundation Degree students prepare to graduate and/ or transfer onto the customized BA award I talked with them about this chapter and about the fact that we will do research together on the course with the aim of documenting their experience and on how the university might improve the course for others. The students were all very enthusiastic and motivated to take part.

Three-quarters of them have benefited from the course already by becoming employed, being promoted within the same organization, moved on to a better job at a different organization, or had their position made permanent. My students are clever, sensitive, busy, committed individuals who are well aware of the dilemmas and contradictions of their education. One student was very adamant that the course's success should not be overly identified with these changes in their employment. She said that what was most important is that "we now know how to talk to our employers and to the people we work with, we know how to engage with them in ways that they now listen to our views."

The students also organized themselves into focus groups to discuss barriers to their education. For them the main problem they encounter over and again with the university is financial. The student financial support systems are not geared to individuals who may have to find their fees from a range of sources. Also the students have complained bitterly about the amount of and/or demeaning nature of paper work required to be considered for financial support. Another barrier frequently discussed is childcare and the general prejudice they encounter when they attempt to bring their young children onto the campus, for example into the libraries. In other words while our department does what it can to support the students and to create an atmosphere conducive to the needs of adult learners not used to higher education, their encounters with the mainstream part of the university often leaves them bruised.

Further work will privilege their voices, in the meantime here are two interviews that I did in June 2008 for a brochure that promoted our course. The students consented to their use in this chapter. I have however changed their names to protect their privacy.

My intention is to draw attention to the way in which these students come to the university with set goals and mature experiences of the world of work and family. They come to us after hearing about us—in other words it is our reputation in the local community that has drawn individuals to the course. They stay with us because we are supportive of their goals—at work, but also in relation to their families and communities. The best way to widen participation may be through our careful listening to their stories and to more stories of individuals who are like them.

INTERVIEW 1

Fatima, How did you become interested in community work?
I left school at sixteen without qualifications—I just wanted to get out and make some money. I wasn't sure really what I wanted to do but I was involved with community projects from when I was sixteen, too. But it was when I got a job as a family support worker that I realized that community work was definitely the path for me. At school I never had role models, but in the field of community work over the years I found I was really impressed and motivated by a lot of the powerful women I got to see doing good work.

Why did you come onto "Working with Communities" at Sheffield University?
I knew that it made sense to get formal qualifications even though I was already working in the field for awhile. And this

course was convenient, in terms of when the classes are and where it's located. When I heard about the course from a friend of mine at first I was unsure because I did not know what to expect. But when I had the interview I was put at my ease and I felt really comfortable. That was it for me. I knew then that the course was for me.

How has being on the course helped you with work?
It's helped me a lot. I was in one post when I started the course and now I have been able to get a better position and I definitely believe that that was because of the course. My co-workers are impressed with how I do things, how I think about issues.

My colleagues think I am on my way to becoming an expert in the field. And now they want to come onto the course too!

What are you currently working on in your job?
I'm part of a team that is working to help deliver race equality in relation to mental health. It's a really exciting project! I am now in a place where I feel I can make a big difference in the mental health and well being of black and minority ethnic communities.

How has the course impacted on your family and friends?
In general everyone has been very supportive. For instance my father cannot wait for graduation! On the other hand I've had the odd one-off experience when someone asked me what was I doing at university: "'Ain't it a bit late?" she said. And I said "no, it's never too late to learn." Also I found that I did have to clear away relationships that were not working out anyway.

What else would you like to say to anyone thinking about coming onto this course?
I would say do it. First of all it is easier than you think! In the first year you spend your time writing about what you know- just learning to do it an academic way. As long as you have a vision -a goal for yourself as someone who works in the community then do it, do it for yourself and for your community.

INTERVIEW 2

Jill, What qualifications did you leave school with?
I had four 'O' levels but I had no interest in school at all! I wanted to travel but I wasn't really able to pursue that. I fell into the health field and went for a Diploma in Nursing. I did two and a half years of nurse training but had to leave with only six months to go. That really affected me, not so much having to leave but that no one from the institution ever got in touch

to find out what had happened to me. For a long time it left me with a bad taste in my mouth when it came to education. I then went into the civil service and spent seven years with my children while they were young. When I got divorced I knew I needed to get clear about my future and I went on the Introduction to Community Development Health Course and from there I then went on the trainer's course associated with that programme.

Why did you choose to come onto the "Working With Communities Course?"
I was involved with the MOSAIC research programme that was at Surestart and information about the course was available. So I came to the taster day that had been organized. The subjects that we talked about drew not only on my workplace experience but on other parts of my life as well. I was particularly excited because of the way the course tries to help women cope with the various barriers that still exist when trying to get into Higher Education. It can be a struggle to balance work, home life especially when you have kids, but it is possible.

How has the course impacted on your working life?
Perceptions of me have definitely changed since being on this course. I am now seen as someone who has knowledge about issues, an expert! That means that I have more responsibility. The course has also deeply affected my practice. When I interview people and work in outreach with communities I think a lot harder about the implications of what I am doing. I'm horrified when I think back on some of the things I used to do before I came on the course! I'm now a much more informed worker, more ethically aware- and that benefits the organization and the people I'm working with.

How does being a student affect your friends and family?
One of the things I like about the course is that I have made new friends in addition to still having my old friends. The course also has had a nice effect on the relationship between me and my children. I was a bit worried at the start that studying might take me away from them but instead I use my independent study time as time to make homework a family event. We all sit around the table doing our studying together. They really enjoy it.

Any tips for others contemplating doing "Working With Communities?"
It's not just that course has changed my life and given me new goals for my life—the course has affected my expectations for my children. Actually it has affected their expectations of themselves! I am the first one in my family to do a degree but I won't be the last!

CONCLUSION

This chapter has looked at how the work of creating a new course with a barely recognized qualification with the aim of widening participation presents specific challenges to traditional universities, like the University of Sheffield. In this case it has been the more marginalized area of the university, that is its adult education center which has been given the role of widening participation. Having been certain of its middle-class core funders for years, we were able to widen participation alongside providing adult learning for the already well educated. But the Equivalent Level Qualifications (ELQ) policy has come as a cruel blow. In order for adult education to survive we have positioned ourselves at least for now as the part of the university that widens participation. This is done via Foundation Degrees and similar awards which will combine the vocational with the academic. The first course to venture into this difficult terrain survives though it felt many times that the project would not come to fruition. But the views of my students keep me fighting for its survival and development. At the same time the Foundation Degree has also been a timely development, coinciding with the arrival of new forward thinking committed to moving the university forward. I am looking forward to it!

REFERENCES

DfES. (2003). *Foundation Degrees: Meeting the Need for Higher Level Skills.* London: DfES.

DfES. (2004). *Evaluation of Foundation Degrees Final Report.* York: York Consulting.

Dodgson, R., Whitham, H. (2005). *Learner Experience of Foundation Degrees in the North East of England: Access, Support and Retention.* Sunderland: Aimhigher Associates, North East/Universities for the North East.

Doyle, M. (2003). Discourses of employability and empowerment: foundation degrees and "third way" discursive repertoires. *Discourse: Studies in the Cultural Politics of Education*, 24(3): 275–288.

Foskett, R. (2005). Collaborative partnership in the higher education curriculum: A cross-sector study of foundation degree development. *Research in Post Compulsory Education*,10(3): 351–372.

Franklin, A. (1999). "Interfaces of race, gender, class and nation," in C. Zmroczek and P. Mahony (Eds *International Perspectives on Women and Social Class.* London: Taylor and Francis.

Franklin, A. and Channer, Y. (1995). Black participation in higher education. *Journal of Further and Higher Education*, 19(3) Autumn: pp. 32–46.

Gorard, S. (2008). Which students are missing from HE? *Cambridge Journal of Education*, 38(3): 421–437.

Gorard, S., Smith, E., May, H., Thomas, L., Adnett, N., Slack, K. (2006). *Review of Widening Participation Research: Addressing the Barriers to Participation in Higher Education.* A report to HEFCE by the University of York, Higher Education Academy and Institute for Access Studies, Stoke-on-Trent.

HEFCE. (2000). *Foundation Degree Prospectus.* Reference 00/27.

House of Commons Innovation. (2008, March). Universities, Science and Skills Committee. March 2008. (http://www.publications.parliament.uk/pa/cm200708/cmselect/cmdius187/187.pdf

Learning and Skills Council. (2008). *Yorkshire and the Humber Regional Commissioning Plan 2008—09.* Coventry: Learning and Skills Council Publications.

Martin, A. (2003). Adult education, lifelong learning and citizenship: Some ifs and buts. *International Journal of Lifelong Education,* 22(6): 566–579.

Scott, P. (1995). The Meanings of Mass Higher Education. Buckingham: SRHE/Open University Press.

THES. (2000, April 14). Stopped by the unsound barrier. *THES.* Available at: http://www.timeshighereducation.co.uk/story.asp?storyCode=151198&sectioncode=26.

THES. (2004, October 29) Black intellectual seems an oxymoron in England. *THES.* Available at: www.timeshighereducation.co.uk/story.asp?storyCode=192064&sectioncode=26

Trow, M. (2000). From mass higher education to universal access: The American advantage. Research and Occasional Paper Series: Center for Studies in Higher-Education 1.00. University of California, Berkeley. Available at: http://repositories.cdlib.org/cshe/CSHE1-00.

Webb, S., Brine, J. & Jackson, S. (2006). Gender, foundation degrees and the knowledge-driven economy. *Journal of Vocational Education and Training,* 58(4): 563–576.

12 Community Perspectives on Poverty and Poverty Alleviation in the Caribbean

Patricia Ellis

INTRODUCTION: THE CONTEXT

> *Nothing is being done here . . . I don't know what they are doing . . .*
> *Nothing they do so far making any difference . . . the poor still poor!*
> (Participant at focus group discussions)

This chapter draws upon empirical research conducted within communities in the English speaking Caribbean that are experiencing the effects of poverty. The Caribbean region is comprised of countries stretching from the tip of Florida in the north to the northern coast of South America in the south. The countries of the English speaking Caribbean are Anguilla, Antigua and Barbuda, the Bahamas, Barbados, Belize, the British Virgin Islands, The Cayman Islands, Dominica, Grenada, Guyana, Jamaica, Montserrat, St Kitts and Nevis, St Lucia, St Vincent and the Grenadines, The Turks and Caicos Islands, and Trinidad and Tobago.

These countries were all colonies of England and Anguilla, The British Virgin Islands, The Cayman Islands, Montserrat and The Turks and Caicos Islands are still British dependencies. The others are independent states and although their education systems are modeled after the British system, curricula have been reformed to reflect Caribbean culture and to respond to Caribbean needs.

George Beckford, a Caribbean economist, in his seminal work *Persistent Poverty* (1972), advanced a theory of underdevelopment in plantation economies which drew attention to how the legacies of colonialism continue to persist within contemporary structures and discourses about development. According to Beckford (1972: 216), "major social and political obstacles to development that are directly attributable to the plantation influence include (inter alia) weak community structure and loose family organization that prevent the emergence of viable local and regional units of administration and control." Here Beckford refers to the development of colonized societies in which the very foundations of the relations between state and society is a rehearsal of "social diseconomies" (Beckford, 1972: 177). As Beckford argues "a general pattern emerges. In all cases the social diseconomies find ultimate expression in a rather unique combination of resource underutilization alongside under-consumption and poverty among the majority of people in plantation society" (Beckford, 1972: 177).

The general case made by Beckford and other Caribbean economists (Best, 1968: Levitt, 2005; for example) is that "in the Caribbean the root causes of persistent poverty is the persistence of class structures and mental attitudes carried over from plantation slavery" and internalized by middle-class elites (Levitt, 2005: 70). Consequently, the "social diseconomies" of which Beckford speaks, find expression in the lived experiences of economic inequality, landlessness, inadequate access to social resources and persistent and expanding unemployment, all occurring within communities that become dispossessed.

Because of concern about existing levels and severity of poverty in some Caribbean countries, several attempts are being made, through the conduct of Country Poverty Assessments to identify underlying causes and factors contributing to the persistence of this phenomenon, and initiatives that are being taken to alleviate it.

This chapter draws on data obtained from Country Poverty Assessments undertaken over the last decade in several countries including Antigua and Barbuda, Grenada, St Lucia, and St Kitts and Nevis. The information was provided by residents in twelve communities in Antigua and Barbuda, seventeen communities in St Lucia, ten communities in St Kitts and ten communities in Nevis. It emerged from and through resident's participation in interviews, focus group discussions and community workshops conducted during Participatory Poverty Assessments undertaken in several communities in various countries.

In their own voices residents in the communities relate their experience of poverty and its impact on their lives, of discrimination, exclusion, and deprivation of rights, and of their vulnerability and the risks that they take in order to survive and sustain their livelihoods. The collective voices of various communities are represented through composite thematic narratives. These narratives seek to convey the nuances of the lived individual and collective experiences and allow insights to be gleaned into the challenging circumstances of communities that have been historically, politically, economically and socially marginalized, and ignored and kept in states of underdevelopment.

The chapter also identifies some initiatives taken to alleviate poverty and to improve living conditions in poor communities, and it identifies residents' needs and their views about the change and actions that must be taken to ensure that people living in poverty in poor communities can enjoy a better standard of living and a better quality of life.

Consequently, the chapter constructs a notion of community through a set of Caribbean lenses and engagements of working and researching with communities. Such engagements foreground a commitment to collaborative practice in which subjectivities of the lived experience of participants in the research process are recognized, respected and acknowledged as sites knowledge production. In this light, it can be argued that the persistence of poverty among some communities has historical, political, economic and social significance that is worthy of social inquiry. Finally, the issue of poverty requires a commitment to unpacking and unearthing the complexities of how marginalization works to reduce capability and perpetuate cultures and communities of silence.

COUNTRY POVERTY ASSESSMENTS (CPAs)

During the last decade, the Caribbean Development Bank with assistance from other development agencies, has facilitated the conduct of Country Poverty Assessments (CPAs) in several Caribbean countries. The aim of the Assessments was to ascertain the nature, extent and severity of poverty; identify the factors that create, contribute to, generate and maintain poverty; assess the impact of poverty on the most vulnerable groups in the society; identify the coping and survival strategies that people living in impoverished communities use to sustain their livelihoods; and identify initiatives taken by government agencies, and civil society organizations to alleviate poverty and to improve living conditions in poor communities.

KAIRI Consultants Ltd, a regional consulting firm, with which I was involved, has carried a significant number of the CPAs each of which includes a Macro Socio-Economic Analysis, A Standard of Living Survey, A Participatory Poverty Assessment and an Institutional Analysis. The firm's multi-disciplinary team consists of a Development Economist, a Sociologist/Social Assessment Specialist, a Community Development/Training Specialist, a Natural Resource Management Specialist, a Statistician/Statistical Analyst, and a Data Analyst/Electronic Data Processor. The team has developed and refined a research methodology that incorporates quantitative and qualitative approaches, and that uses methods and techniques designed to assess the multi-dimensional nature of poverty from various perspectives (KAIRI Consultants, 2004).

THE PARTICIPATORY POVERTY ASSESSMENT METHODOLOGY

Negotiating access with the communities was undertaken on the basis of working with them through dialogic spaces where they were encouraged to rethink their lived experiences. Our engagements with communities was developed around an understanding that to reclaim communities required methodological endeavors that provided opportunities to enhance human capabilities and functioning (Levitt, 2005; Sen, 1999). In this light, poverty was interpreted to be a form of disenfranchisement which involved capability deprivation (Sen, 1999), and what was required was to allow communities to forge their own agenda that would provide them with real opportunities for personal and social development.

The inclusion of Participatory Poverty Assessments (PPAs) in the CPAs provided opportunities for individuals and groups to reflect on their experience of poverty and its impact on their lives, to identify factors that have contributed to their living in impoverished conditions, and to suggest actions that in their view would alleviate poverty and improve their living conditions. In order to ensure that the various PPA activities were well conducted and would produce high quality data, Field Research Facilitators in each country were exposed to intensive training in the theory, practice, and use of a Participatory Research methods and techniques.

Specific selection criteria were used to ensure that communities selected in each country were among the poorest and that they were representative of all of the types of communities existing in the countries, including among other things, geographic location, population size, economic activity, and level of poverty and wealth. Purposive sampling was used to identify community leaders, households, and poor individuals to be interviewed, but all residents were invited to participate in relevant focus group discussions and in community workshops.

Over a period of several months, a pair of field research facilitators observed community life and living in each community, interacted and held informal discussions with community residents, conducted separate focus group discussions with men, women, young people under twenty-five years of age, elderly persons over sixty-five years of age, unemployed people, and people with disabilities. They also facilitated community workshops and identified poor households and individuals to be interviewed by the consultants.

Researchers and consultants listened to the voices of community residents and obtained significant amounts of qualitative data that highlighted the lived experiences and perspectives of people living in poor communities. The qualitative data from the PPAs were combined with quantitative data generated from the Surveys of Living Conditions, and this has deepened understanding of poverty and of its impact on those living in impoverished conditions (Melville and Wint, 2007).

POVERTY IN COMMUNITIES

Beckford (1997) claims that the persistence of poverty in the Caribbean is inextricably linked to legacies of colonial underdevelopment perpetuated by the continuities of "the plantation" is an important one and worthy of reiterating. Since colonial times poverty has existed in Caribbean communities and it still exists in several today and this is recognized by those communities experiencing such poverty. According to a participant in one of the community workshops "I know this is a poor community; look at the conditions we living in!" This in spite of the fact that over the years community development has been seen as a strategy for alleviating poverty, for improving the living conditions, the standard of living and the quality of life of community residents.

The implementation of infrastructural and housing projects, provision of utilities, facilities and essential services over time was intended to address public and material community poverty. On the other hand, in order to address private, individual, and income poverty, job opportunities were made available and citizens were encouraged to participate in income generating projects so as to be able to meet some of their basic needs.

At the same time programmes were also designed to provide residents with the knowledge and skills that would enable them to improve the conditions under which they were living. In addition the implementation of large numbers of cultural and social programmes and activities fostered social interaction, community spirit and cooperation among residents, increased residents' awareness about social problems, and stimulated ideas about social change (Ellis, 1994).

POVERTY AND DEPRIVATION

It is now generally acknowledged that poverty is not only multi-dimensional but that deprivation is a significant characteristic of poverty (Ludi and Bird, 2007). Recent studies of poverty and well-being have looked at the links between different types of deprivation and poverty (Camfield, 2006; McGregor, 2006).

Residents in some communities who studied in recent CPAs in the Caribbean, also saw poverty as deprivation not only of an income and of the means to meet basic needs, but also of access to resources, of equal opportunity and choices, of access to resources, of representation, of a voice, of a good life and a sense of well-being and of rights. Prolonged lack of opportunities and resources has resulted in loss of capability, exclusion from productivity, and has prevented people from participating in and benefiting from essential societal processes, as well as from acquiring the means to move out of poverty. According to a male participant in the focus group discussion "*Opportunities not there. . . . I going dead poor!*"

Residents involved in PPA activities identified ways in which deprivation had caused them to live in poverty, and prevented them from improving their standard of living and enjoying a sense of well-being. These male participants in focus group discussions revealed, "Poverty is being deprived of a good start" and that it "deprived [them] of a good life." They further noted that "opportunity not distributed fairly, people who better off get preference in everything."

While the majority of people in every society take certain rights for granted, information provided by many of those who participated in the PPAs in the Caribbean showed that people living in poverty were being deprived of several rights. Among these were the right to an education that would equip them with the knowledge and skills needed to obtain employment and earn an income that would enable them to meet basic needs and to enjoy an acceptable standard of living a good quality of life. They also experienced deprivation of resources and of opportunities to voice their views, opinions and needs; and were not able to participate in decisions that would affect their lives.

The issue of deprivation through poverty is central to concerns about human rights and the right to participate in full citizenship. Many residents in the identified communities in which PPA activities were conducted believed that they had no voice, that they were ignored and that what they said was not important. They felt left out and that they had no control of their lives. For example this collage of statements from focus group discussions reflects the depth of loss felt as a result of such disenfranchisement:

> *We have no voice . . . No one listens to us, they don't take on what we say . . . Nobody don't take on what we say even if it important . . . They leave us out, everything is for the youth . . . I poor I have no choice I can do nothing about it.*

Poverty studies in several countries world-wide suggest that people living in poverty experience a sense of ill being and powerlessness, and that they are often excluded from participating in or benefiting from societal resources and processes (DfID, 2005; Narayan et al., 2000a, 2000b; UNDP Croatia, 2006).

Inequality and discrimination are built into, reinforced, and perpetuated by social structures and systems that contribute to isolation and social exclusion. Data from Poverty Assessments in the Caribbean have shown that social exclusion of vulnerable groups, including poor women, men, children, the elderly and people with disabilities, results not only from low incomes and lack of access to resources, but also from cultural traditions, societal structures and discriminatory practices (Melville and Wint, 2007).

Some community residents who participated in focus group discussions in recent PPAs in various countries felt strongly that this was the case. They cited instances where they were unable to access some available resources because of such factors. Their various responses from interviews and focus group discussions have been shaped into a narrative that illustrates a collective consciousness of how they experience exclusion:

> *If you poor you can't get a loan 'cause you don't have the deposit . . . I try to get a house but they always turn me down . . . It seems like if the set up things to keep us poor . . . They put you on file and never get back to you . . . The society design so who poor will stay poor . . . Poverty is when you keep down by the system . . . Poverty is perpetuated by the government, they develop programmes that exclude us . . . Poverty is*

*like a system to keep poor people subservient and in a different class
... Wealth is not shared equitably, only one set of people benefiting...
People should be treated equally whether they are rich or poor.*

Participants in focus group discussions in several communities also agreed
that stigmatization and prejudice contribute to a lack of acceptance, loss
of status and power, and ultimately to marginalization. They claimed that
*"They make you feel less than a person . . . People don't want me to accept
me for what I am . . .* [There is] *the stigma of being poor."*

VULNERABILITY

Data from the PPAs also showed that because for children, the elderly, and
single female parents, the negative effects of poverty are more severe, these
groups are more vulnerable and are in danger of falling into deeper poverty or of enduring long term, persistent poverty. Moreover because they
often lack the resources and the capability to respond to crises, shocks and
threats to their livelihoods, several members of these groups admitted that
in order to survive and sustain their livelihoods, they sometimes have to
engage in activities that leave them open to exploitation, and to take risks
that threaten their security.

One of the women in the focus group discussions said "It risky going
from man to man, you could get AIDS." However another woman who
is a head of the household and single parent stated *"It not* economical to
have all your children from one man, that is how I survive." These seemingly contradictory statements present the real dilemmas of daily survival
for these communities. On the other hand, the concern for security among
young people had to do with crime and their involvement. "Crime pays, but
it risky," said one young man in the focus group discussions. According to
another young man, "Crime pays but if the police catch you . . . I does sell
drugs but is a chance I taking."

At the same time residents in some communities also constructed their
vulnerability in political terms and identified instances in which they were
exploited by politicians and in which their appeals for assistance from the
latter were turned down because they not party supporters. "It ain't right
that we should be living so," one participant stated. "Only at election time
they promise to help us . . . They only help if you belong to the party,"
claimed another young man.

Consequently, the survival of members of many poor households can be
threatened by changes in the economy, crises, illness, loss of income and
debt. For example, an elderly participant lamented "I have high blood pressure and it getting worse but I can't afford the medication." However because
of lack of resources they see themselves as powerless and may lack the ability
and the motivation to respond effectively and this makes them vulnerable.

PERCEPTION AND MEANING OF POVERTY

To explain poverty one has to live it.

This statement by a head of a household who was interviewed is a reminder that an understanding of poverty must be based on the lived experience of those who are experiencing poverty and on listening to them as they describe the impact of poverty on their lives.

Residents in the deprived communities that were studied are very much aware that poverty is multi-dimensional and that there are different kinds of poverty.

> *There are different kinds of poverty. . . . Poverty has a physical and a mental part . . . There is spiritual poverty . . . Poverty is a state of mind . . . Even your words are poor . . . Poverty is a psychological state.*
>
> *Poverty is emotional pain, it eats us.The pain that poverty brings, it difficult to speak about . . . Financial stress can bring your spirit down . . . Poverty affects relationships in the family . . . It worse when you poor and get sick and can't afford the medicine.*

While residents in all of the communities studied agreed that lack of income was a common characteristic of poverty, they were also aware of the social, emotional and psychological dimensions of poverty. They recognized that lack of good health and of education, social problems, poor relationships, poor quality of life and a sense of ill-being contributed to and were consequences of poverty.

Single female parents spoke of the absence of emotional as well as of financial support from children's fathers and the psychological trauma they experienced when they are solely responsible for providing for and managing children, especially teenagers. "It hard, is me alone, no support from the fathers or anyone else," said one interviewee. Elderly persons spoke of neglect and abandonment, lack of love and care, feelings of loneliness and absence of support systems—"No one to take care of me . . . Nobody to talk to, nothing to do, no where to go." Yet, their articulations served to provide insights into the complexity of poverty and illuminate how the experience of the conditions of poverty are manifested at multiple levels—individual, at the household and at the community level.

Individual Poverty

Participants in the study of all ages admitted that poverty can make people become destitute and that lack of money can prevent them from acquiring food, clothes, and adequate shelter, and from being able to plan or to achieve their goals. Their representations of the experience of poverty at an individual level point to a sense of resignation yet frustration about such deprivation and their seeming inability to move on with their life dreams.

Interviews with elderly persons highlighted the link between poverty and ageing and between economic deprivation and deterioration in health. A significant number of individuals, including young men, felt hopeless and powerless to achieve anything or to change their situation; that their lives were insignificant; and some even questioned whether it was worth living. Their stories unfold in the following excerpt:

> *Look at my clothes, they old but I can't afford to buy new ones, I have no money . . . I wanted to be a nurse but I had no money . . . I have no money so I can't plan for the future . . . I have nothing. I own nothing. No money to buy anything . . . I am old I need food clothes and a better house . . . Look how I living, I sick so I can't work and no body don't help me . . . Things worse now I old . . . The only money I have is what I get from welfare and it small . . . Medication expensive so I can't always afford it . . . I get the medication free. The doctor say to take it after meals, but I don't have anything to eat and you can't take medicine on a hungry belly . . . Too poor to move on . . . I poor already I can't do nothing about it so I have to accept it . . . What is the sense of living I better off dead!*

Household Poverty

It is in households that poverty is felt most keenly. Many household heads believed that they were poor and live in impoverished conditions because they had insufficient or no money to meet the basic needs of their families. Data from interviews with household heads show that single parent female-headed households, multi-generational households and elderly single person households were among the poorest. Food security is essential to ensure the survival of household members, but lack of money coupled with high cost of living threatens the food security of many poor households.

In many of the households interviewed no adult was employed, and in others those employed were doing odd jobs or working in low-skilled, low-status jobs for small wages that were insufficient to meet their basic needs. Information provided in interviews with heads of households confirmed their belief that unemployment, deprivation of job opportunities, and employment which paid low wages, contributed to poverty.

Among the strategies that poor individuals and households use to survive is dependence on remittances from relatives and friends abroad and while for many poor households these are important resources, they often are not large or regular. Moreover dependency, especially if it is the main means of survival can damage self-esteem and rob a person of dignity. Their stories are revealed thus:

> *No work, no money, no food, nothing . . . I can't afford, the cost of living too high . . . We can't eat everyday . . . Unemployment contributes to poverty . . . Nobody in here working . . . Is a year now I not working*

> *... Jobs hard to get they want experience ... I need a job ... The house in bad condition, it leaking, it want fixing but I can't afford ... The house so bad it leaking sun ... There is no privacy, the children getting big and we need more space ... If not for family abroad we would be in a worse position. ... I feel like a beggar always having to depend on people for things ... A neighbor does help me out sometimes but I feel bad asking ... I too old to work I have to depend on my children.*

Community Poverty

Poor communities are characterized by the absence of physical infrastructure and public facilities and services, and many of the communities that were studied during the PPAs lacked these in some degree. At the same time, while residents in many communities had access to schools, health centers, and recreational facilities, facilities for the elderly and people with disabilities were conspicuous by their absence.

In focus group discussions and community workshops with community residents they stressed that their ability to access, use and benefit from community facilities and services did not only depend on their availability, but also on distance, cost, the quality of the services being offered, and the attitude of providers.

> *We live in a poor community ... The roads bad and very few facilities ... No community center, no library, no recreational facilities ... We need a day care center or a preschool ... Nowhere for us to meet and nothing for us to do ... The clinic too far ... You have to go to too many people before you get what you want ... The service not good ... Their attitude poor ... Health care available but the quality poor.*

IMPACT OF POVERTY

The PPAs provided opportunities for different groups to describe and share their experiences of poverty and its impact. Most residents and community leaders believed that because children and elderly people depended on others for their survival, they felt the impact of poverty most keenly.

Information provided in focus group discussions and interviews showed that in addition to being deprived of food, children in poor households were also being deprived of a stable family life, of love, care and supervision, and of a good education. "We don't always have food, I always hungry," said a young person. Others declared, "My mother and father always quarreling and fighting ... Sometimes I hate my mother when she can't give me what I want." A female single parent stated that she worked two jobs and has to leave her children alone often.

Because poverty is gendered, males and females experience its impact in significantly different ways. Data from the PPAs show that poverty prevents men and women from performing their gender roles and from meeting society's expectations. According to men, poverty decreases their power and status in the household, affects their relationships with women and threatens their sense of manhood. Some of the claims expressed by young men were "I can't provide for my children, I don't feel like a man . . . My girlfriend left me and went with another man 'cause I couldn't give her the things she want."

On the other hand, poor women, especially those with large numbers of children, were concerned about their inability to feed their families and to send their children to school everyday: "I feel bad when I have no food to give the children . . . I can't send the children to school everyday, no food and no money for bus fare."

Women also admitted that poverty affected their relationships with men, left them open to sexploitation, caused them to have relationships with several men, and to endure domestic violence and abuse. Some of the statements heard from these women were, "Some women go from man to man . . . When things real bad my partner and I does quarrel and fight . . . To get the job you have to let the boss feel you up."

Data from the PPAs also showed that many young people in poor communities experienced stigma and discrimination and were shunned and ostracized by their peers. Because rejection had damaged their self-esteem several had joined gangs and become involved in illegal activities to gain respect.

THE ROLE OF EDUCATION

Everyone who participated in the PPAs believed that deprivation of education contributed to poverty and that education is essential to be able to move out of poverty. Many of the young people were also very aware that poverty had deprived them of education and had limited their opportunities, choices and life chances. However they criticized the education system and an irrelevant academic curriculum that did not provide them with the skills needed to gain employment. Thus, while acknowledging that "education is the key, if you don't have education you can't get away from poverty" and that "only education can break the cycle of poverty," participants also recognized the role of the community to "encourage the young people to make the most of their education so that they would be in a better position [in life]."

In the Caribbean a great deal of emphasis is placed on certification, especially as a mechanism for obtaining a job. Data from Standard of Living Surveys conducted in some countries have revealed that between 50% and 80% of the poor had no certificates compared with 34% to 54% of the non-poor, and data from PPAs show that lack of money has prevented some poor children from completing secondary school and obtaining certificates (KAIRI, 2007).

While education is viewed as a strategy for moving out of poverty, data from the PPAs show that availability of education alone is insufficient to ensure accessibility, regular and consistent participation or benefits from education, or that education is used to bring about change in living conditions. Many residents stressed the need for a more relevant curriculum, a change in some teachers' attitude towards poor children, and for more supportive systems to provide more assistance to poor families and their children.

Information obtained during interviews with parents indicated that some poor children were not always able to access or benefit fully from available educational opportunities. Among the reasons identified for this were the low levels of parents' education; the latter's inability to meet the costs of lunch, bus fare and school books; irregular attendance and high drop out rates; and some teachers' attitude to children living in poor communities. Because several parents were unable to provide lunch and transportation daily, or to purchase books and other school supplies, irregular attendance and high drop rates among children in primary and in secondary schools existed in many of the communities studied.

It is now accepted that the higher the level of parent's education the less likely it is that they and their children will live in poverty. However, interviews with heads of households in several communities show that while a few of them had some secondary education, some of these had not completed, that the majority had only primary education, and that few if any were participating in adult education programmes.

In some households girls had dropped out in either form two or three (ages thirteen though sixteen) because of pregnancy and in a few cases they were sometimes kept home to look after younger siblings, and in some households boys had to leave school early in order to work and contribute to the household income.

In focus group discussions several young people described the treatment they received by their peers and by some teachers because they were poor or lived in a poor community. They spoke about being insulted, ridiculed and ignored. Stigma, discrimination and exclusion not only had a devastating effect on them, made them feel ashamed, and eroded their self-esteem, but they also created an atmosphere in the classroom that was not conducive to learning. They expressed that they were stereotyped because of the community of origin: "The teacher say since I live in . . . X . . . community I will come out a drug pusher . . . The teacher always insulting us and saying how we poor . . . It difficult to learn when you feel shame because you not like other children . . . She [the teacher] ignore me she only take on the rich children . . . They look down on you and treat you different."

Because many conditions of poverty remove full access to knowledge, information and the capacity to be analytical, adult and continuing education programmes are critical to provide a second chance for those who did not complete or benefit from formal schooling. Such programmes can provide adults with information and equip them with skills that they need to sustain their livelihoods, and can empower them and give them the confidence to act to change their situation.

However the data from the PPAs suggest that many of the existing programmes were not "pro-poor," had not considered the specific educational needs of individuals living in poverty; they were not designed to help them to reflect on and critically analyze their experience of poverty and to identify the structural and institutional factors that contribute to them living in poverty, and did not provide those who participated with skills that they needed to initiate and manage change. Absence of appropriate programmes not only deprives poor adults of opportunities to knowledge and skills, but it limits their life chances, and robs them of the possibility of moving out of poverty.

The majority of adults who participated in PPA activities in the communities studied did not participate in any adult education programmes either because they did not know of any, had no time or believed that such programmes were for young people.

On the other hand, several of the available programmes focused on skills training for youth, and while residents recognized the need for these, many of them said that they were more interested in programmes that taught them things that they would be useful in their everyday lives. Among other things they identified the need for programmes in adult literacy and parent education, for programmes to teach them how to market the craft items they produced, and for training programmes that would empower them. However it was observed that "There are no programmes for people who can't read" and that there was a need to "organize motivational programmes to empower people."

Through their involvement in Participatory Research people are engaged in a process of education and learning. Through participation in the various PPA activities, residents in all of the communities studied were involved in an educational process through which they had opportunities to increase their knowledge and understanding of factors that contribute to the conditions in which they live; and of the societal structures and institutional arrangements that reinforced and perpetuated inequality, oppression and discrimination of the poor. Participants in several of the community workshops expressed the need and desire for more adult education programmes with the type of activities done in these workshops. They expressed that "the workshop was very good, I learn a lot about poverty and the community . . . We need adult education programmes . . . Parent education and counseling programmes . . . More workshops like this one."

POVERTY ALLEVIATION INITIATIVES

Concerned about the existence of poverty in their countries, several Caribbean governments have taken initiatives to alleviate and reduce poverty. They have formulated pro-poor policies and projects to improve community infrastructure, and facilities and services being offered to poor and to vulnerable groups. They have also taken steps to increase employment opportunities and to build the capacity of community residents to manage their own development.

However an examination of some of these initiatives suggests that emphasis appears to have been placed on the physical and material aspects of poverty. At the same time several elderly persons and people with disabilities in some countries have benefited from the introduction and/or expansion of social assistance programmes. In addition in several countries meals, books and uniforms are being provided to children from poor households and while this has enabled more children to attend school more regularly, in some cases those children most in need did not always benefit from these initiatives.

In some countries, building the capacity of community residents was facilitated through more consultation with community residents and the implementation of series of training programmes and special projects. However although residents in several communities studied in the PPA had identified the need for specific types of adult education programmes, not many of these were implemented.

While it is clear that some poor communities and residents in some countries have benefited from poverty alleviation programmes, PPA data suggests that many of the programmes were short-term and not well targeted, and were generic and did not respond to the specific practical and strategic needs of poor individuals and vulnerable groups. As a result while some participants in workshops in several communities said that nothing had been done for them and their communities, others believed that initiatives taken by government and other agencies had not made a difference to people living in poverty or had not improved the condition of those who were destitute.

CONCLUSION

PPAs conducted in the Caribbean have highlighted the hardships, struggles and challenges that people living in poor communities face in order to survive and sustain their livelihoods. PPAs also created a vehicle through which the voices of the poor were heard, but the data obtained from the various activities suggest that pro-poor policies and poverty alleviation initiatives in the past had not always taken the specific needs and views of poor individuals and groups.

The data from the PPAs conducted in various countries also highlight poor people's understanding of the role that education can play in alleviating poverty and of the need for adult education and community-based programmes as well as for a more diverse and appropriate curricula than that currently in use in schools in the formal education system.

The challenge for policy makers and practitioners in the Caribbean is to formulate policies that will result in a change in the practice of education and poverty alleviation, and in a change and improvement in living conditions in poor communities. Policy makers and practitioners must also implement programmes designed to meet particular and specific needs of poor communities and their residents, and to create mechanisms to provide support and assistance to poor individuals, families and vulnerable groups.

The agenda however, needs to move beyond provision and support to embrace communities in setting the agenda for change and allowing the change to evolve through participatory practices that seek to interrupt traditional power relationship between social groups. This way, adults and children alike who experience the conditions of poverty will be able to be architects of their own futures, where they will not only obtain maximum benefits from the wide range of available educational opportunities and poverty alleviation initiatives, but will also be able to create new opportunities for sustained development that seek to transform the conditions of poverty in which they live, and so in turn will they reclaim their communities.

REFERENCES

Beckford, G. (1997). *Persistent Poverty: Underdevelopment in Plantation Economies of the Third World*. Barbados: The University of the West Indies Press.

Best, L. (1968/September). Outline of a model of pure plantation economy. *Social and Economic Studies*, 3: 283–326.

Camfield, L. (2006). The why and how of understanding "subjective" wellbeing. Exploratory work by the WeD Group in Four Developing Countries. WeD Working Paper 26. ERSC Research Group on Wellbeing in Developing Countries. December 2006: ESRC. Available at: http://www.welldev.org.uk/research/workingpaperpdf/wed26.pdf.

DfID. (2005). Reducing poverty by tackling social exclusion. A DFID Policy Paper. September 2005. DfID: London. Ellis, P. (1994). *Community Development in the English Speaking Caribbean: Experiences in the Windward Islands*. St Philip: Pat Ellis Associates.

KAIRI Consultants. (2004). *Technical Proposal for Consulting Services For Country Poverty Assessment—Antigua and Barbuda and St Lucia. Republic of Trinidad and Tobago*. Report prepared by KAIRI Consultants, Tunapuna, Republic of Trinidad and Tobago.

KAIRI Consultants. (2007). *Final Reports—Country Poverty Assessments St Lucia. Antigua and Barbuda. Republic of Trinidad and Tobago*. Report prepared by KAIRI Consultants, Tunapuna, Republic of Trinidad and Tobago.

Levitt, K. (2005). *Reclaiming Development: Independent Thought and Caribbean Community*. Kingston: Ian Randle Publishers.

Ludi, E. and Bird, K. (2007). *Brief No 1—Understanding Poverty*. Available at: www.poverty-wellbeing.net.

McGregor, J. A. (2006). Researching wellbeing: From concepts to methodology. WeD Working Paper 20. ESRC Research Group on Wellbeing in Developing Countries. September 2006: ESRC. Available at: http://www.welldev.org.uk/research/working.htm#wed26.

Melville, J. and Wint, E. (2007). *A New Perspective on Poverty in the Caribbean: The Strength of a Participatory Approach.* Caribbean Development Bank. Kingston: Ian Randle Publishers.

Narayan D., Patel, R., Schafft, K., Rademarcher, A. and Koch-Schulte, S. (2000a). *Voices of the Poor: Can Anyone Hear Us?* New York: Oxford University Press.

Narayan D., Chambers, R.,Shah, M., Petesch, P. (2000b). *Voices of the Poor: Crying out for Change.* New York: Oxford University Press.

Sen, A. (1999). *Development as Freedom.* Oxford: Oxford University Press.

United Nations Development Program (UNDP), Croatia. (2006). *Poverty, Unemployment and Social Exclusion.* Zagreb, Croatia: UNDP.

13 "I Am a Certain Person When I Am Here, It Is Not Who I Am"
Refugees' Voices within Communities of Change

Judith Szenasi

INTRODUCTION

This chapter describes a small-scale ethnographic research project concerning refugees when they first arrived in a small city based in the East Midlands in the UK and the continuous displacement they experienced in their attempts to integrate into new communities. The research journey emerged from my experience of working as a community development practitioner, working with principles of inclusion, social justice, participation and empowerment. The project has contributed towards creating a "refugee standpoint" research approach, seeking to understand refugee theories from the perspectives of refugees and connecting knowledge and power discourses that have potential to contribute towards developing theories of refugee justice. Questions that emerged from the research focused on the processes involved in identity formation of a small group of refugees and how the "self" is constantly re-negotiated and reconstructed through the experience of displacement. The research identified a number of exclusionary and oppressive immigration policies, practices and procedures in the UK that have caused acute forms of exclusion. The combination of policies and practices with experiences of racism and discrimination has impacted on the way that refugees have been able to reconstruct the self within communities. Possibilities of community as expressed through informal friends networks experienced by the participants involved in this study are important factors in reducing some of the isolation that the refugees experienced when they first arrived in their new communities. The implications of the discussion for those working to supporting the inclusion of refugee children and young people into schools and their wider communities are easy to visualize.

The research journey began when I worked as a community development practitioner in an urban Sure Start programme. The Sure Start programme in the UK was devised by New Labour in 1998 to deliver improved outcomes for pre-school children, parents and communities within education, health and employment by working with communities in local neighborhoods around issues that were most pertinent to those communities.

I aim within all of my work to adopt a critical and therefore a radical approach towards practice rather than a functionalist or consensus approach. A radical approach within community development emphasizes that transformative change needs to occur in the structures of society that are the root causes of oppression through a process of critical consciousness (Ledwith, 2005). A functionalist or consensus approach to community development is disembodied from the political process (Shaw, 2005: 3). As a community development practitioner my personal values, and principles of social justice and equality actively contribute towards a critical praxis in my work and my preferred identity as a researcher and therefore it connects the knowing and doing. It is essential therefore, for me as a thinker and practitioner, to be reflective and self-reflective. In the study involving refugees, I aimed to create a space for excluded voices to be heard which connects people to their communities through a process of critical consciousness which has the potential to bridge the gap between social justice and exclusion.

CONTEXT

The small city where the study is based has benefited from diverse multi-ethnic and multi-lingual communities before becoming a dispersal area for refugees and asylum seekers in 2001. The most recent census identified sizeable Pakistani, as well as Indian and African Caribbean communities (Szenasi, 2008). A number of local as well as regional studies e.g., Fox (2006) and Aldridge and Dutton (2006) confirm that there are no exact numbers of asylum seekers and refugees available. Refugee Action estimates that around 150 people are in receipt of "Section 4 Support" this means that people are either waiting to hear if their claims have been accepted by the Home Office or they have agreed to return to their countries of origin "voluntarily" (Szenasi, 2008). Most recent arrivals from the African Continent, and the Middle East have formed their own community groups and associations in the city based on notions of shared identity, interest, culture and language.

Local studies have focused on the needs of refugees and on gaps in service provision in education, employment, housing, health, language and interpreting and leisure. However, at the time of the research there were no local qualitative studies on refugees when they first arrive in the UK and the continuous displacement they experience in their attempt to integrate into new communities. Furthermore, no local studies have explored the impact of displacement on refugees' identities and the role and potential strength of community in the process of negotiating new identities. A two-day Open Space consultation event organized by community development practitioners in 2008 sought to address some of these concerns asking "how can we ALL work together to improve services for refugees/asylum seekers?" (Szenasi, 2008). The event was attended by refugee community groups, individual refugees and local service delivery organizations. The event identified a number of common themes of concern to refugees including reporting restrictions and destitution, access to further education, employment and health. It also highlighted that refugees experienced multiple forms of social exclusion in relation to the labor and housing markets, from community, education and social services, from political engagement and from participation in organizations (Szenasi, 2008). Refugees in the town where this research took place are actively displaced from social, community and political arenas and this limits their assertion of new reconstructed identities and control over their future. It is therefore important to briefly explore the politics and policies that contribute to refugees' exclusion.

POLICY AND POLITICAL LANDSCAPE

The policy environment around refugees' arrival in the UK has dramatically changed since 1993 (Amas, 2008). Before this date refugees benefited from the same rights and welfare entitlements as British nationals, however, with the introduction of the 1999 Asylum and Immigration Act, enacted in 2000, a National Dispersal Scheme was initiated that displaced new arrivals to twelve designated regions within the UK (Amas, 2008). It also introduced detention centers, where asylum seekers are detained in prison camp conditions, a voucher system of "welfare in kind" and severely limited rights in respect of legal appeals (Gibney, 2006). The introduction of the Act also constructed two distinct identities within the concept of new arrivals "asylum seekers" and "refugees." Asylum seekers are awaiting their Home Office decision and are severely restricted in accessing welfare rights and civil and political engagement (Lister, 2008). Asylum seekers survive on meager welfare handouts, are not entitled to work and often have to wait a number of years for a decision by the Home Office (Castles and Miller, 2003). They often find themselves "in drawn-out limbo situation, since determination procedures and appeals may take many years" and in the UK more than 90% of asylum applications are rejected (Castles and Miller, 2003: 102). However, Gibney (2006: 144) indicates that Western states have devised a number of "non arrival measures" to prevent asylum seekers from even reaching the borders where they would be entitled to claim protection and this has contributed towards the construction of a "Fortress Europe." Such exclusionary measures as moving entrance decisions away from Western borders to consular offices and foreign airports, and empowering unaccountable officials, have meant that the "hypocritical nature of state practices have been conveniently placed out of the public gaze" (Gibney, 2006: 146).

Refugees have received a positive decision from the Home Office; refugee status denotes a person "granted asylum status" and connects contested notions of citizenship about rights, responsibility, belonging and participation (Lister, 2008). Notions of citizenship are contested because although refugees when they are granted "status" are considered UK citizens within the legal discourse (the right to reside in the UK), the experience of "achieving" full citizenship rights is deemed exclusionary and oppressive in the way it is often described as "a conspiracy against outsiders"—a mechanism for keeping migrants and asylum seekers out and for bestowing inferior rights on those who manage to enter the UK (Lister, 2008: 1). According to Lister it is oppressive when successive governments place too much emphasis on "obligations over rights and make rights totally conditional on the discharge of those obligations" (2008: p.1). Citizenship within a policy and political landscape, which connects notions of citizenship with "acceptable integration" practices into the UK, emphasizes social control rather than social justice in the way that refugees are forced to assimilate within "cohesive" communities based on misplaced notions of shared values and norms, citizenship tests and "oath of allegiance" as purported by New Labour immigration policies (Alexander, 2007).

Cohen (2006) acknowledges that there is often confusion between the terms "refugee" and "asylum seeker" that has been compounded by political and legal discourses that operate in a culture of disbelief. Policy responses are often supported by a hostile media that labels refugees and asylum seekers as "economic migrants"; people escaping economic disadvantage in their home countries, in order to take advantage of the benefits of the welfare state; or, as has become more apparent after September 11, 2001, as "potential terrorists or security threats" (Gibney, 2006: 146). However, refugee communities within grassroots organizations, individuals within the focal study and community development practitioners all consider the term "refugee" as an inclusive term that denotes both asylum seekers and refugees. The social construction of two distinct identities for refugees and asylum seekers is bound up with a number of powerful discourses and this became apparent within this small-scale research project.

THE RESEARCH PROJECT

Community development practice evolves from a strong ideologically situated value base of equality and trust (Ledwith, 2005). It takes a considerable amount of time to build up relationships of mutual respect and trust and it raises critical questions of the rights of the "outsider" to undertake research, and responsibilities that emerge from the privileged position as a researcher (Smith, 2006). Essential within the research I was embarking on was the continuous need to reflect on my own position within the multifaceted relationships of "researcher" and "researched" and to be aware of the implication this had in the production of knowledge (Ledwith, 2005). As a community development practitioner working within a critical praxis of participation, inclusion, equality and trust it was essential to develop approaches in relation to research *with* communities (Gilchrist, 2004). It was important to ensure that I had a historical and social connection with the participants before I embarked on the research project. It is clear that from a community development perspective an anti-positivist and anti-oppressive approach towards research needed to be adopted that challenges power relations within an awareness of dominant and imposed values and belief systems (Ledwith, 2005). Critical within this thinking is that a participatory and collaborative approach is adopted that involves participants fully in all aspects of research design and process based on notions of "empowerment" and "voice" (Armstrong & Moore, 2004).

I was involved in working with a newly formed community self-help group for African refugee women and children in 2002. This group was developed by active members of recently arrived African refugee women with the support of a community development worker colleague from the local Sure Start programme. While working with women in the African Women's project over a number of years, I became a familiar and trusted person to the group. This working relationship consisted of supporting the group in their development of becoming sustainable and independent from the local programme (Twelvetrees, 2002), and involving individual members in the group in the management and direction of the local Sure Start programme and the wider community (e.g. linking members to regeneration initiatives related to refugees). In this sense a phase of 'entering the research field' started long before the research project I am writing about was discussed and agreed with the group. A small research group was established within the early stages of the project which consisted of members of the African Women's Group, the Sure Start community development worker, a community development practitioner who worked with mental health service receivers in Delivering Race Equality; a Department of Health initiative, and a previous member of the African Women's Group who was a community development student at the local university with an interest in research. The purpose of the research group was agreed as follows:

- To agree a broad theme or focus for the research
- To discuss issues of confidentiality and ethical concerns related to the research
- To agree the design of the methodology
- To agree a dissemination strategy

The research group discussed in detail the issues of confidentiality and ethical practice. We agreed that participants taking part in a small-scale study could easily be identified from their narratives and protecting people's identity was therefore a prime concern. Piper and Simons (2005: 58) highlight the complex social and political relationships involved in conducting ethical research and argue that an "ethical discourse of social justice" is an essential ingredient of reflective practice. Jacobsen and Landau (2003: 187) question, however, whether any refugee field research is conducted in an ethical way. They claim that many studies fail to address the ethical problems of researching "vulnerable communities," failing to adequately consider how research "puts their subjects at risk." This is pertinent in areas "where the displaced are highly vulnerable" (Jacobsen & Landau, 2003: 193). However, by labeling one particular group—here, refugees—as particularly "vulnerable" researchers risk implicitly constructing "an identity of the excluded other" (Armstrong & Moore, 2004: 5). The research group could not resolve all of these tensions but we hoped that commitment to an ethics of care as part of the research methodology could go some way towards minimizing such risks.

Research questions evolved over a period of time and eventually focused on how refugees experience their arrival and integration in the UK and how these experiences impact on refugees' sense of self, and possibilities of community in reclaiming and re-negotiating aspects of refugees' identities.

DEVELOPING METHODOLOGY

Participatory and collaborative action research *with* communities involves bringing a critical lens to all aspects of research design, production and process in order to create conditions for possibilities of transformative change with communities that is not oppressive (Ledwith, 2005). Such an approach to research can have multiple starting points where specific research questions evolve over a period of time which may not necessarily follow a rigid and orderly pattern associated with traditional action research methodologies through progressive cyclical stages (Noffke & Somekh, 2005). The production of knowledge is not viewed as a "neutral' activity" (Smith, 2006). Instead, it is recognized that knowledge is produced through language and is a cultural and social construct located within existing social relations and institutions subject to power relations (Denzin, 2001). Knowledge production in this instance privileges particular interests and standpoints (Thomson & Gunter, 2007). Early on in the research process I wanted to privilege refugee knowledges often constructed as "other" within traditional positivist refugee studies on forced migration (see Jacobson & Landau, 2003; Kramer, 2005). I wanted to value and acknowledge the validity of refugee voices. Following Thomson and Gunter (2007) I realize that this type of "standpoint" approach does not produce research that speaks for *all* refugees. I felt, however, that a small-scale qualitative research project which worked hard to include refugee voices might enable understanding of refugee theories from the perspectives of refugees that seek to challenge, explain and analyze the causes of oppression and inequalities refugees experience and could therefore contribute towards developing theories of refugee justice (Burns & Walker, 2005). I suggest that for the purpose of this project, refugee standpoint research could be viewed as:

- Addressing issues of importance and relevance to refugees—so that the research promotes the interests of refugees
- Working collaboratively and participatory *with* refugees in developing research design and processes *together*
- Requiring researchers to continuously reflect on their own position in respect to the multifaceted relationships of "researcher" and "researched" and to continually consider the implications of these relationships in the production of knowledge
- Taking an anti-positivist and anti-oppressive approach towards research that challenges power relations within an awareness of dominant and imposed values and belief systems
- Enabling refugee voices to be positioned as critical within methodology and analysis
- Making a positive difference in the lives of refugees
              (Model adapted from Thomson & Gunter, 2007: 331)

Within the research project I attempted to utilize ethnographic approaches to produce rich narratives through the fieldwork (Goldbart & Hustler, 2005). There are many divergent perspectives revealing potential epistemological ambiguities within ethnographic research (Coffey, 1999; Clifford & Marcus; 1986), however, as Goldbart and Hustler suggest (2005: 16) the characteristics of ethnography are rooted in "enriching descriptions of culture." The research participants and the research group chose to gather data through:

- Two ethnographic participant observations of the African Women's self-help group recorded through brief notes and transcribed as field notes
- Interviews with three African women refugees, using a tape recorder, and transcribing the tapes word by word
- An interview with the Community Development facilitator of the African Women's self-help group, transcribing notes from the interview

The interviews were based on a spontaneous developmental approach where questions were used as prompts or aide memoirs in order for participants' perspectives, feelings and memories to emerge, and to enable them to own the discussions and process of the interview. In all aspects of the research we were trying to put refugee voices at center stage in order to challenge, explain and analyze the causes of oppression and inequalities refugees experienced from their own perspectives. We had found that an absence of theories related to refugees' experiences and their first contact with the immigration system was stark and felt it was therefore important to examine aspects of immigration procedures, policy and legislation as these were the dominant discourses with the participants' narratives.

THE CONSTRUCTION OF REFUGEE IDENTITIES

> I am a certain person when I am here, it is not who I am, I am not able to be myself, because I am not around people who speak my language, who eat my food, who understand my humor, my jokes. There is a part of me that is hibernating, the person that is me is not existing right now. It is a persona in a sense, because it is about fitting in. It is something I had to do back home too, it is part of history, the colonialism, how white people want to see us . . . I think my displacement hasn't just started with the refugee experience, it is the whole colonial thing.
>
> (Nataizya, 2008)

All participants in this study lived in former British colonies (Sierra Leone, Zambia and Zimbabwe). The devastating effect of colonialism did not disappear with the former colonies achieving independence, rather, according to Said (1978, 1993), the social, political and economic structures which were developed during colonial rule, continue to impact on the cultural, political and economic lives of people today. The legacies and histories of colonialism continue to marginalize and oppress people in former colonies within their home countries and when they arrived as refugees in the UK. A history of colonialism has also ensured a continuous process of displacement, where identities are disavowed, reclaimed and re-negotiated and the relationship between homeland and Diaspora are situated within contradictory positions of places and spaces of belongingness and sites of struggle. Displacement therefore, as expressed by Nataizya, creates a fluidity of a self where refugees are caught up in many histories and where identities are unraveled (Smith, 2006).

Participants in this study vividly recounted their arrival in the UK. They were subjected to confusing and often frightening immigration procedures and at a loss of what was expected from them. Two participants, who arrived at London airports experienced hostile attitudes from immigration officials, where they had to wait for long periods in unsuitable waiting areas where they were searched, photographed and underwent compulsory medical tests:

> And then they call you and take you to another room; two immigration officers, they took me to the back of the airport, put gloves on and empty every little thing from my bag, every scrap of paper they

took out, it was terrible. They did not explain, they had to search me. Whatever were they looking for? So they took me to a room for x-rays to see if I had TB.

(Nataizya, 2008)

Nataizya was moved to a detention center from the airport: "They give you badges with your photo and a number, no names." The practice of providing photo identification, subsuming people's names with numbers can be viewed as a powerful way of erasing people's identity and sense of self and used as a means of control and discipline in what Foucault (2007) describes as "formulas of domination," as a way of organizing people or "bodies" in large institutions such as psychiatric hospitals, prisons and arguably detention centers. Names are essential parts of people's identities and are tied up with cultural and historic meanings (Smith, 2006). The practice of taking away people's names in the detention center, serves as a powerful reminder to people that their sense of self and their identities are insignificant to the officials, and institutions within the immigration process. The process allows for the erosion of the self, whereby people are rendered invisible, therefore the numbering rather than naming of individuals can be perceived as part of a de-humanizing process of stripping away any sense of individuality and personhood in the same way as prisoners when they are detained in prisons. Detention centers are often run by private companies and contracted by the Home Office. A number of recent critical inspection reports by the Chief Inspector of Prisons indicate intimidating, aggressive and racist bullying behavior by staff towards refugees in detention centers (Athwal, 2007), as narrated by Nataizya:

We were fenced in; there was barbed wire all around the building, all electrified. You had roll call every morning around 6.30am this alarm would off from the PA system. It was like a prison camp and the worst thing the most annoying thing was, they would put on loud music or drum music, or shout Wake up, Wake up! So you had to get up even though your child is sleeping.

(Nataizya, 2008)

As mentioned earlier, the 1999 Asylum and Immigration Act, had a dramatic impact on the rights and welfare entitlements of refugees seeking asylum in the way that people were given welfare through a voucher system, limited access to legal appeals and were dispersed to designated areas within the UK (Gibney, 2006; Amas, 2008). The dispersal process was confusing and frightening for the women who took part in this study; they were not given a choice where they were moved to, and no consideration was given with regards to the networks of family or friends they may have had. One of the women was able to make friends in the short space of time whilst at her temporary accommodation in London sharing with other African women the experience of displacement from home and family and most importantly, through this friendship, she was able to reconnect and reclaim essential elements of her identity from home such as African food and African people:

> I made friends with one lady and three boys from The Gabon and Sierra Leone and this other lady. One of them brought me some chilies and some African food.
>
> (Martha, 2008)

Two women were allocated solicitors in London; their dispersal away from London was particularly stressful, as they were unsure how their legal case would progress whilst being relocated away from London. It is acknowledged by refugee community organizations that the reduction in legal aid and access to quality immigration and asylum support services have left many refugees without legal representation (Szenasi, 2008). Refugees who have exhausted all rights of legal appeal are offered very limited support, which is subject to strict eligibility criteria. A Home Office decision of refusal is enacted in the legal discourse of "no recourse to public funds." Withdrawal of financial support results in many people adopting "a survival lifestyle," relying on informal friendship networks, often made up of refugees for main sources of support such as food, safety and accommodation (Szenasi, 2008). Finda experienced destitution early on within the asylum process, which resulted in enduring hardship for her and her children:

> They turned my asylum down. I was then asked to leave the house. They give you nothing, apart from three weeks of vouchers even though I was pregnant.
>
> (Finda, 2008)

The imposed identity of "destitute" did not just apply to Finda, but as she suggested, it particularly related to her son who was often unwell and required regular medical treatment and hospitalization. She actively positioned her son within the dominant discourse of destitution reminding "officials" that the construction of such identity includes children which are often left out of dominant refugee research studies which privilege the constructed narratives of single male asylum seekers in political exile (Dumper, 2008).

> They said they would help me under Section 4. I said "it is not about me, it is about my child. He is most destitute because of his condition."
>
> (Finda, 2008)

It is clear that the UK's immigration policies particularly in relation to destitution, and Section 4, act as a multi-dimensional exclusionary process, whereby various forms of exclusion are combined: access to housing, welfare rights, and benefits, education and legal support for example are all restricted creating "acute forms of exclusion" (Madanipour et al., 1998: 22). The combination of these exclusionary processes that refugees and their children experienced, caused invisibility in the way that refugees are denied access to economic, cultural and political processes of the mainstream culture. All refugee women in this study experienced continual displacement as they were constantly moved from one area to another, which made it difficult to settle into neighborhood communities. Continuous displacement also involved being located in predominately white areas of the city where racist incidents are not uncommonly targeted at new arrivals such as refugees (Burnett, 2008).

> It was a white area, you can't see Asians it was for white people. People said "why do they have to send these people (refugees) here? They have to send them somewhere else." You could not see black people if you are walking for a day.
>
> (Finda, 2008)

Racism is also directed at people who have gained refugee "status." who are living in ethnically diverse neighborhoods, bringing up children and participating in education and employment. Martha, who gained her refugee "status,", experienced a challenging transitional phase where her new identity as a "refugee" was questioned with suspicion:

> I had a lot of problems getting a National Insurance number. I went to the job center for this but my only form of identification was my Home Office papers, which has your photo on it, and I had just come in and my hair was different, I had braids then. The job center considered my papers a fake; they said 'she looks different'. So this guy came and had a look and decided that no, I was not that person in the picture
>
> (Martha, 2008)

Nataizya related persistent discriminatory behavior and attitudes of members within her neighborhood, when they "discovered" her refugee identity. The consequence of this unwanted exposure has meant she has not been able to privilege her refugee identity; instead, her identity in this sense is implicated and dislocated by social narratives outside her own wishes and desires. In particular, this had an impact on her identity as a mother and relates to strong notions of protectiveness towards her children:

> They delivered one of my Home Office letters next door and the lady she opened it. And it was soon around in the neighborhood that I was a refugee. Whenever they say something about immigrants, you are that person that it is directed at. I am scared of the situation when my daughter will get bullied because her mummy is a refugee.
>
> (Nataizya, 2008)

She has attempted to privilege and reclaim her identity as an African woman whilst living in the UK. Her journey of discovering and claiming this important aspect of her identity has not been without struggle. The pain and sadness of being forced to leave family, friends, work colleagues, from home and country become journeys of exile, where new identities are constructed, negotiated and reclaimed and old ones are painfully dissolved. The dislocation of the self creates continuous displacement and a sense of not having any roots, and the search for belonging carries on much like migration itself:

> I never had a desire to live in this country. Never! It is not my dream to live in the UK. I am feeling more and more that I am anxious to go home. To be in Africa at least. It is too much! The prejudices and the everyday things and the more you are exposed to it, the harder it gets. But the situation in my home country is awful, I left my home behind and it is never going to get better in my country. And it is the bereavement process that I am going through with my family members and I lost my home so I am a sort of refugee for life now, because there is nothing to go home to.
>
> (Nataizya, 2008)

THE POSSIBILITY OF COMMUNITY

The Immigration and Asylum Act 1999, as already discussed, brought with it significant policy changes impacting on the way the UK Government responded to refugees within the international obligations of the 1951 Geneva Convention (Zetter & Sigonal, 2005). Dispersal of refugees to designated areas away from the South East and London where traditionally, a number of refugees had settled and established Refugees Community Organizations which enabled people to reconstruct their identities and reconnect with communities, "has fractured the connection between refugees/asylum seekers and their well-established frameworks of community support" (Zetter & Sigonal, 2005: 172). Refugees arriving in areas with no previous significant histories of refugee migration found that the experience of settling into communities brought with it isolation:

> . . . at that time there were not many African people here and isolation was high and people wanted to meet each other with the same colour and African culture, to be part of that community and talk to each other.
>
> (Martha, 2008)

The local Sure Start programme where this research took place, identified refugees as a potential new group who did not access and engage with mainstream services and community networks. The programme employed a small team of community development workers:

> We noticed a number of African women with children who were very isolated. Some of the women met up very informally in one woman's house. We brought toys and talked to the women about their needs. It was mainly about giving information and recognizing the important mutual support network of women in the community. This was the start of one of the first refugee community groups here.
>
> (Emma, 2008)

The notion of "community" is contested by many writers (Bauman, 2001; Gilchrist, 2004; Ledwith, 2005; Shaw, 2007), particularly in the way it can be viewed as a convenient way of legitimatizing and justifying exclusionary social policies (for example; refugee "integration") through a process of appropriation. The notion of community can however, also provide a site for solidarity, social justice, collective interest and identity (Shaw, 2007). The African Women's group has brought a number of women together, and developed collective responses to identified needs. Furthermore, in the process of continuous displacement that individual refugee women faced in their desire to integrate into communities, the group provided an important cultural place and space where identities were reclaimed and reconstructed through shared experiences:

> One day in my village on the South East side of Kenya, you may not know this but Kenya is a beautiful country with many colors; many different greens, yellows and browns from the vegetation; trees, bushes, grasses so many colors, there are large mountains too which look orange in a certain light, and then of course all the different shades of red, blues, pink and orange from our beautiful African skies, my grandmother who was very wise told me this story when I was about seven or eight years old . . .
>
> The start of the story as told by one of the African women in the group

These stories from "home" are told and shared among the women and children in the group; however new stories are told in the form of English folk songs and children's rhymes, creating hybrid spaces (Bhabha, 1994):

> Emma gives up on the idea of going outside as it starts to rain, and announces to the group to do some singing. The women and children sit in a circle and the worker asks each mother and child what songs they would like to sing, suggestions come forward: "Old McDonald, Incy Wincy Spider, Row-Row-Row your Boat . . ."
>
> (Participant Observation Notes, 2008)

The group accessed a variety of funding sources and delivered informal adult learning activities on health and education, as well as art workshops for women and children. They planned, delivered and organized cultural community events such as festivals, carnival, and campaigns. Women in this study made important friendships within the group and this has helped in reducing some of the isolation that refugee women experienced when they first arrived in the community. For the women participating in this study, the group represented safety, security and an invaluable network of support:

> The group was the first time I was able to meet other women with children and start having a life.
>
> (Finda, 2008)

> It is good to go to the group, when I am at home I think too much.
>
> (Martha, 2008)

> There is a lot of support amongst us. The group is great.
>
> (Nataizya, 2008)

CONCLUSION

A combination of exclusionary and oppressive immigration policies and practices, together with experience of racism and discrimination, have impacted on the way that refugee women who took part in this study have been able to reconstruct the "self" within communities. However, refugee women have strived to exercise control over the events in their lives in their attempt to reclaim essential aspects of identities and culture that are restructured and repositioned within prevailing discourses of "vulnerability," and the "excluded other." Possibilities of community as offered by the African Women's Group, where refugee voices, experiences and knowledges are valued and celebrated, are vital for allowing people to reconstruct their identities within new communities.

The approach I have taken in this exploratory work is based on community development principles of inclusion, social justice, participation and empowerment which have made it essential to center the voices of the refugees involved in the study. The "refugee standpoint" research approach which unfolded has at its starting point the involvement and perspectives of refugees through which can be built relevant theories of refugee justice. The children of women such as those represented in this chapter typically "spend their evenings and weekends in the cramped imprisonment of bed-and-breakfast accommodation—not knowing if they will be deported in the morning" (Garner, 2002). Refugee stand-point research to explore the experience of displaced children may offer the possibility for these children to resist the isolation and oppression that women refugees have recounted.

REFERENCES

Aldridge, F. and Dutton, Y. (2006). *Counting Up: A Study to Estimate the Existing and Future Numbers of Refugees in the East Midlands Region.* Leicester: NIACE.

Alexander, C. (2007). Cohesive identities: The distance between meaning and understanding, in M. Wetherall, M. Lafleche and R. Berkeley (Eds.) *Identity, Ethnic Diversity and Community Cohesion.* London: Sage Publications.

Amas, N. (2008). *Housing, New Migration and Community Relations: A Review of the Evidence Base.* London: Information Center about Asylum and Refugees.

Armstrong, F. and Moore, M. (Eds.) (2004). *Action Research for Inclusive Education: Changing Places, Changing Practices, Changing Minds.* London and New York: Routledge.

Athwal, H. (2007) Asylum deaths. Briefing Paper number: 4 (November). London: Institute of Race Relations.

Bauman, Z. (2001). *Community—Seeking Safety in an Insecure World.* Cambridge: Polity Press.

Bhabha, H.K. (1994). *The Location of Culture.* London: Routledge.

Burnett, J. (2008). *Racism, Destitution and Asylum.* Briefing Paper umber: 6 (June). Leeds: PAFRAS.

Burns, D. and Walker, M. (2005). Feminist methodologies, in B. Somekh and C. Lewin (Eds.) *Research Methods in the Social Sciences.* London: Sage.

Castles, S. and Miller, M. (2003). *The Age of Migration: International Population Movements in the Modern World.* New York: Palgrave MacMillan.

Clifford, J. and Marcus, G. (Eds.) (1986). *Writing Culture—The Poetics and Politics of Ethnography.* London: University of California.

Coffey, A. (1999). *The Ethnographic Self: Fieldwork and the Represenation of Identity.* London: Sage Publications.

Cohen, S. (2006). *Deportation is Freedom!: The Orwellian World of Immigration Controls.* London and Philadelphia: Jessica Kingsley Publishers.

Denzin, N.K. (2001). *Interpretive Interactionism.* London: Sage.

Dumper, H. (2008). Navigation Guide: Women Refugees and Asylum Seekers in the UK. London: Information Center about Asylum and Refugees.

Foucault, M. (2007) *Madness and Civilization.* Oxon: Routledge.

Fox, S. (2006). *Filling the Gaps.* Derby: Refugee Action and Refugee Housing.

Garner, L. (2002). Triumph of our "refugee school." London: *Evening Standard.* Thursday 2 May. Available at: http://lists.becta.org.uk/pipermail/eal-bilingual/attachments/20020508/b9d5fa71/attachment.html.

Gibney, M. J. (2006). A thousand little Guantanamos: Western states and measures to prevent the arrival of refugees, in K.E. Tunstall (Ed.) *Displacement, Asylum, Migration.* Oxford: Oxford University Press, pp. 139–169.

Gilchrist, A. (2004). *The Well-Connected Community: A Networking Approach to Community Development.* Bristol: The Policy Press.

Goldbart, J. and Hustler, D. (2005). Ethnography, in B. Somekh and C. Lewin (Eds.) *Research Methods in the Social Sciences*. London: Sage.

Jacobsen, K and Landau, L. (2003). The dual imperative in refugee research: Some methodological and ethical considerations in social science research on forced migration. *Disasters*, 27(3): 185–206.

Kramer, S. (2005) Getting closer: Methods of research with refugees and asylum seekers, D. Ingleby (Ed.) *Forced Migration and Mental Health: Rethinking the Care Refugees and Displaced Persons*. New York: Springer Science + Business Media, Inc., pp 97–114.

Ledwith, M. (2005). *Community Development—A critical Approach*. Bristol: The Policy Press.

Lister, R. (2008). Citizenship. Unpublished paper for the Women and Migration: Art, Politics and Policy Conference. Loughborough University: 20 June, pp. 1–10.

Madanipour, A., Cars, G. and Allen, J. (Eds.) (1998). *Social Exclusion in European Cities*. London: Jessica Kingsley.

Marcus, G. (1986) Contemporary problems of ethnography in the modern world system, in J. Clifford and G. Marcus (Eds.) *Writing Culture: The Poetics and Politics of Ethnography*. London: University of California.

Noffke, S. and Somekh, B. (2005). Action research in B. Somekh and C. Lewin (Eds.) *Research Methods in the Social Sciences*. London: Sage.

Piper, H. and Simons, H. (2005), Ethical responsibility in social research, in B. Somekh and C. Lewin (Eds.) *Research Methods in the Social Sciences*. London: Sage.

Said, E. (1978). *Orientalism*. London: Penguin.

Said, E. (1993). *Culture and Imperialism*. London: Chatto & Windus.

Shaw, M. (2005). Political, professional, powerful: understanding community development. Transcript of introductory presentation at the Community Development Exchange Annual Conference 2005. (23–25 September) Leeds.

Shaw, M. (2007) Community development and the politics of community. *Community Development Journal*. 43(1): 24–36.

Smith, L. (2006). *Decolonizing Methodologies: Research and Indigenous Peoples*. London and New York: Zed Books Ltd.

Szenasi, J. (2008). *How Can We ALL Work Together to Improve Services for Refugees/Asylum Seekers Living in Derby?* Unpublished Open Space report commissioned by The Community Safety Partnership, Derby City Primary Care Trust, and Job Center Plus: Derby (June, 2008).

Thomson, P. and Gunter, H. (2007). The methodology of students-as-researchers: Valuing and using experience and expertise to develop methods. *Discourse: Studies in the Cultural Politics of Education*, 28(3): 327–342.

Twelvetrees, A. (2002), *Community Work*. London: Palgrave.

Zetter, R, Griffiths, D. and Sigona, N. (2005). Social capital or social exclusion? The impact of asylum-seeker dispersal on UK refugee community organisations. *Community Development Journal*, 40: 169–181.

Conclusion
Aspirations for Cross-Cultural Perspectives on Policy and Practice—Decolonizing Community Contexts

Jennifer Lavia and Michele Moore

In our introduction to this book we hoped the thirteen chapters to follow would respond to questions of "othering," difference, marginalization, exclusion and communities of silence through rich and diverse reflections on education, community and change. Looking back through the chapters we find that it is possible, through the chapters, to engage with a range of education practices and changing community contexts which raise seldom heard voices to reveal a wealth of possibilities for forging new agendas of social justice and community development and for bridging gaps between social justice and exclusion. Diverse topics and frameworks have been presented which sometimes reveal deeply held uncertainty about ways of experiencing and reflecting upon communities.

Different conceptualizations of both education and community are evident through the pages of this book as the link between education and community is explored. Coherent themes have been addressed within the chapters; perceptions of injustice and oppression are articulated which generate strong recurring ideas for decolonizing practice through the valuing of indigenous knowledge and perspectives. Authors have referred to and explored ideas about culturally and morally ethical research practice in projects that seek to alter struggles for change. They have not been afraid to expose practical problems, theoretical contradictions and transgressive thinking embedded in their work. Discernible global shifts that impact on the decolonization of education and communities have been interrogated in conjunction with local boundaries and tensions that influence and shape change, so that in contrast with coherent themes, there are also hugely different images of community inscribed in each chapter.

CROSS-CULTURAL WINDOWS ON EDUCATION AND COMMUNITY

The mango trees under which Paulo Freire reflected on the role of education for critical consciousness and community are evoked through many connections authors make to the work of the innovative and influential Brazilian thinker (Freire, 1998). The sights and sounds of small towns in the mid-western United States are conjured up as is the invidious imprint of the history of colonialism in the lives of indigenous people in the East Caribbean and South Africa. The challenges rural communities grapple with in the face of climate change in rural Australia and the hopes of those living and working in deprived communities in an English city made up of red brick terraced housing and council owned flats are tangible through the chapters. The ongoing liberation struggle faced by black academic teachers in universities in the Free State province of South Africa can be read alongside the discoveries of families living in the poorest households of Jamaica. The experience of groups who have often been objectified—children, refugee women, students, disabled people and those living with poverty for example is represented in newly respectful ways throughout the book and now becomes more open to deconstruction and change. There are representations of struggle and pain made explicit through immensely different kinds of experience stretching across children's reflections on the death of their pets to women's recollections of homes they have been parted from and the aching legacy of apartheid. While no one who has been involved personally or professionally in any struggle against oppression could read these accounts without experiencing some emotion, especially when reading some of the situations of the world's children, the authors have avoided the pitfalls of writing in a sensational way. They are continually reflective and respectful of the people they are working with and at pains to test their own assumptions against the lived experiences of others. There are also sites for celebration in the book as children and young people realize they can be agents of change in their own communities or pro-poor policies or enabling practices of teaching and learning start to surface and transform lives.

In our role as editors we have been struck by the rich and evocative views of community life, education and struggles which the authors reveal and the transparency they have offered in terms of their own changing perspective as the project of engaging with communities unfolds and changes our own view of the world. Through the chapters comes a sense of hope mixed with uncertainty as the authors set out to capture and describe possibilities for understanding analyzing and commenting upon perspectives, policies and practices which shape the vastly different community contexts in which they are working.

CROSS-CULTURAL PERSPECTIVES AND MULTIPLE IMAGININGS

Some very different gazes on education and community come alive through the pages of this book. In some of the chapters there is a detailed and unflinching exploration of the effects of oppression and regulation in communities. Others signal the importance of the questions raised in interpreting and theorizing our engagements—which reach far beyond the role of academics in transforming societal values and practices. We found it was not possible to organize the chapters in a progressive way or to collect particular stances or discourses on community or cultures into neatly designated themes. We have enjoyed the contributions to the book for the breadth of reflection on education, community and change which each author enables the reader to encounter. Each chapter however, in its own way, also reminds us of the vastness of the project of decolonizing community contexts with which we are all differently engaged. In the end we have opted to hope that the different forms of consideration each chapter has afforded will have encouraged wide-ranging reflection of each reader's own shaping in its own right. We have not sought to subordinate the cross-cultural perspectives on policy and practice which each author has shared to a single unifying analysis but nonetheless, a unifying agenda for decolonizing community contexts is captured through the text.

There is collective resistance to the regulation of knowledge and to the suppression of indigenous voices. Commitment to unearthing new alliances, and to locating new opportunities for deepening the connections between education and community, is obvious. A willingness to create new possibilities for enquiry and particularly to advocate new strategies for listening to unheard voices, to see previously unseen commentators, to reach out and to learn from them in ways which refuse to collude with dogmatic methodological practices that have previously given no legitimacy to insider perspectives and which have therefore denied them a place in policy making and practice adds an extremely exciting dimension in this book. Yet we realize that whilst some parts of the book inspire great confidence for forging new alliances in changing community contexts, in others an open discourse of considerable uncertainty dislocates the path of our theorizing. And so we hope the book seizes the imagination of its readers and might add to our individual collective and repertoires of possibilities for "daring to think otherwise" about education policy making and practice and its connections with community (Allan, 2003). We present the book as a resource through which debates on the essential ingredients for decolonizing community contexts can be re-considered in relation to contemporary cross-cultural glimpses of a wide range of education and community matters.

In this book we have tried to make plain that a willingness to be engaged with communities seeking radical change is clearly not something that can be contained within the academy and all of the writers see themselves as concerned with an activist agenda that often fractures and always disturbs both academic and political ways of thinking, researching, writing, speaking and listening. A high level of personal reflection has consequently been invested by all authors in their production of the chapters which make up this book and each chapter identifies multi-faceted issues to be considered by those embarking on research with communities.

Two points seem central as we look back over the contents of this book. First, the chapters exemplify the complexity of understanding community, and it is in the process of unpacking such complexity that decolonizing agendas emerge and are understood. Second, the complexity to which we refer here presents challenges and opportunities for examining closer the relationship between education and community. By extension educational research can adopt a "decolonization" vantage point to provide insights in this complex and contested relationship. We are inspired, but to echo the words of writer and civil-rights activist Maya Angelou, we have learned through the accounts within this book, that we still have a lot to learn.

REFERENCES

Allan, J. (2003), Daring to think otherwise? Educational policymaking in the Scottish Parliament. *Journal of Education Policy*, 18(3): 289–301.
Freire, P. (1998). *Pedagogy of the Heart*. New York: Continuum International.

Contributors

Evelyn Abram is Deputy Headteacher at Sharrow School in Sheffield. She has worked tirelessly to build the school's reputation for excellence as it tries to ensure equal opportunities for all children, with due regard for gender, race, religion, class or disability, and as it has adamantly opposed to racism of any kind. The school has undergone radical transformation in recent years and is now one of the greenest and most inclusive schools to be found. She has been involved in research and dissemination of the schools successes for many years.

Contact details: Sharrow Primary School, South View Road, Sheffield, S7 1DB, UK. Tel: +44 (0114) 2551704 Fax: (0114) 2551704 Email: info@sharrow.sheffield.sch.uk

Vanessa Andreotti, is a senior lecturer at the School of Māori, Social and Cultural Studies in Education at University of Canterbury, New Zealand. She is also a research fellow at the University of Ireland, Galway and at the Centre for the Study of Social and Global Justice at the University of Nottingham, UK. Vanessa's research focus is on building bridges between contemporary theories and debates around globalization and diversity and pedagogical practices in educational contexts.

Contact details: School of Educational Studies and Human Development, University of Canterbury, Private Bag 4800, Christchurch, New Zealand. Tel: +64 3 364 2987 ext 8841 Email: vanessa.andreotti@canterbury.ac.nz

Felicity Armstrong is a Reader at the Institute of Education, University of London here she directs the Inclusive Pedagogy (MA in inclusive education); Inclusive Education: Theory and Practice (MA in Special Education, Inclusion; and Disability Studies). Her research interests include policymaking and the ways in which different policies and practices contribute to processes of inclusion and exclusion in education in sometimes contradictory ways. She is committed to working with practitioners to bring about change in their own work contexts through different kinds of action research.

Contact details: Dept. of Educational Foundations and Policy Studies, Institute of Education, University of London, 20 Bedford Way, London WC1H 0AL. Tel: +44 (0)20 7612 6300, Fax: +44 (0)20 7612 6366, Email: f.armstrong@ioe.ac.uk

Len Barton is Emeritus Professor of Inclusive Education at the Institute of Education, University of London. He is internationally known for his outstanding contributions to disability studies and for his pioneering work to advance the struggle for inclusive education. He is the founder and editor of the leading journals *British Journal of Sociology of Education* and *Disability and Society*. His interests lie with the development of a sociopolitical perspective on disability issues and education. Current research projects examine the development of inclusive policies and practices in schools and LEAs and he has published extensively on these matters.

Contact details: Dept. of Educational Foundations and Policy Studies, Institute of Education, University of London, 20 Bedford Way, London WC1H 0AL Tel: +44 (0)20 7612 6750, Fax: +44 (0)20 7612 6636, Email: len_barton@sky.com

Tsitsi Chataika is currently a Postdoctoral Research Fellow in the Centre for Rehabilitation Studies at Stellenbosch University working on the African Policy On Disability and Development (A-PODD) Project. She is also a Research Fellow in the Centre for Global Health at the University of Dublin, and in the Research Institute for Health and Social Change (RIHSC) at Manchester Metropolitan University. Tsitsi recently received her PhD from the University of Sheffield, UK, and her focus was on the personal experiences of disabled students in higher education in Zimbabwe. Tsitsi is on the Overseas Editorial Board of the Disability & Society.

Contact details: Centre for Rehabilitation Studies, P.O Box 19063, Tygerberg, 7505, South Africa Tel: +27 (0)21 938 9816. Fax: +27 (0)21 938 9855. Email: tchataika@sun.ac.za

Barbara Comber is Professor and Key Researcher of the Centre for Studies in Literacy, Policy and Learning Cultures and the Hawke Research Institute for Sustainable Societies at University of South Australia. She teaches literacy education and educational research programs for practicing educators at all levels of schooling. Barbara has directed a number of competitively funded research projects concerned with literacy development, teaching and socioeconomic disadvantage. She has developed or contributed to language and literacy teacher education materials in a number of Australian states, the U.S. and Canada. She has edited seven books and published numerous articles and chapters for teachers and teacher educators in critical literacy, teacher development and social justice.

Contact details: University of South Australia, Division of Education, Arts and Social Sciences, Hawke Research Institute, Magill Campus, MH1–03, C1–75, South Australia Tel: +61 8 830 24229; Fax: +61 8 830 24212 Email: Barbara.Comber@unisa.edu.au

Antonia Darder is a Professor of Educational Policy Studies and Latino/a Studies at the University of Illinois at Urbana-Champaign. She taught as a Visiting Professor at the University of California Irvine (2001–2002), a Professor of Education and Cultural Studies at Claremont Graduate University (1990–2001) and at Pacific Oaks College where she developed the first graduate program in Bicultural Development. She has also taught at California Polytechnic University and the Massachusetts Institute of Technology and served as a Distinguished Professor at New Mexico State University, Las Cruces. Her current work focuses on comparative studies of racism, class and society. Her teaching examines cultural issues in education with an emphasis on identity, language, and popular culture, as well as the foundations of critical pedagogy, Latino/a studies, and social justice theory.

Contact details: University of Illinois, Urbana-Champaign, Educational Policy Studies College of Education, 360 Education Building, MC-708, 1310 South Sixth Street Champaign, Illinois 61820,USA. Tel: (217) 244–4741. Email: adarder@gmail.com

Jane Dodman is currently Vice President, Corporate and Human Resource Services, at the International University of the Caribbean (IUC). She is the administrator of the University of Sheffield's Caribbean Programme in Jamaica. She previously functioned as the Principal of the Mel Nathan College, one of the constituent Colleges of the IUC. She has worked at the Mel Nathan Institute for Development and Social Research for twenty-five years. She has published articles on determining priorities in rural communities in Jamaica and widening and deepening participation in academic and policy research in Jamaica (with David Dodman).

Contact details: International University of the Caribbean, 47 Old Hope Road, Kingston 5, Jamaica, West Indies. Tel: +876 754 1921. Email: hr.corporatevp@iuc.edu.jm

Pat Ellis is a consultant and education researcher. She is one of the co-founders of the adult education movement in the Caribbean and is actively involved in community action research throughout the region. Her recent work involves poverty research for community participation within Country Poverty Assessments funded by the Caribbean Development Bank. She is internationally known for her work in adult and community education.

Contact details: Pat Ellis Associates Inc., 15 Standford, St. Philip, Barbados, West Indies Tel: (246) 423–8115, Email: patellis@sunbeach.net

Anita Franklin is Director of the Working with Communities programme at the University of Sheffield, UK. Her teaching and research interests include gender policies and practice, feminist theory, and theories of difference. She has written widely in these areas highlighting the conditions of immigrants and the interfaces of race, gender, class and citizenship. Her research has also extended to inquiry into the relationship between Sheffield City Council and the Yemeni Association, African Caribbean

Enterprise Centre and the Sheffield Positive Action Training Consortium. She has also written for the BBC.

Contact details: The Institute for Lifelong Learning, School of Education, The University of Sheffield, 196–198 West Street, Sheffield S1 4ET, Tel: +44 0114 2227115 Email: a.franklin@sheffield.ac.uk

Jennifer Lavia is a Lecturer in Education in the School of Education at the University of Sheffield. She is director of the School's Caribbean Programme and is on the curriculum team for the School's Working with Community: identity, regeneration and change, undergraduate and postgraduate courses. Her research involves perspectives of the "colonized": to foreground the conditions that determine professional and transnational identities; to explore the relationship between education and development; and to reinterpret current understandings about globalization and pedagogies for creating futures. She is also interested in emancipatory approaches to educational practice.

Contact details: University of Sheffield, School of Education, 388 Glossop Road, Sheffield, S10 2JA, United Kingdom. Tel: +44 0114 222 8097; Fax: (+44) (0)114 279 6236; Email: j.lavia@sheffield.ac.uk

Lynn Ley is Headteacher at Sharrow School in Sheffield which serves children from many cultures and welcomes the multi-ethnic nature of its pupil intake. Under Lynn Ley's stewardship Sharrow school has become a *community* building where teaching and learning takes place in the widest sense. She has been involved in research to support students and communities for several years, most recently taking the story of the development of a bright, colourful, welcoming school at the centre of a deprived inner city area to a wider audience through university presentations and writing.

Contact details: Sharrow Primary School, South View Road, Sheffield, S7 1DB, UK. Tel: +44 (0114) 2551704 Fax: (0114) 2551704 Email: info@sharrow.sheffield.sch.uk

Sechaba MG Mahlomaholo is research professor in the School of Education at North West University in Potchefstoom, South Africa. He is an emerging organic intellectual whose work is informed by the emancipatory agenda, located in a spectrum of theoretical positions ranging from Critical Theory, Postcoloniality, Feminist and Critical Race Theories. According to him, because all learners deserve better, education should thus foster self-respect and respect for others. To achieve this objective he attempts to create empowering learning environments through analysis of learners' discourses in his research.

Contact details: P.O. Box 6228, Baillie Park-2526. The Republic of South Africa. Tel: +27 18 200 4770 Fax: +27 18 299 4712 E-mail: 21606900@nwu.ac.za

Lynn Mario T. Menezes de Souza is a Professor at the University of Sao Paulo, Brazil and a UNESCO consultant for indigenous education. Lynn works interdisciplinarily and has researched and published widely in the areas of education, linguistics and postcolonial studies. Lynn is the chief editor of the journal *Critical Literacies: Theories and Practices*, published by the Centre for the Study of Social and Global Justice at the University of Nottingham.

Contact details: Al. Badejo, 392, Alphaville 11, Sao Paulo, 06500.000, Brazil. Tel: 55 11 30915052. Email: mdesouza@usp.br

Michele Moore is Senior Lecturer in the School of Education at the University of Sheffield. Her research is concerned with the multiplicity of issues around inclusion, including disability, disadvantage, children and young people's participation, family support and school and community life. She is interested in examining the interconnections between identity, regeneration and change to generate fresh insights about what can be done within communities to recognize and support those who feel and articulate that they matter less than their contemporaries. She is Deputy Editor of the leading journal *Disability & Society*, Founder and Member of the Editorial Team of the journal *Community Work & Family*.

Contact details: University of Sheffield, School of Education, 388 Glossop Road, Sheffield, S10 2JA, United Kingdom, Tel: (+44) (0)114 222 8132 Fax: (+44) (0)114 279 6236. Email: m.p.moore@sheffield.ac.uk

Kate Pahl is Senior Lecturer at the School of Education, University of Sheffield. She is director of the MA, Working with Communities and teachers and researches in the area of language and literacy. She has published a number of articles in this area, and co-authored a book with Jennifer Rowsell titled *Literacy and Education: The New Literacy Studies in the Classroom*. She is on the editorial boards of *Literacy*, the United Kingdom Literacy Association journal *UKLA*, and *The Journal of Early Childhood Literacy*. . She is an Editorial Advisory Board member of *Reading and Writing: Journal of the Reading Association of South Africa*, co-editor of the Taylor and Francis on-line literacy abstracts database and Reviewer for *Discourse, Reading Research Quarterly, Linguistics and Education, Language and Education, Literacy* and *The Journal of Early Childhood Literacy*.

Contact details: University of Sheffield, School of Education, 388 Glossop Road, Sheffield, S10 2JA, United Kingdom, Tel: (+44) (0)114 222 8112, Fax: (+44) (0)114 279 6236, Email: k.pahl@sheffield.ac.uk

Judith Szenasi is a community development worker, currently undertaking a number of projects including work with a mental health service users/ receivers organization researching and writing reports on Delivering Race Equality in Mental Health, identifying new projects and developing funding proposals. Recently she has been commissioned by the Community Safety Partnership, The Primary Care Trust and Job Centre Plus to work with Refugees and Asylum Seekers. She is an Associate Lecturer on Working With Communities programmes at Derby University and at the University of Sheffield.

Contact details: 124 Stenson Road, Derby DE 23 1JG Tel: +44 01332 763361 Email: Judithszenasi@googlemail.com

Zeus Yiamouyiannis is an educational consultant. He received his PhD in Philosophy of Education from Syracuse University in 1998. His research addresses how emotions, specifically self-esteem, affect learning. He has published widely on topics ranging from non-traditional math and science education to reflective teaching to moral education and has spent many years in various aspects of education reform, development, and policy.

Contact details: 622 66th Street, Oakland, CA 94609, Tel: 510–428–2797 (home); 510–684–9379 (cell)

Index